DCPL000

D0229495

Historical Novels by Philippa Gregory

The Cousins' War
The White Queen
The Red Queen
The Lady of the Rivers

The Tudor Court
The Constant Princess
The Other Boleyn Girl
The Boleyn Inheritance
The Queen's Fool
The Virgin's Lover
The Other Queen

The Wideacre Trilogy

The Wise Woman
Fallen Skies
A Respectable Trade
Earthly Joys
Virgin Earth

Books by David Baldwin

Elizabeth Woodville: Mother of the Princes in the Tower
The Kingmaker's Sisters: Six Powerful Women
in the Wars of the Roses
The Lost Prince: The Survival of Richard of York
Stoke Field: The Last Battle of the Wars of the Roses
Robin Hood: The English Outlaw Unmasked

Books by Michael Jones

The King's Mother: Lady Margaret Beaufort, Countess
of Richmond and Derby
Bosworth 1485: The Psychology of a Battle
Agincourt 1415
Total War: From Stalingrad to Berlin
Leningrad: State of Siege
The Retreat: Hitler's First Defeat
Stalingrad: How the Red Army Triumphed

'The Women
of the
Cousins' War

The Women of the Cousins' War

The Duchess, the Queen and the King's Mother

PHILIPPA GREGORY

DAVID BALDWIN & MICHAEL JONES

SIMON &
SCHUSTER

London · New York · Sydney · Toronto · New Delhi

A CBS COMPANY

First published in Great Britain by Simon & Schuster UK Ltd, 2011
A CBS COMPANY

Copyright © Philippa Gregory, David Baldwin and Michael Jones, 2011

This book is copyright under the Berne Convention.
No reproduction without permission.
All rights reserved.

The right of Philippa Gregory, David Baldwin and Michael Jones
to be identified as the authors of this work has been asserted by them in accordance
with sections 77 and 78 of the Copyright, Designs and Patents Act, 1988.

1 3 5 7 9 10 8 6 4 2

Simon & Schuster UK Ltd
1st Floor
222 Gray's Inn Road
London WC1X 8HB

www.simonandschuster.co.uk

Simon & Schuster Australia, Sydney
Simon & Schuster India, New Delhi

Every reasonable effort has been made to contact copyright holders
of material reproduced in this book. If any have inadvertently been overlooked,
the publishers would be glad to hear from them and make good in future editions
any errors or omissions brought to their attention.

A CIP catalogue record for this book is available
from the British Library.

ISBN HB 978-0-85720-177-5
ISBN TPB 978-0-85720-178-2

Typeset in Plantin by M Rules
Printed in the UK by CPI Mackays, Chatham, ME5 8TD

CONTENTS

BATTLES IN THE
COUSINS' WAR

◎ Lancaster victories
⬠ York victories

Skye
Inverness
Aberdeen
Dundee
Stirling
Glasgow
Edinburgh
Hedgeley Moor
1464
Carlisle
Hexham
1464
Isle of Man
Lancaster
Towton
1461
York
Preston
Ferrybridge
1461
Wakefield
1460
Lincoln
Caernarfon
Chester
Blore Heath
1459
Stoke
1487
Losecote Field
1470
Shrewsbury
Ludford Bridge
1459
Bosworth
1485
Northampton
1460
Aberystwyth
Edgecote
1469
Fishguard
Mortimer's Cross
1461
St Albans
1455, 1461
Ipswich
Swansea
Cardiff
Tewkesbury
1471
Barnet
1471
LONDON
Bristol
Dover
Winchester
Lewes
Calais
Taunton
Southampton
Hastings
Exeter
Chichester
Plymouth
Dorchester
FRANCE
Penzance
ENGLISH CHANNEL

NORTH SEA

IRISH SEA

The Women
of the
Cousins' War

INTRODUCTION

Philippa Gregory

Leabharlanna Poibli Chathair Bhaile Átha Cliath
Dublin City Public Libraries

This is a new sort of book for me; a collection, written by myself and two other historians, of three short 'lives' of three extraordinary women: Jacquetta Duchess of Bedford, Margaret Beaufort, and Elizabeth Woodville. This book came about because so many readers ask me for the 'true' stories on which I base my novels, and there is nothing readily available for these three: *The Lady of the Rivers* (2011), *The Red Queen* (2010), and *The White Queen* (2009). The existing biographies of Margaret Beaufort and Elizabeth Woodville were out of print when I started my research, and so I worked from rare second-hand copies. I invited the authors, David Baldwin and Michael Jones, to each write a short essay on their subject for us to jointly publish here.

There was no biography at all of Jacquetta, and I realised that if I wanted to find out about her life I would have to do my own original research from the early documents, and trace the brief references to her that occur throughout other histories. As a woman who was present at many great events, and a kinswoman of both royal houses of England, she is often mentioned in the histories of her time; but her story has never before been told. To trace her life I had to read accounts of the lives of her contemporaries and of her times, forever looking out for a reference to her, her husbands or her family. This way I have managed to trace her from her childhood in

English-held France, to her family home of Luxembourg, through her first marriage into the royal House of Lancaster, into her second marriage, when she lived at the royal courts of Lancaster and York and to her country house in England. If she was present at a great event she was sometimes mentioned by name; once or twice she was one of the primary actors. Most of the time the record does not speak of her and I can only speculate as to what she was doing.

In the course of writing the biography of a woman who was present at the events but all-but missing from the record, a woman who is 'hidden from history', I had to think about what it means to write the different forms of history-based writing. In one week I wrote some of this non-fiction biography, some pages of the novel, and a synopsis for a drama screenplay that is based on the novels. All of these are grounded on the few known facts of Jacquetta's life, and all of them (including the history) are works of speculation, imagination and creativity.

WHY WRITE A HISTORY
OF THESE WOMEN?

Why should one bother to write the history of a woman such as Jacquetta Duchess of Bedford? Or of Elizabeth Woodville? Or of Margaret Beaufort? Does Jacquetta's absence from the records of her own time indicate that she is no great loss to the history books of today? Of course not. Jacquetta is absent from the records of her time because the letters, chronicles and journals written then mostly told of public events, and as a woman, excluded from formal political power and military service, Jacquetta was not a primary actor. Occasionally, she was at the forefront, and then we find her recorded, for instance accused of witchcraft, or kidnapped to Calais; sometimes she was an actor representing the queen or king, sometimes she was in a conspiracy and her work is still secret. So she does have a presence in the historical records if they are carefully examined.

But the interests of medieval chroniclers were not the same as ours. Historians today are interested in women, in the dispossessed, in the marginal, in the powerless. In particular we are interested in women's history – women as a group, and individual women. Historians would now agree that an account of a society which does not look at the lives of half of the population is only half an account. Jacquetta's life, as a prominent medieval woman, can tell us much about the queen's court, about elite life, about marriage, loyalty, social mobility, sex, childbirth and survival. She is interesting as a representative of her time and class as well as her gender. The medieval historians do not record such things; we have to look for them through the records, reading between the lines.

The histories of the other two women of this book are little better known; but Elizabeth Woodville's life story has been told largely in terms of her second husband Edward IV, and the tragedy of her son Edward V. She is often slandered – as a social climber, as an abuser of power and as morally corrupt – on a biased reading of very little evidence. Margaret Beaufort, on the other hand, has been made into a stereotype of virtue. There is very little written about her, and even less that sounds realistic. We can read about her piety and self-sacrifice, almost nothing about her ambition, conspiracy and passion. Much of the work she undertook for her son was done in secret, the collaborators sworn to silence and any documents destroyed. It is almost impossible to reconstruct the history of her life's work: it was a secret she kept to the grave.

And finally, to me these women are interesting as individuals. They are my heroines, they are my foremothers. To paraphrase Ecclesiasticus 44:1, 'Let us now praise famous women, and our mothers that begat us ...' If a woman is interested in her own struggle into identity and power then she will be interested in other women. The lives of these, and other women, show me what a woman can do even without formal power, education, or rights, in a world dominated by men. They are inspirational examples of the strength of the female spirit.

WHAT IS HISTORY?

History is not a simple factual record though it depends on the facts. There are sciences underpinning the making of history; for instance, the sciences of archaeology, forensics, genetics or geography; but history itself is not a science. There may be historical explanations which can be expressed in forms other than prose: in formulae, in statistics, or in maps. But most history is written in prose; and the selection of the material, the organisation into narrative and the choice of language show that it is a created form, an art.

Selection is inevitable. No history can include all the known facts of any event, even a single small limited event. There is simply too much material for one description. This is now so thoroughly agreed that the very idea of a total history – a

History of the English Speaking Peoples sort of history — is regarded by historians as impossible. We all understand that under such inclusive titles there were massive exclusions by the historian, sometimes unstated, sometimes unconscious. These days we understand that only a partial story can ever be told, and there is no longer any expectation that a historian will tell the whole of history, or even explain the full context. Historians select what story they are going to tell, then they select what facts they are going to use to illustrate and prove this story. They make this selection on the basis of what they think is most relevant to their subject, and on what is most interesting to themselves. Just because it is factual does not mean it is innocent of artifice. It is structured: the process of selection, assembly, description, consideration and ranking of facts shows that. There is no such thing as an unbiased unprejudiced history. The very act of selection of the subject introduces a bias. The author's preferences and opinions are the basis of the history that he or she writes, though sometimes readers – reading only one account or perhaps watching only one historian on television – think that this single view represents the totality of the subject. It does not, it cannot. It only ever represents the totality of the view of one historian. Someone else, even someone looking at exactly the same facts, might read them differently to a different conclusion, or start with a different view.

The writing of a history book is a personal process, a creative process, undertaken inside the strict innate rules of a craft form. Historians only rarely explain their process and their prejudices; these are rightly concealed under the smooth narrative of the story they have chosen to tell. They almost never discuss their writing style. Reviewers and readers tend to look at the content, but hardly ever question the narrative technique of a history. It is interesting that the convention of how histories are written is almost never challenged; though it is a powerful unstated convention, almost universally applied. Almost all histories are almost always written in the third person. Very occasionally, histories are written in third-person present tense – a device to give the illusion of intimacy. You will often see this in promotional material trying to entice readers into studying a history which the publicist secretly fears is too old and too dull: 'Mary Queen of Scots is in flight from rebels in Scotland and puts her trust in her cousin Elizabeth.'

Most histories are written in third-person past tense with a concealed narrator – the magisterial voice, a tone most powerful in conveying information without inviting challenge: 'For Elizabeth, Robert Dudley had one supreme advantage over all her other male admirers. He could not offer her marriage.'

As readers we are accustomed to accepting information from a concealed narrator. It is also the form used to convey instruction in everyday life: 'During rapid heat-up, do not place any food in the cooking compartment.' And, of course, it is the form usually used for orders: 'Jews will not be permitted to employ female citizens of German or kindred blood as domestic servants.'

In short, the concealed narrator is the one who reassures the reader that he is an authority to be trusted, or whose commands should be obeyed. The historian, fallible, biased, prejudiced, sometimes ignorant – above all, singular with a singular point of view – writes in a form which sounds universal, authoritative, certain. And – significantly – the form conceals his or her very presence. How much less powerful is the phrase 'I think that, for Elizabeth, Robert Dudley had one supreme advantage over all her other male admirers. He could not offer her marriage ...' than the authority of the sentence when the historian's thought process is unstated, and the historian herself is invisible.

History is a personal creative craft, not a science; it is an account made by each historian, not a body of facts which exists independently of them. Indeed, there is no such thing as a 'body' of accepted facts – it is more like an 'amorphous flock' of accepted facts of which the individuals come and go. E.H. Carr, answering this very question, discusses how a fact discovered by one historian might become an accepted 'historical' fact, and be admitted to the general body of known historical facts, changing the narrative. He suggests a fair admission policy would be when a fact has been cited by three different historians.

Equally, I suppose, a historical fact might fall out of the historical record. Perhaps Anne Boleyn's vestigial finger (almost certainly a fallacy invented by her detractors) may disappear in time. It was 'common knowledge' when I was at school; it has now disappeared from reputable scholarly histories, lingering only in popular belief. Perhaps another decade will see it disappear altogether. History is a created narrative which tells a story stepping from one agreed fact to another, with gulfs of unknown between each step, bridged only by speculation and imagination.

WHAT IS FICTION?

Fiction is not wholly the creation of an imaginary world, any more than history is the total description of a real one. Even the most unrealistic and fantasy-like fictional creations have a lineage which often stretches back to a reality. The extraordinary creations of science fiction are often rooted in science research, as the work of Isaac Asimov, Arthur C. Clarke and Robert Heinlein demonstrates. Their fiction is rooted in science fact, research or possibility and is called 'hard science fiction' as a result. Other novel forms are also based on reality. Some great classics have even been written to expose a reality of life and stimulate change. Charles Dickens's *Hard Times* is a novel set in the northern manufacturing towns as an appeal for better treatment of the workers. Other novels, such as Charlotte Brontë's *Jane Eyre*, use a real childhood experience as the starting point for the fiction. Some novels are firmly based in the real present world of the author, with fictional characters and story. Jane Austen's *Persuasion* accurately describes Bath and Lyme. Some novels go even further into reality, taking their setting, characters and, even, events from everyday life; and some tell stories of the historical past.

HISTORY AND FICTION

It is odd that – even though history is not purely fact, nor fiction purely imaginary – historical fiction, which openly declares itself to be both fact and fiction, should be denied serious attention. Too many critics think of historical fiction as flawed and unreliable history, written by authors too lazy to check the facts. Others condemn it for being insufficiently imaginative, written by authors too lazy to invent. Some readers want to know the proportion of fact to fiction – as if fact and fiction were not combined in every form of writing, as if historical fiction were a recipe. Some readers want to identify the facts from the fiction; but this is to deny the very form of the novel: something that combines fact and fiction.

As a writer who prefers to read history to fiction – but loves to write history, journalism and fiction – I choose to write historical fiction for love of the form. I find it uniquely satisfying to be able to research real characters in the real past and then speculate about their emotions, motives and unconscious desires, which cannot be discovered from the records they left, but have to be imagined.

There are differences between historians and novelists, of course. But perhaps fewer differences than readers think. Historians, like novelists, have to make things up – make up their view of the character, theorise about the character, imagine the character's inner life. As any biographer will confirm, the subject of a history is created in the mind of the author, built up from anecdotes and facts and snippets and portraits, in just the same way as a fictional character is made in the mind of a novelist. Both writers use their imagination to flesh out and animate their subject. The process of imagining someone who no longer exists is very like the process of imagining someone who has never existed.

Historians have to speculate. There are simply not enough certain facts available to write an unbroken historical account in which everything is known. Historians have to speculate about how one character arrives at a conclusion, who has advised him, how events are caused. When historians speculate, they make it clear they are doing so (at any rate the good ones do!). You will find the essays in this book are full of 'probably's, 'maybe's, and 'likely's. It is frustrating for the historian; but in many instances, when there is no record of what exactly a historical character was doing, the historian has to fall back on what was most likely, what people of the same sort were doing, what would be typical behaviour at this particular time.

Novelists writing historical fiction do the same (at any rate the good ones do!). A nonsensical novelist will make up whatever he likes – but I am not concerned here with what should really be called historical fantasy – when an imagined historical period offers little more than the costume and the excuse for the story, a creation more like a pantomime than a realistic drama. Here I am discussing the serious historical novel in which the author takes the history seriously, researches like a historian, but chooses to write as a novelist. The historical novelist who is serious about his craft will speculate just like the historian, falling back on the most likely of the facts available. The job of the historian is to select the facts, speculate, and then declare the speculation and acknowledge other possibilities. The job of the novelist is to take the facts, speculate, and make such a convincing story-path of the speculation that the reader does not wonder if there was any other route. The novelist cannot allow the reader to escape from the spell of the novel; the reader cannot be allowed to unpick the history from the fiction until the book is closed at the very end of the story. To write a successful novel, the historical fact, the history-based speculation and the pure fiction have to blend.

The novelist has all this to do; and more. The novelist has to write something that is pleasing on the page and the ear. The very words are chosen with care not just for what they mean; but also for what they conjure, perhaps even for how they sound, or what they look like on the page. Far more than the historian the novelist is concerned with extraneous detail: costume, saddlery, food, hobbies, weather. The novelist is also concerned with the inner life: secrets and the unconscious.

And a novel, unlike a history, has a choice of narrators. A novel can be written from many points of view. Most often a novel is written in the style called omniscient narrator or concealed narrator, in which the story is narrated by a disembodied voice, someone who sees everything and describes it with apparent neutrality, just like the usual style of a history. When the novel is narrated by the omniscient narrator, the rule generally is that the narrator has to be omniscient and stay omniscient: this narrator knows everything. The omniscient narrator cannot write as a historian who is honour-bound to acknowledge the limits of the research. Readers of history are accustomed to a break in the narrative when the historian explains that the facts are missing and that at this point we are inside the realm of informed speculation. Sometimes the historian will even step into the third-person prose to say why he or she personally cannot be certain about a fact. But this is not possible for the novelist. The reader of a novel doesn't want to start with a world view, a god's view, which suddenly breaks down and says 'actually we don't really know the facts here, but the most likely thing is . . .' The reader wants to be captured by the narrator, and the reader wants to stay captured.

Not all novels are told by an omniscient narrator. They can come from an authorial voice, whose presence is understood by the reader and who sometimes directly addresses the reader. They can be written as if by one of the characters, looking back over their lives. As I have developed my own writing I have come to love the narrational device of writing in the first person, present tense, as one of the characters reporting on the events from her own viewpoint, as they happen. The advantage of this is to put the reader in the shoes of the protagonist, seeing the world from her viewpoint:

I touch the milestone once more, and imagine that tomorrow the messenger will come. He will hold out a paper
sealed with the Howard crest deep and shiny in the red wax.
'A message for Jane Boleyn, the Viscountess Rochford?' he
will ask, looking at my plain kirtle and the dust on the hem
of my gown, my hand stained with dirt from the London
milestone.

'I will take it,' I shall say. 'I am her, I have been waiting forever.' And I shall take it in my dirty hand: my inheritance.

The present tense also has the advantage of avoiding the
hindsight of historians who know what is going to happen
and whether or not it was a success. Some of my favourite
scenes have been when the narrator expected the 'wrong'
history: thinking that something would happen, that did
not, in the end, take place. This challenge has been very
stimulating for me as a novelist and sometimes even led to
new conclusions for me as a historian. For example, I suggested that Mary Boleyn in *The Other Boleyn Girl* was
certain that her sister Anne would escape execution. The
history indicates this. Anne made an agreement, mediated
by the Archbishop of Canterbury, Thomas Cranmer, to
accept that her marriage with Henry VIII was null and void.
She was probably expecting retirement to a nunnery.
Historians have not paid much attention to this agreement
since they write from the point of view of knowing the end
of the story: that the agreement did not save her, and Anne
was executed. From the point of view of the history of what
happened, the agreement is not very interesting – it made
no difference to the outcome, it can be safely all-but forgotten.

But for me thinking as a historian about what might have
happened, or what Anne might have hoped and planned,

these days become tremendously interesting. By thinking about them as 'live' negotiations and putting aside the eventual outcome, I came to realise the importance of those last days in the Tower. That Anne should have struggled for her life, should have been prepared to set aside her position as queen and the inheritance of her daughter is a most important historical insight. For me as a novelist, writing 'in role' as the doomed woman's sister, this is also tremendously interesting. This is a moment where I (speaking as Mary Boleyn) am absolutely convinced that my sister will survive, that my former lover Henry VIII will let her go. The tension and then pathos of the execution scene are based on the history; but draw all their energy from the fact that it is written from the point of view of Mary, who is expecting a pardon not a death. To write this scene as a novelist, I had to 'forget' what I knew of the history.

'Thank God,' I said, knowing only now how deeply I had been afraid. 'When will she be released?'

'Perhaps tomorrow,' Catherine said. 'Then she'll have to live in France.'

'She'll like that,' I said. 'She'll be an abbess in five days, you'll see.'

Catherine gave me a thin smile. The skin below her eyes was almost purple with fatigue.

'Come home now,' I said in sudden anxiety. 'It's all but done.'

'I'll come when it's over,' she said. 'When she goes to France.'

Interestingly, readers captured by the novel, and by the controlled delivery of the information, seem to accept the convention, and 'forget' the history they know. Many people have told me of the sense of great tension in the novel at the prospect of the execution though, of course, we all know that Anne will die.

A novel about Anne Boleyn need not end with her death – though every biography does so. Most histories aim for a complete account of their subject and so a traditional biography starts with the birth of the subject and ends with the death. History, as a study of time, tends to be written in a narrative line that follows time from the furthest past to the most recent. But a historical fiction need not do this. It can obey, instead, the requirements of the novel-form to open with a powerfully engaging scene, and this can be a foreseeing, or a flashback, or an event outside ordinary time, or outside the story altogether. Over the years this has become a signature technique for me. I try to make the opening scenes of my novels a powerful insight into the entire story, a vivid freeze-frame moment: a gestalt moment. The first scene for me does not just start the narrative – it symbolises it. My novel *The Other Queen* opens with Mary Queen of Scots breaking out of Bolton Castle by climbing down a rope made of sheets, a factual event and an act of typical adventure, courage and recklessness, that the more traditional and sentimental portraits of the doomed queen deny. The man who is going to fall disastrously in love with her sees her captured, circled with torches, lit like an angel, ringed with fire like a witch.

In *The Red Queen* the novel opens with a dream sequence, the dream which inspires Margaret Beaufort to her life's work, and which warns her that exceptional women face exceptional dangers. *The White Queen* opens outside of time altogether, with the myth of Melusina, the water goddess, which is threaded through the novel as both a traditional story and one of the themes of the book: the different worlds of men and women. *The Lady of the Rivers* opens with the young Jacquetta meeting Joan of Arc, a girl who sees visions and speaks with angels, just as Jacquetta sees visions and hears the singing of spirits.

THE RECIPE

But how much fiction should there be in a historical novel? And how much fact? All historical novelists would give their own answer. Personally, I would say: as little fiction as possible in the chronicle of events. A chronicle is a simple narrative that says: this happens and then this happens. I believe that the chronicle should form the structure of the historical novel and it should be as solid as the historical record allows. If we know that a battle happened at Bosworth in 1485 and we know how it was fought and who won, then this must be the fact in my novel as it is in the history book. But what it was like, and how it felt to people at the time: this is where a historical novel can be a far more exciting, inspiring, poignant and beautiful form than a factual account.

But however vivid and powerful the historical novel, I believe it should be based on the recorded facts and never deviate from them when they are available. How few facts are available for some periods and lives, and how much the historian has to speculate to tell a coherent story is perhaps demonstrated in this collection of three essays: the factual basis that underpins my first three novels of 'the cousins' war'.

WOMEN AND HISTORY

When I consider how significant a role these women played in their times, the interest of their own lives, and the importance of their children, it amazes me that their histories have not already been thoroughly explored and recorded. Why are there not many histories of the three women of this book, when one was a queen, one was a royal duchess and the other the founder of the best-known line of monarchs in the world? Why are these three women, and so many of the other women that I write about, either absent from the historical record altogether, or hardly mentioned? Michael Hicks, the medieval historian, explains:

> Historians used to suppose that there could be no history of women; especially medieval women, and certainly none that was worth the recounting. Initially, perhaps, this was because historians (especially male historians) had no wish to write about members of the other sex. They subscribed to the presumption that history was about politics, in which women have traditionally played little part. Women's failure to participate in what really mattered in the past meant that women themselves were unhistorical and unworthy of the historian's attention.

When women do emerge into the historical record, why are they viewed so negatively? Why was Mary Boleyn all-but invisible to history, when the story of her life and her family was so extraordinary? And why is Anne of Cleves almost forgotten, or remembered only as the fat smelly one?

I believe that women are excluded from medieval history as historical characters because of the traditional view at the time of the nature of women, which was that women were innately incapable of major public acts: 'The Church provided two models for women: Eve the temptress and Mary, the Mother of God; thus society viewed women as either pure and virginal or filled with the carnal lust of the deceitful Eve. In either case the culture stereotyped them.'

We can see the consequences of viewing women as Eve the temptress, or Mary the Virgin, when we look at women who have entered the historical record and been firmly categorised as one or the other. Later historians revise in vain; some stereotypes are very tenacious. For instance, Katherine Howard, the young fifth wife of Henry VIII: 'She was beheaded on 13 February 1542, only nineteen or twenty years old. The drama of her execution lends gravity to a brief life which would otherwise pass unnoticed.'

Actually, I think that Katherine Howard's brief life is very worthy of notice, and her beheading is not the only interesting thing about her. But of all the Henry queens she is the one most likely to have been promiscuous, and this ruined her reputation in her own times, and even today inspires a sort of smug tolerance:

Then there is the question of her sensuality. The long withdrawing roar of Victorian morality inhibited generations of historians from treating this with anything other than disapproval and distaste. But we are past that now. We can confront sex as a fact, not as a sin. We can even, if pushed, see a sort of virtue in promiscuity.

Katherine benefits enormously from this shift in moral

values. True, she was a good-time girl. But like many good-time girls she was also warm, loving and good natured.

It seems extraordinary to me that I should be stepping up to defend the reputation of a young woman who was executed in 1542. But new research indicates that – born between 1524 and 1527 – she was even younger at her first sexual experience than was previously thought. So, since her first so-called sexual encounter with her music teacher took place when she may have been a little girl of just eleven years old, this incident cannot be regarded as evidence of female promiscuity; more likely, it is evidence of coercion. Then, at the age of perhaps twelve, in an ill-chaperoned household she made a secret betrothal with an older, sexually experienced, man – Francis Dereham – who may have seduced her for his sexual pleasure and to promote his social advancement. At around fifteen years old she was placed in an arranged marriage to the 49-year-old Henry VIII. It is unlikely that her affections were engaged by this bad-tempered man, old enough to be her grandfather. And then she fell in love with Thomas Culpepper and perhaps became his lover. She wrote to him: 'it makes my heart die to think what fortune I have that I cannot always be in your company.'

Surely, these are not the words of a good-time girl seeking a romp? These are the passionate words of a very young woman in love for the first time. So her well-recorded 'promiscuity' amounts to inappropriate behaviour by her teacher when she was eleven years old, one incident of grooming at the age of twelve, and one possible love affair. This hardly makes her a 'good-time girl'. Executed at seventeen, she had no time to establish her own style or morality as a woman.

The reputation of Anne of Cleves, the king's fourth wife, is also a slander, but the source of it is the king himself: 'I liked her before not well but now I like her much worse. She is nothing fair, and have very evil smells about her. I took her to be no maid by reason of the looseness of her breasts and other tokens, which, when I felt them, strake me so to the heart that I had neither will nor courage to prove the rest. I can have none appetite for displeasant airs.'

One glance at the Holbein miniature of Anne shows a pretty young woman, not particularly dark or slack-skinned. It is unlikely that she carried 'evil smells' – the ladies of her bedchamber would not have allowed her to go unwashed to the king's bed on her wedding night, and no one but the king ever mentioned this. But on that wedding night, when the king found himself impotent, he was quick to blame her.

At this time Henry VIII was grossly overweight, painfully and regularly constipated with outbreaks of wind, and with an ulcerous sore from an old wound on his leg which had to be kept open to allow the pus to drain. There was indeed a fat stinking unsexy person in the Cleves/Henry VIII bed; but it was not the 24-year-old woman who knew that her future depended on pleasing her 49-year-old husband – a sick man, old enough to be her father. Henry's tyrannised court had no option but to take his word, against the evidence of their own eyes, and agree that the new young queen was so ugly as to prohibit sexual intercourse. Interestingly, historians have blindly followed this line, taking the word of the divorcing man against the evidence of his wife: not for the first time; nor, I expect, the last.

Very few women escape this powerful stereotyping. Great queens like Elizabeth I and Victoria receive a huge amount of positive attention, and are cast in the role of the 'Mary the Virgin' character. Indeed, admiration of Elizabeth is such a rule that historians are uncomfortable when they want to challenge the heroic myths; as the editor of a collection of essays on Elizabeth discovered: 'I encountered several versions of the startled response of one scholar, "Oh!" he exclaimed. "I really wouldn't want to say anything bad about Elizabeth."'

The disadvantage for historians celebrating the chastity of historical women is that, just as they cannot see Anne of Cleves or Katherine Howard for the young women they were, because they are dazzled by their bad reputation, they also cannot understand the women that they overly praise. Such historians are uncomfortable about examining women's personal lives, their lives as normal women. Queen Victoria's clearly expressed sexual desire for her husband Albert was suppressed until recently, and her loving relationship in widowhood with her servant John Brown was only fully examined in 2003. Queen Elizabeth's sexual life with a succession of favourites has been blandly described as 'courtly love' by historians, who are uncomfortable at the evidence that she satisfied her powerful sexual drive in serial exaggerated flirtations, and sexual play.

For historians who cannot bring themselves to ascribe active sexuality to respectable women, the controversy of the Katherine of Aragon divorce becomes quite incomprehensible. They want to believe that Katherine of Aragon, an outstandingly pretty princess, sixteen years old, spent five months in Wales with her young handsome husband on a prolonged honeymoon, without once having sexual intercourse though they had been publicly married and publicly put into bed together. This unlikely claim is Katherine's own, to defend herself against an attempt by her second husband, Henry VIII, to declare his marriage to her as null – he argued that they would have been too closely related to marry, if she had consummated the marriage with his elder brother Arthur. Katherine had a series of defences: a contradiction in the Bible texts, the opinion of the majority of theologians, a dispensation from the Pope; but she fell back on the simplest argument – that she was not in too close affinity to Henry VIII because her marriage with his brother was never consummated. Despite having been married to a healthy young man for five months, she claimed she had been a virgin-widow.

Historians, overawed by Katherine's piety, cannot bring themselves to believe that she would have had sex and then denied it. Instead, they argue that she was a virgin, inexplicably refusing sex with a handsome young husband to whom she had been betrothed from the age of four. They have to believe that she defied everyone by refusing to consummate a vitally important marriage, as arranged by her parents and blessed by the Pope, after the young couple had been publicly commended to be fruitful, and put into bed together. And also that nobody at the time – not the Spanish ambassador, nor the churchmen, nor the duennas – observed that the new Princess of Wales was refusing her husband his legal marital rights and so jeopardising the alliance between England and Spain which was the reason for the marriage.

WOMEN EXCLUDED FROM HISTORY

Whether a woman is being regarded as Eve the temptress or Mary the Virgin, this is still to view her in relation to her sexual activity with men, and this is private activity, not a public or historical act. Women were not seen as having a public nature; they were not often observed performing visible, significant and historical acts. When a woman broke this taboo and was clearly involved in public acts, the medieval historians of her time were forced to see her as a stereotype or – at the worst – hardly a woman at all. If she was neither Eve nor Mary, then she must be a man. So too the playwrights:

> LADY MACBETH: The raven himself is hoarse
>   That croaks the fatal entrance of Duncan
>   Under my battlements. Come, you spirits
>   That tend on mortal thoughts, unsex me here,
>   And fill me from the crown to the toe topful
>   Of direst cruelty!

Traditional historians do not look for energetic, effective women; and when they cannot blind themselves to the vibrant presence of such a woman, rather than amend their views of women, they define her instead as so exceptional as to be a pseudo-man.

One of the early written histories of England, commissioned by Henry VII, father to Henry VIII, written in Latin by Polydore Vergil sometime from 1507, describes the reigns of Henry VI and Edward IV but has more to say about a woman – Margaret of Anjou – than about any other character of the times. Vergil's difficulty in describing her is that her reality challenges this view of woman's passive private nature. For him, as for so many historians who came after him, a woman cannot be a historical figure. If she acts powerfully, she is really a man: 'A woman of sufficient forecast, very desirous of renown, full of policy, council, comely behaviour, and all manly qualities . . .'

This is the start of the interrogation of Margaret of Anjou's femininity that has gone on until our own times. In a very little while this queen who fought so courageously for her son, her husband and her House would become not even a man but a beast, a 'she-wolf':

She-wolf of France, but worse than wolves of France . . .
Women are soft, mild, pitiful, and flexible;
Thou stern, obdurate, flinty, rough, remorseless

Many historians in the past 600 years had difficulty in describing women making history, taking events into their own hands and being agents of change, because they simply could not believe that it could be done. If it was done, then it must have been done by someone who was in some way male. Amazingly, this view of women was not left in the medieval period: 'The coverage of Hillary Clinton's presidential campaign, for example, has been notable for its emphasis on her appearance, with endless scathing comments on her unwomanly ambition and her coldly tenacious style.'

The UK's first woman prime minister attracted the same unease in 1988: 'In criticizing Mrs Thatcher as a surrogate man, feminists mean she has betrayed women – not only politically but spiritually. Antifeminists mutter the same thing. She is abhorrent, anathema, unfeminine. She is herself destroying what is most precious and treasured about womanhood in pursuit of mere manly power.'

Women were not only missing from history because of the blinkered vision of male historians, they were excluded because of the tradition of the historical record. Before history started to research the stories of social minorities, the lower classes, the excluded, the less visible, it had always focused on the documented decisions and doings of the great people – almost always men. Since women of the pre-modern world were excluded from public life, they were not likely to perform major public acts that would have entered the record books. Since women were banned from political power almost everywhere in the world until they won the right to vote, mostly in the first half of the twentieth century, they are bound to be absent from any political history. Since they were banned from combat, or segregated into women's services in the UK until the 1990s, they are mostly absent from military history. Forced to hand over land or any wealth to a husband on marriage until 1870 in the UK, there are few women entrepreneurs or capitalists in the histories of farming or industry. Barred from gaining degrees at Oxford and Cambridge until – incredibly – the late 1920s, educated in separate colleges in the USA, potential women scientists, doctors, mathematicians, literary and social critics were not educated and so are absent from the magisterial nineteenth-century records of pioneers and experts. As late as the 1960s, professional and graduate schools in America imposed a quota that there should be no more than 10 per cent of women on their courses. Since women were not allowed to earn, study or train, how could they ever become notable? How could they ever get into the historical record for their achievements? Why would anyone ever remember them?

The 1895 editors of a history of law praise the 'sure instinct' of the law in excluding women: 'On the whole we may say that, though it has no formulated theory about the position of women, a sure instinct has already guided the law to a general rule which will endure until our own time. As regards private rights women are on the same level as men, though postponed in the canons of inheritance;

but public functions they have none. In the camp, at the council board, on the bench, in the jury box, there is no place for them.'

'There is no place for them' – how that echoes down the years! Instinctively – not thoughtfully – the law knew that women should be excluded. And so it is done, and not just in the law. In the fine arts women were present as models but not as artists: in 2007, women artists had created 2 per cent of the pictures of the National Gallery in London, but women's faces, and their bodies – often naked – are everywhere on the walls. Women's bodies are clearly art, of interest to the museums; but their vision is not. Again, this is because women were effectively banned from training. The Royal Academy schools in the UK only admitted women from 1861, and then they were not allowed to draw nudes. Only in the twentieth century did most schools allow women artists to study in life classes, and look at the naked body.

Female musicians were also discouraged. Although Abraham Mendelssohn trained his talented daughter Fanny, he compared her with her brother: 'Perhaps for Felix music will become a profession, while for you it will always remain but an ornament; never can and should it become the foundation of your existence.'

Almost all great orchestras banned women performers until 1912 when four women joined the New Queen's Hall Orchestra, London. Progress has not been swift. The Vienna Philharmonic only decided to accept women as full members in 1997, and by 2008 had recruited one: a harpist.

Women could not hope to succeed in any art when they were banned from education and training, when they could not earn or inherit money to purchase fine-art equipment or musical instruments. They lacked the networks and support of colleagues; they were especially vulnerable to physical and sexual abuse. Like all young artists they needed a patron or senior mentor and this was an especially difficult relationship for a young woman to manage.

There were many heartening exceptions to this general exclusion of women from the arts and the sciences. Gifted women taught themselves, working quite alone, unaware that they were actually part of a tradition of lone female scholars. Generous men shared their education: mentored female scholars, or educated their daughters. Women used the patriarchal Church to finance and protect their studies. Powerful women stepped into positions of leadership; clever women found ways to make and keep a fortune from their husbands. In the arts and in the sciences, in the Church and in the world, exceptional women in exceptional circumstances managed to win the expensive and exclusive training, equipment, time and opportunity to practise their art, craft or science, and thus achieve the level of skill needed to create a work so good that later critics would overcome their own prejudices and rank it alongside male achievements. Of course they were very few. Virginia Woolf suggested that no woman could effectively write unless she had an annuity and a room of her own. Hers was a bleak assessment; but she was right: it is almost impossible to complete great work isolated from one's peers, without income, without space, without equipment and without training.

But there is another sense in which women were barred from history. They were excluded as the producers of history, as writers. They failed to become historians. When we read 'well-behaved women don't make history' we must understand that not only were women barred from acting on events, denied the recognition they deserved, and explained away; they were also barred from recording events. Women are not in the record and they were not allowed to write the record. In this dual sense, history has always been made by men.

Why this should be, is quite transparent. It is no mystery. History is written or commissioned by victorious men to tell their own version of their lives. One of the spoils of victory is to be the one who tells the story. Defeated men, such as Richard III, lost both the battle and the telling of the history. The story will be that of a triumphant male, in which women (if they appear at all) are either his supporters or his victims. The victors of events prior to our own century are almost always male. As late as 1961 E.H. Carr's definitive musing on the nature of history referred consistently and exclusively to male historians and only to male historical figures: 'The knowledge of the historian is not his exclusive personal possession: men, probably, of many generations and of many countries have participated in accumulating it. The men whose actions the historian studies were not isolated individuals acting in a vacuum: they acted in a context . . .'

Every scholarly history that was written before 1920 was written by a man who had been taught by a man, whose thesis would be examined by a man, and whose book would be published by a male publisher, and reviewed by a male critic. This could not change until women were admitted to universities and colleges. When women could train as historians in the universities, they could for the first time research, write and publish scholarly history. The arrival of professionally trained women historians became a driving part of the new scholarship of history that looked for the first time at the minorities, at the marginalised, at the persecuted and at the working class. Women historians joined with left-wing and labour historians in opening up archives with questions about the lives of those that history had previously overlooked. When women started to write history they took an interest in women's history and started to discover the women whose stories had been neglected, and they started to analyse the traditional history and offer an alternative to the male stereotyped views of women. They were part of a rise of historians questioning the accepted views and the canon of traditional history who critically examined issues of bias in gender, race, culture and nationality.

From the late 1950s we see the rise of women's studies, created by the new generation of women graduates. We see the publishing of realistic and fair histories of women written by women historians who were actively seeking evidence, and – when they found it – describing it, not explaining it away. We see research into early female artists and musicians, scientists and mathematicians. Now you can search in any library, or look in any university or local-history group and find that this pioneering work has become mainstream. Women are becoming so well established in the historical record, both as historians and as subjects, that their very struggle is being forgotten.

When women are allowed to study and become historians they bring a more realistic view to the subject. Individual women, working as historians, know the range of their own experiences and capabilities and thus know what other women can do and be. Women who know themselves, know that their gender is not especially or exclusively saintly. They know it is not especially promiscuous or especially wicked. Women know that they are neither Eve nor Our Lady. Once women start to write about women a new realism creeps into the writing, and – as you see from the two co-authors of this book about women – this realism is shared by men.

THREE WOMEN OF THE COUSINS' WAR

This book is part of the ongoing process of seeking and describing women in history. It examines the three women who were the heroines of the first three novels in the series I have called 'The Cousins' War'. This was the name given at the time to the series of battles and skirmishes which later historians would call the Wars of the Roses. But the name 'the cousins' war' is the name that was used at the time and it describes the family nature of the conflict: an armed quarrel between brothers and then their sons – the cousins – over which descendant of Edward III should become King of England. It has been military history and political history which have dominated the accounts of these times, and since few women fought, and since no woman had any political rights, it is not surprising that their lives and experiences were ignored by most historians. But the three historians in this book have chosen to look at three women of the time and have uncovered extraordinary stories of networking, conspiracy, influence, power-grabbing and self-sacrificial courage which mean that we have to adjust our view of the times and include these women as effective actors on the historical stage.

The first character in the book is Jacquetta Duchess of Bedford, whose full biography has not yet been written. I started to study her for my novel *The Lady of the Rivers* and found an absence where a biography should be. Though she was a duchess of England, the mother of a queen, and the leading light in the court of Lancaster and then of York, nobody had thought to research Jacquetta.

There are gaps in her history that perhaps later scholars will study. We know next to nothing about her private life with her husband Sir Richard Woodville. We glimpse her in the historical record only when he serves as a military commander for the House of Lancaster, and when she serves as the primary lady-in-waiting to Margaret Anjou. We know only approximate dates of her confinements, especially those babies who may have died young: the account I give here is from my own research and from lengthy discussions with David Baldwin; it is not definitive. We are more sure about the deaths of her adult children than their birth dates because the adults later became siblings to the Queen of England and entered the historical record.

I think I can speculate with some confidence about some aspects of Jacquetta. I think she was loyal: for she served the House of Lancaster and Margaret of Anjou until the final defeat at Towton, when Margaret fled from the battle. I am sure she was passionate: for she married for love and paid a high price to do so. I know she was something of a scholar: for she kept the library inherited from her first husband; she raised a son who was a poet, a writer and an editor. Her daughter and her son sponsored the first printing press in England and edited the first ever book printed in England. I can speculate that her daughter's court was the model for Thomas Malory's vision of Camelot; but there is as yet no solid proof as to whether Jacquetta herself was an educated, scholarly woman, and if it was her love of learning which descended to her grandson Henry VIII and her great-granddaughter the studious Queen Elizabeth I.

We know little about Elizabeth Woodville before she made her ambitious second marriage to the young King Edward IV. Her first marriage to a relatively obscure country gentleman left few traces. She is visible on the record during her time as queen; but we know less about the months when she saved herself and her daughters from Richard III, living in sanctuary. Did she really release her second son into his care when he had kidnapped her first? Did she really believe that Richard III had murdered her sons and yet bring herself to reconcile with him, putting her daughters in his care – where their brothers had been? Why did she first conspire against him; but then order her son home from the court of Henry Tudor to reconcile with him? We know very little of what she was doing after the accession of Henry VII and the marriage of her daughter to the new king. Can it be that she really joined a plot against the incoming Tudor king, her own son-in-law? And why would she have done that?

Margaret Beaufort's official story is powerfully bland. We have few details about her magnificent organisation of the so-called Buckingham rebellion. Perhaps we can read much into the fact that at the time the rebellion was named the Beaufort rebellion – for her, the kingpin plotter at the centre of dangerous intrigue. It was later historians who re-named the plot and so helped to obscure her shocking treason against an ordained king of England and the betrayal of his queen – her friend. We know almost nothing about her relationships with her three husbands, nor with her daughter-in-law, who was of the rival house and the daughter of her enemy. We can only reconstruct her passionate and intimate relationship with her son from small snippets of gossip, and the architecture of the royal palaces that they designed together to give themselves, in every place, a small personal shared room.

Our lack of knowledge about these women is caused by the scarcity of any records at all. The records that survive from this period are scanty. The vast majority of people were not literate, and those who did write letters, diaries or journals did not preserve their work. There are so few documents that they can be listed here: four chronicles, covering different, often short periods of time and often arguing different viewpoints; a few collections of private family letters, of which the Paston Letters are best known; the recorded impressions of a few foreign visitors; and the commissioned 'History of England' written by Polydore Vergil at the request of Henry VII.

As one might expect, the chronicles and the 'History' are all written by men, the foreign visitors are all men too, and these are all men who share the medieval view of the nature of women; some of them – as celibate churchmen – are professionally remote from women. They tell us what has happened in their world, and they tell us what they believe is the nature of that world. They do not expect to see women working effectively and powerfully, and when this is the case they often fail to report it. When they do see an ambitious and powerful woman like Margaret of Anjou they often report her negatively, or as if she were, in some way, manly. Other women, like Margaret Beaufort, appear as saints.

None of the women of this book escapes these stereotypes. Jacquetta's story is nowhere fully told; but she is sometimes slandered as the sexually driven, secretly married wife of a socially ambitious nobody, and as the suspect witch who put her daughter to bed with a young king by enchanting him. Her daughter Elizabeth Woodville is seen as the woman who seduced a younger man and upset the order of the court. Her greed put her in conflict with the Earl of Warwick and brought war to the kingdom, and her ambition drove her to send her daughter to seduce the probable murderer of her sons, and poison his wife. Margaret Beaufort is an example of the saintly stereotype. There is no evidence of her having sex after her first brief marriage which gave her a son; historians suggest that her third marriage was a celibate union, and depend heavily on the descriptions of her in the history commissioned by her son, as a pious thoughtful woman who prayed for the victory of her son and wept in moments of joy for her realisation that all worldly success is fleeting. Her jockeying for power at her son's court, her meticulous business sense, her brilliant political strategy, and her cool-headed cold-hearted alliances are not mentioned, let alone celebrated in traditional histories of this founding mother of the Tudor house.

There is one further gap in the record that I would like to mention here, as an invitation to further study. Traditional historians have not only missed the nature of women and the range of their experiences; they have also missed the networks of women that we can see only when we start to look. Margaret Beaufort was lady-in-waiting for years to Elizabeth Woodville, and godmother to Elizabeth's daughter. Then she was friend and chief lady-in-waiting to Queen Anne, wife of Richard III, until she betrayed her loyalty and her friendship by conspiring with Elizabeth Woodville, who was herself Anne's sister-in-law. Then Margaret and Elizabeth were co-grandmothers to the Tudor heirs: Arthur, who died; and Henry, who would become Henry VIII. Margaret lived long enough to be a powerful influence on the young Henry VIII and to see him married to Katherine of Aragon.

Elizabeth's mother, Jacquetta Duchess of Bedford, was a lifelong friend of Margaret of Anjou, serving her until the marriage of Elizabeth to Edward IV meant that she became chief lady of the rival court of York. Margaret of Anjou was briefly mother-in-law to Anne Neville, who married her son Prince Edward of Lancaster until widowed at Tewkesbury, when Anne went on to marry Richard Duke of Gloucester, and become sister-in-law, and then successor and enemy to Elizabeth Woodville. There are some amazing connections here among women competing and co-operating that have been hidden from the history along with the characters and actions of these women.

As this is a book for the general reader we three authors decided against footnoting our work but we have each included an account of our sources that you will find at the foot of each section.

A book like this could not be written without the work of fellow scholars. I have to thank firstly the pioneers of women's rights and women's history. Without the former I would not have been allowed a place at a university; without the latter I would not have had the material which has illuminated my life. I thank my mother, from my heart, for her determination to get me an education and a trade, and for knowing that these are skills that a woman must have. My warm thanks to David Baldwin and Michael Jones for writing about these wonderful women in the first place, and for writing about them with me.

NOTES AND SOURCES

The phrase 'hidden from history' which so precisely describes the unmentioned presence of women in the past is from Rowbotham, S. *Hidden from History: 300 years of women's oppression and the fight against it*, London: Pluto Press, 1973. The Bible, Ecclesiasticus 44:1 says 'Let us now praise famous *men ...*'

The encouraging account of Mary Queen of Scots in present tense is from the back-jacket copy of my novel *The Other Queen*, London: Harper Collins, 2008, and the description of Elizabeth and Robert Dudley from Alison Weir's *Elizabeth the Queen*, London: Pimlico, 1999. The instructional tone is from the booklet which came with my new cooker: Neff instructions for use B46W74.0GB; and the chilling voice of Nazi authority is drawn from Noakes, J. and Pridham, G. *Documents on Nazism 1919–1945*, NY: Viking Press, 1974, pp. 463–7.

The scene as narrated by Jane Boleyn comes from my novel *The Boleyn Inheritance*, London: HarperCollins, 2006, and the subsequent passage is from the viewpoint of Mary Boleyn: Gregory, P. *The Other Boleyn Girl*, London: HarperCollins, 2001. Michael Hicks's exceptionally honest explanation of why women are missing from medieval history is helpfully clear: Hicks, M.A. *Anne Neville, Queen to Richard III*, Stroud: Tempus, 2006.

The views of women, Eve as a temptress, is quoted by Levin, C. and Watson, J. *Ambiguous Realities: Women in the Middle Ages and Renaissance*, Wayne State University Press, 1987. The lack of interest in Katherine Howard was expressed by a woman historian, Mary Hays: *Female Biography; or, Memoirs of Illustrious and Celebrated Women, of all ages and cultures*, facsimile reprint 1803, but this unfortunate view of Katherine Howard comes from David Starkey: Starkey, D. *Six Wives, the Queens of Henry VIII*, London: Chatto & Windus, 2003. Joanna Denny provides an empathetic biography that also has new evidence as to Katherine's date of birth. I quote Katherine's letter from Denny's book *Katherine Howard, A Tudor Conspiracy*, London: Portrait, 2005.

Henry VIII's lack of pleasure in his wedding night with Anne of Cleves is quoted from Weir, A. *The Six Wives of Henry VIII*, London: The Bodley Head, 1991. The reluctance of scholars to criticise the Virgin Queen is cited: Walker, J.M. *Dissing Elizabeth, Negative Representations of Gloriana*, London: Duke University Press (1998); Queen Victoria's widowhood was examined in Lamont-Brown, R. 'Queen Victoria's "secret marriage"', *Contemporary Review*, December 2003. Lady Macbeth's speech is from Shakespeare's *Macbeth*: Act 1, Scene v, 38–43.

Polydore Vergil's history has been edited and republished: Vergil, P. and Ellis, H. *Three Books of Polydore Vergil's English History Comprising the Reigns of Henry VI, Edward IV and Richard III*, Kessinger Publishing Legacy Reprint, 1971. Shakespeare's critical account of Margaret of Anjou comes from *Henry VI: Part III*, Act 1, Scene iv, 111 – 141/2. Later she-wolves include Hillary Clinton: Feldman, S. 'Gender traitors', *New Humanist*, Vol. 123, No. 4 (August 2008), accessed: http://newhumanist.org.uk/1816/gender-traitors, and Margaret Thatcher: Gale Group: *Washington Monthly*, Vol. 20 (May 1988) *Is Margaret Thatcher a Woman? No woman is if she has to make it in a man's world*, accessed: http://www.thefreelibrary.com/Is+Margaret+Thatcher+a+woman%3F+No+woman+is+if+she+has+to+make+it+in+a...-a06676349.

Laura Ulrich cites many exclusions of women in Ulrich, L. T. *Well-behaved Women Seldom Make History*, New York: Knopf, 2007; Levin and Watson defended the absence of women from the law: Levin, C. and Watson, J. *Ambiguous Realities: Women in the Middle Ages and Renaissance*, Detroit: Wayne State University Press, 1987. The absence of women artists was noted by the *Guardian*, 27 March 2007. Abraham Mendelssohn predicted the importance of music for his son in preference to his daughter, cited by Diana Ambache in *Women of Note*, accessed: http://www.ambache.co.uk/; and the slow progress of the Vienna Philharmonic to gender-free hiring is demonstrated in Oxford University Press, *Timelines in music history: Women in music*, accessed: http://www.oxfordmusiconline.com/public/page/womentimeline. Virginia Woolf is a definitive author on these matters of creativity and the difficulties put in the path of women: Woolf, V. *A Room of One's Own*, London: Hogarth Press, 1929. E.H. Carr considers the creation of history but not the gender of the historian in Carr, E.H. *What Is History?* London: Macmillan; New York: St Martin's Press, 1961.

BIBLIOGRAPHY

Amt, E. *Women's Lives in Medieval Europe*, New York: Routledge, 1993

Baldwin, D. *Elizabeth Woodville: Mother of the Princes in the Tower*, Stroud: Sutton Publishing, 2002

Barnhouse, R. *The Book of the Knight of the Tower: Manners for Young Medieval Women*, Palgrave Macmillan, 2006

Bramley, P. *The Wars of the Roses: A Field Guide and Companion*, Stroud: Sutton Publishing, 2007

Carr, E.H. *What is History?* London: Macmillan; New York: St Martin's Press, 1961

Castor, H. *Blood & Roses: The Paston family and the Wars of the Roses*, London: Faber, 2004

Cheetham, A. *The Life and Times of Richard III*, London: Weidenfeld & Nicolson, 1972

Chrimes, S.B. *Lancastrians, Yorkists, and Henry VII*, London: Macmillan, 1964

Cooper, C.H. *Memoir of Margaret: Countess of Richmond and Derby*, Cambridge: Cambridge University Press, 1874

Denny, J. *Katherine Howard, A Tudor Conspiracy*, London: Portrait, 2005

Duggan, A.J. *Queens and Queenship in Medieval Europe*, Woodbridge: The Boydell Press, 1997

Field, P.J.C. *The Life and Times of Sir Thomas Malory*, Cambridge: D.S. Brewer, 1993

Freeman, J. 'Sorcery at court and manor: Margery Jourdemayne, the witch of Eye next Westminster', *Journal of Medieval History*, 30: 343–57, 2004

Godwin, W. *Lives of the necromancers: or, An account of the most eminent persons in successive ages, who have claimed for themselves, or to whom has been imputed by others, the exercise of magical power*, London: F.J. Mason, 1834

Goodman, A. *The Wars of the Roses: Military Activity and English Society, 1452–97*, London: Routledge & Kegan Paul, 1981

Goodman, A. *The Wars of the Roses: The Soldiers' Experience*, Stroud: Tempus, 2006

Gregory, P. *The Other Boleyn Girl*, London: HarperCollins, 2001

Gregory, P. *The Boleyn Inheritance*, London: HarperCollins, 2006

Griffiths, R.A. *The Reign of King Henry VI*, Stroud: Sutton, 1998

Grummitt, D. *The Calais Garrison, War and Military Service in England, 1436–1558*, Woodbridge: Boydell Press, 2008

Haswell, J. *The Ardent Queen: Margaret of Anjou and the Lancastrian Heritage*, London: Peter Davies, 1976

Hays, M. *Female Biography; or, Memoirs of Illustrious and Celebrated Women, of all ages and cultures*, facsimile reprint, 1803

Hicks, M.A. *Anne Neville, Queen to Richard III*, Stroud: Tempus, 2006

Hicks, M. *Warwick the Kingmaker*, London: Blackwell Publishing, 1998

Hipshon, D. *Richard III and the Death of Chivalry*, Stroud: The History Press, 2009

Hughes, J. *Arthurian Myths and Alchemy: The Kingship of Edward IV*, Stroud: Sutton Publishing, 2002

Jones, M.K. and Underwood, M.G. *The King's Mother; Lady Margaret Beaufort: Countess of Richmond and Derby*, Cambridge: Cambridge University Press, 1992

Karras, R.M. *Sexuality in Medieval Europe: Doing unto Others*, New York: Routledge, 2005

Kelly, J. *Women, History and Theory*, Chicago: University of Chicago Press, 1984

Lamont-Brown, R. 'Queen Victoria's "secret marriage"', *Contemporary Review*, December 2003

Laynesmith, J.L. *The Last Medieval Queens: English Queenship 1445–1503*, Oxford: Oxford University Press, 2004

Levin, C. & Watson, J. *Ambiguous Realities: Women in the Middle Ages and Renaissance*, Detroit: Wayne State University Press, 1987

Levine, N. 'The Case of Eleanor Cobham: Authorizing History in *2 Henry VI*', *Shakespeare Studies* 22: 104–21, 1994

Lewis, K., Menuge, N.J. and Phillips, K.M. *Young Medieval Women*, Stroud: Sutton Publishing, 1999

MacGibbon, D. *Elizabeth Woodville 1437–1492: Her Life and Times*, London: Arthur Baker, 1938

Martin, S. *Alchemy and the Alchemists*, London: Pocket Essentials, 2006

Maurer, E. *Margaret of Anjou: Queenship and Power in Late Medieval England*, Woodbridge: The Boydell Press, 2003

Neillands, R. *The Wars of the Roses*, London: Cassell, 1992

Newcomer, J. *The Grand Duchy of Luxembourg: The Evolution of Nationhood*, Luxembourg: Editions Emile Borschette, 1995

Péporté, P. *Constructing the Middle Ages. Historiography, Collective Memory and Nation Building in Luxembourg*, Leiden and Boston: Brill, 2011

Phillips, K.M. *Medieval Maidens: Young women and gender in England, 1270–1540*, Manchester University Press, 2003

Prestwich, M. *Plantagenet England 1225–1360*, Oxford: Clarendon Press, 2005

Ross, C.D. *Edward IV*, London: Eyre Methuen, 1974

Rowbotham, S. *Hidden from History: 300 years of women's oppression and the fight against it*, London: Pluto Press, 1973

Rubin, M. *The Hollow Crown: A History of Britain in the Late Middle Ages*, London: Allen Lane, 2005

Seward, D. *A Brief History of the Hundred Years War*, London: Constable, 1973

Simon, L. *Of Virtue Rare: Margaret Beaufort: Matriarch of the House of Tudor*, Boston: Houghton Mifflin, 1982

Starkey, D. *Six Wives, the Queens of Henry VIII*, London: Chatto & Windus, 2003

Storey, R.L. *The End of the House of Lancaster,* Stroud: Sutton Publishing, 1999

Thomas, K. *Religion and the Decline of Magic,* New York: Weidenfeld & Nicolson, 1971

Ulrich, L.T. *Well-behaved Women Seldom Make History,* New York: Knopf, 2007

Vergil, P. and Ellis, H. *Three Books of Polydore Vergil's English History Comprising the Reigns of Henry VI, Edward IV and Richard III,* Kessinger Publishing Legacy Reprint, 1971

Walker, J.M. *Dissing Elizabeth, Negative Representations of Gloriana,* London: Duke University Press, 1998

Ward, J. *Women in Medieval Europe 1200–1500,* Essex: Pearson Education, 2002

Warner, M. *Joan of Arc: the image of female heroism,* London: Weidenfeld and Nicolson, 1981

Weinberg, S.C. 'Caxton, Anthony Woodville and the Prologue to the "MorteDarthur"', *Studies in Philology,* Vol. 102, No. 1: 45–65, 2005

Weir, A. *The Six Wives of Henry VIII,* London: The Bodley Head, 1991

Weir, A. *Lancaster & York: The Wars of the Roses,* London: Cape, 1995

Williams, E.C. *My Lord of Bedford, 1389–1435: being a life of John of Lancaster, first Duke of Bedford, brother of Henry V and Regent of France,* London: Longmans, 1963

Wilson-Smith, T. *Joan of Arc: Maid, Myth and History,* Stroud: Sutton Publishing, 2006

Wolffe, B.P. *Henry VI,* London: Eyre Methuen, 2006

Woolf, V. *A Room of One's Own,* London: Hogarth Press, 1929

ONLINE SOURCES

English History, *Katherine Howard*: englishhistory.net/tudor/
monarchs/howard.html

Feldman, S. (2008) 'Gender traitors', *New Humanist*, Vol. 123,
No. 4, August: http://newhumanist.org.uk/1816/gender-traitors

Gale Group: Washington Monthly Company (1988) *Is Margaret
Thatcher a Woman? No woman is if she has to make it in a man's
world*: http://www.thefreelibrary.com/Is+Margaret+Thatcher+
a+woman%3F+No+woman+is+if+she+has+to+make+it+
in+a...-a06676349

Mendelssohn, A. cited by Diana Ambache in *Women of Note*:
http://www.ambache.co.uk/

Oxford University Press, *Timelines in music history: Women in music*:
http://www.oxfordmusiconline.com/public/page/womentimeline

JACQUETTA OF LUXEMBOURG

1415/16–1472

Philippa Gregory

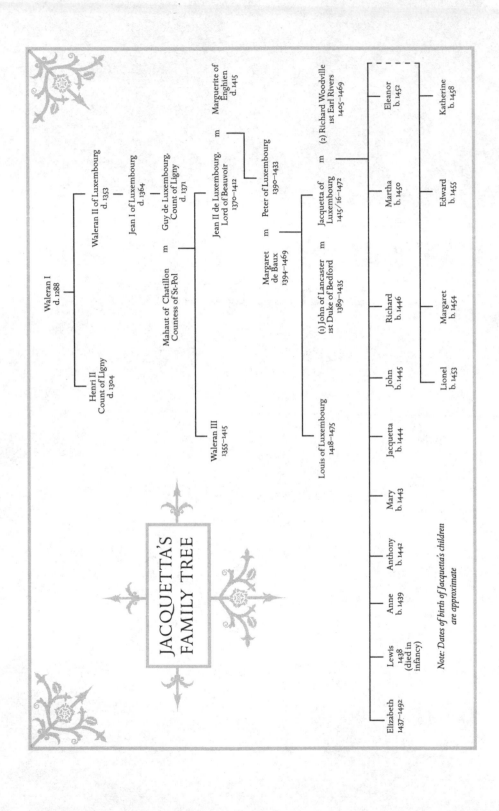

JACQUETTA'S FAMILY TREE

Waleran I
d. 1288

Henri II
Count of Ligny
d. 1304

Waleran II of Luxembourg
d. 1353

Jean I of Luxembourg
d. 1364

Guy de Luxembourg,
Count of Ligny
d. 1371

Mahaut of Chatillon m
Countess of St-Pol

Marguerite of
Enghien
d. 1415

Jean II de Luxembourg, m
Lord of Beauvoir
1370–1412

Waleran III
1355–1415

Margaret m Peter of Luxembourg
de Baux 1390–1433
1394–1469

Louis of Luxembourg
1418–1475

Jacquetta of m (1) John of Lancaster m (2) Richard Woodville
Luxembourg 1st Duke of Bedford 1st Earl Rivers
1415/16–1472 1389–1435 1405–1469

Elizabeth
1437–1492

Lewis
1438
(died in
infancy)

Anne
b. 1439

Anthony
b. 1442

Mary
b. 1443

Jacquetta
b. 1444

John
b. 1445

Richard
b. 1446

Martha
b. 1450

Eleanor
b. 1452

Lionel
b. 1453

Margaret
b. 1454

Edward
b. 1455

Katherine
b. 1458

Note: Dates of birth of Jacquetta's children
are approximate

CHILDHOOD

Jacquetta of Luxembourg was born, perhaps in one of her family's chateaux in France, probably in the year 1416. This uncertainty as to her date of birth is not uncommon for women of this period: none of the three women of this book had the date of their birth recorded. Girls were not valued in the fifteenth century, and nobody could have predicted that the oldest daughter of the heir of Luxembourg would be a leading English woman through two reigns and two regencies, a witness to some of the most significant events of two wars, the mother of a queen and the founder of a royal dynasty, and a powerful actor in her own right.

She was the second child born to a noble family, in a world that had been at war for so long that neither her father nor her grandfather had known a reliable peace. She spent her childhood in the beautiful castles and fortified chateaux of northern France, which then belonged to England.

The English had inherited northern France through the marriage of a French princess to England's King Edward II. But many of the French denied the right of a woman to inherit and argued that the throne should belong instead to the male heir of the junior royal family of France: the Valois. Hostilities started in 1337 and continued, with occasional periods of peace, for more than a century – earning the interminable battles the name 'the Hundred Years' War'. Although armies were small and battles had only a local impact, the entire

Medieval Luxembourg, as imagined in the nineteenth century

country was disrupted by the shifting borders, the assault on towns, the brigandage of the regular forces, the anarchy of the private armies, and the impoverishment of trade – all this amid the normal day-to-day lethal uncertainty of medieval life. The four-generations' war blighted the disputed territories and impoverished all of France.

It damaged England too. The overseas wars were an unbearably expensive drain on what was little more than a subsistence economy, distracted everyone from building prosperity and peace, and rewarded those who were opportunistic, militaristic, or even outright lawless. There was a constant sacrifice of life and fortune:

... close the wall up with our English dead!
In peace there's nothing so becomes a man

As modest stillness and humility;
But when the blast of war blows in our ears,
Then imitate the action of the tiger;
Stiffen the sinews, summon up the blood,
Disguise fair nature with hard-favour'd rage;
Then lend the eye a terrible aspect.

The time of Jacquetta's birth were the glory days for England as the young king, Henry V, invaded France in 1415 and won a tremendous victory at the battle of Agincourt, rolling out English power. The English and their allies occupied most of the northern half of the lands we now call France, including Paris. This was in addition to the traditional English holdings in the west of the country, around Bordeaux. These rich lands were the dowry of Eleanor of Aquitaine when she married Henry II of England, and a celebrated English possession for the previous 300 years.

Jacquetta's family, as counts of Luxembourg, were neighbours to France and vassals to the Duke of Burgundy. They had to choose sides in this conflict that had already absorbed the energies of England and France for seventy-eight years. Naturally enough, they chose to follow their ducal cousins to side with the English and feud against the Valois. Perhaps the Luxembourg family believed the English were morally right, perhaps they thought they would profit most from English neighbours, or perhaps the English simply looked like the stronger side and the safer bet.

In 1420 the French King Charles VI signed away the rights of his son Charles, and gave his daughter Catherine of Valois in marriage to the conquering Henry V of England, to seal the Treaty of Troyes. He made Henry V of England his heir, and the young English king, with a new-born son to follow him, must have thought that he had secured his lands

ENGLAND

Calais

Rouen   Rheims

Paris

Troyes

Dijon

Chinon   Nevers

French lands

English lands   FRANCE

Burgundian lands

Bordeaux

The lands of France in 1429

in France for ever. But, aged only thirty-four, he died of dysentery after laying siege to Meaux in 1422, and the English lands in France, and the claim to the entire kingdom, were inherited by a nine-month-old baby: Henry VI. The country faced a long regency headed by the baby's two uncles: Humphrey Duke of Gloucester, who ruled in

England; and John Duke of Bedford, who was Regent of France.

When Jacquetta was a little girl of six years old, her uncle Louis of Luxembourg was making his way from France to England to congratulate the baby boy who had so precociously inherited the throne of England and France. Louis de Luxembourg would go on to serve John Duke of Bedford as his chancellor for ten years from 1425–35, and was so reliable and trustworthy that Bedford named him as executor of his will.

While the infant Henry VI was in his nursery, his homeland of England was disrupted by the growing powers of the rival nobles who ruled their own lands, disregarding both the young king and the law. In France, the little king's inheritance was threatened by the French claimant: the disinherited Valois son Charles. Charles the Dauphin was an unpromising challenger to the regency of John Duke of Bedford. Named by his own mother as a bastard, disowned by his dead father, scarred by a terrible childhood, he was utterly baffled as to how he might win the kingdom that had been so abruptly given away to England.

The arrival of Joan of Arc at the court of Charles the Dauphin was an extraordinary opportunity for the French cause. Her visionary leadership identified him as God's choice for France, and led the demoralised French army to a string of victories in 1429. Her ambition was to drive the English utterly from the land. She even told them so, in a bold document in which she warned John Duke of Bedford to leave France or face the consequences: 'Surrender to The Maid sent hither, by God the King of Heaven, the keys of all the good towns you have taken and laid waste in France . . . If you do not, expect to hear tidings from the Maid who will shortly come upon you to your very great hurt.'

Claiming that she was inspired by the guidance of angels, riding under a banner of lilies, bearing a sword but never using it, the charismatic girl marched the French prince out of a sense of personal failure into Rheims Cathedral to be crowned and anointed with the sacred oil of the very first king of the Franks, Clovis. She led the French army up to the city walls of Paris and, if the Valois court had supported their heroine, she might have been completely victorious. The court's failure to exploit the fantastic power that Joan of Arc brought them may well have been because they feared – as the English were convinced – that Joan was a witch. Joan's claim to be guided by angels, her healing skills and her good luck were deeply suspicious qualities to her enemies; and even to those who followed her. In the story of Joan of Arc, which was a legend during Jacquetta's childhood and thereafter, Jacquetta would have seen that an exceptional woman attracts attention which can prove to be fatal.

It was another of Jacquetta's uncles – John of Luxembourg – who did the English a once-in-a-lifetime service when one of his vassals dragged Joan of Arc from her horse during a skirmish at nearby Compiègne and brought her in to John's castle at Beaurevoir near Cambrai. Louis, Jacquetta's brother, was staying at the castle, placed with his uncle to learn the ways of the world. John of Luxembourg's stepdaughter Jeanne de Bar was another guest. Jacquetta herself might have been there when Joan was brought in.

John held Joan of Arc for four months while his wife Jehanne de Bethune, his stepdaughter Jeanne de Bar and his great-aunt Jeanne the Demoiselle of Luxembourg pleaded with him not to release 'the Maid' to the English, foreseeing, quite rightly, that it would be to send her to her death. While the Demoiselle lived with her nephew, Joan of Arc was safe;

but when the old lady died in November 1430, John of Luxembourg accepted a fortune of 10,000 livres from the English, and defied the women of his household to send Joan to the Church. As they had feared, the English Regent of France, John Duke of Bedford, insisted on a show trial by the Church, and she was burned at the stake.

THE LUXEMBOURG INHERITANCE

Jacquetta's father, the Count of Conversano and Brienne, was the oldest of the anglophile brothers and so, on the death of the Demoiselle of Luxembourg, he inherited the title and became Count Peter I of Luxembourg and St Pol. The family was well connected in Europe: the Luxembourgs were of the royal family of Bohemia; Jacquetta's cousin was Sigismond, the Holy Roman Emperor. On her father's side she descended from Duke John II of Brittany. On her mother's side she descended from Simon de Montfort. Jacquetta could trace her ancestry back to English as well as European royalty. Indeed, she could go farther than this: her family could trace their line back through recorded history, into myth.

The family city of Luxembourg was founded around a castle developed from a Roman fort built on a rock called 'the Bock' dominating the roads and rivers between France, Germany and the Low Countries. It was famous as one of the most powerful and defensible castles in Europe. The Counts of Luxembourg traced their ancestry back to the first count, Siegfried, who bought the site of the castle in 963 and was said to have married the water goddess

Melusina. It was she who made the castle of Bock magically appear, the morning after her wedding. Their happy marriage lasted until Count Siegfried broke his vow of allowing her absolute privacy each month. Spying on her in her bath, he discovered that his wife was a magical being: half-woman, half-fish, something like a mermaid. He cried out in understandable shock, and Melusina and her bath immediately sank through the solid rock beneath the castle, and disappeared.

Jacquetta would have known of this legend, which is stated as an accepted fact in her family tree, occurs in many versions all across Europe, and was recognised by C.G. Jung as an archetypal myth. Melusina appears as a character in alchemy; she represents water and the moon, the female presence. In adult life Jacquetta owned a copy of a rare manuscript of the history of Melusina, her ancestress, and Melusina may have been a theme at her daughter Elizabeth's wedding, and at royal jousts. Whether Jacquetta regarded Melusina as a real ancestor or not, the metaphor was a deep and powerful one:

GLENDOWER: I can call spirits from the vasty deep.
HOTSPUR: Why, so can I, or so can any man;
    But will they come when you do call for them?

'Will they come when you do call for them?' is perhaps the very question that Jacquetta would have asked herself, that the English Regent of France, John Duke of Bedford, would have asked of her, and that subsequent generations, frightened and attracted by her reputation, would like to know.

FIRST MARRIAGE: ROYAL DUCHESS

Jacquetta may have spent only a little time in the city of Luxembourg. Her father inherited his title when she was a very young woman, at a time when most girls of her class were sent away to stay with noble relations as a sort of 'finishing school'. They would learn the skills and arts necessary for being a great lady by serving as companions or maids-in-waiting in other great houses under the discipline of the lady of the house. When she reached marriageable age, from fourteen years onward, Jacquetta's parents would have arranged a match for their daughter. No young woman of her class would have been allowed to choose her own husband; her preference would probably not even have been consulted. Marriage was designed to confirm an alliance, to consolidate lands, to earn a dowry and to create an heir. The notion of love was a matter for troubadour poetry, or for bawdy jokes; it was not considered a reason for marriage. Jacquetta's marriage was arranged unusually late, and it may have been one of passionate desire – at least on the side of her husband.

Her marriage was arranged by her uncle, the Chancellor Louis of Luxembourg, at the request of his great friend and patron, John Duke of Bedford. Bedford's first wife, Anne of Burgundy, had died of fever in November 1432 after a marriage that had lasted ten years. They too had married for dynastic reasons: their marriage confirmed the alliance between Burgundy and England, and throughout her life Anne was effective in maintaining the friendship of her brother the Duke of Burgundy, and the alliance between England and Burgundy which was essential to the balance of power that guaranteed English success against France. She seems to have been a woman of charm and energy, and generosity to the poor. Indeed, she caught the fatal fever after visiting the sick in the Hôtel-Dieu of Paris. Bedford stayed by her bedside during her illness and made a pilgrimage around the churches of Paris for her recovery. He could not save her. John Duke of Bedford, forty-three years old, weary after years of service in France, may perhaps have felt a great sense of loss and loneliness on the death of his wife. He was scandalously quick to seek comfort. Only five months after his loss he married Jacquetta – twenty-six years his junior. The marriage service was performed by her uncle, Bedford's chancellor and trusted friend Louis of Luxembourg, in his bishop's palace at Thérouanne.

The hugely powerful, enormously wealthy Duke of Burgundy, Bedford's former brother-in-law, was outraged that his sister's widower should re-marry in such a short time. The tradition was that mourning should last a full year – but John Duke of Bedford must have been planning the marriage to his new wife within weeks of burying his first. He had chosen a daughter of the vassal of Burgundy: a snub to the ducal House of Burgundy, and an ill-judged show of favouritism to the House of Luxembourg. It widened the breach between Burgundy and England that undermined the military alliance of the two great landholders in northern France. The alliance between them had held the French at bay: a split would endanger English dominance in France. Perhaps Bedford hoped that the alliance with Luxembourg would replace the alliance with Burgundy; but his hasty second marriage to the seventeen-year-old was regarded as an insult to his first wife and brought him neither territory, nor title, nor dowry. It jeopardised his life's work: English ownership of France. He must have been truly besotted.

Marriage to John Duke of Bedford made the young Jacquetta the first lady of France, and second only to the king's mother in England. It also brought her into immediate contact with the knife-edge politics of the long war. On his way to marry her, John Duke of Bedford paused in Calais to put down a mutiny in the garrison. The soldiers were complaining about arrears of pay. Usually such disputes ended peacefully with pardons and payment of back pay, but on this occasion the duke ordered the execution of four ringleaders. On the return journey, Bedford and his new wife called at the garrison to reinforce discipline. Bedford expelled eighty of the mutinous soldiers, who had to go home to England without any pay at all, and only then could the duke and his bride continue on to Paris.

Here, Jacquetta was to be the mistress of the beautiful palace of the Hôtel de Bourbon, near the royal palace of the Louvre. She saw the extreme contrasts of warring medieval France – the terrible poverty in the streets, where beggars died of hunger, and the luxury and wealth behind the palace walls. Within the palace there was perhaps even a laboratory for alchemy, the mystical science of the medieval period.

The study of alchemy had only been allowed in English lands under a royal licence since 1403, such was the fear and suspicion of this medieval 'science'. But the desperate need for gold had inspired a renewal of interest. One of the promises of alchemy is that the adept might learn how to make the 'philosopher's stone', a substance which refines base metal into gold. Alchemists believed that gold and other minerals were made slowly in the depths of the earth, and that this process could be speeded up, either by the flames of the forge or by the gentle heat of the water bath. John Duke of Bedford licensed alchemists in France to find the formula to make gold to pay his soldiers, and to find the other promised treasure of alchemy: the elixir that would prolong life – perhaps to eternity. Many of the great men of Europe, including Bedford's brother Humphrey Duke of Gloucester, explored alchemy – a form of study which would in time evolve, on the one hand, into modern sciences, and, on the other, into mysticism. But to the medieval mind there was no separation between art, spirituality, magic and the sciences; and the spirit of the alchemist was as much an ingredient as the liquids he or she learned to distil, the metals they forged and the elements they discovered. It was a spiritual exercise as well as a science, and it still has adepts today.

In her new home in Paris Jacquetta also found her husband's famous library: religious texts and thirteen precious volumes of stories about Arthur, the mystical King of England. These were hand-copied manuscripts, made before the invention of printing, of great beauty as well as great rarity. They were to be read not only as entertaining stories, but also as prophecies of the future of England, and as a rule book for the imaginary chivalric world which was a guiding light to every man of honour. They may have made troubling reading for the Regent of France, since the stories emphasised the need for a king to be balanced in his health and temperament. His physical well-being determined the health of his lands. In the medieval world view the state of the body reflected the soul of a man: a man who was physically strong and beautiful would have a beautiful soul. The health of the king reflected the health of the nation: a physically strong and beautiful king would rule over a healthy and fertile land.

As John would have known, there were already rumours that his young nephew the King of England was 'cold' and 'moist' – passive, and too easily influenced, a boy born under the sign of Luna, unlike his father Henry V, who had been 'hot' and 'dry', born under the sign of Mars: a fighting king.

Just two months after her whirlwind wedding, Jacquetta visited England with her husband and met this new royal kinsman, Henry VI. The country was in crisis: the French wars were ruinously expensive, the nobility of England were running their own lands almost independent of any central control, the young king showed no signs of being able to assume the regal power that was his by right, and the growing rivalry between the lords, exacerbated by his favouritism, was a danger to the stability of the Crown. The king was under the influence of two rival family members: his uncle Humphrey Duke of Gloucester, a most astute and determined politician; and his great-uncle Cardinal Henry Beaufort, the son of John of Gaunt and his mistress (and later wife) Katherine Swynford.

Bedford and his wife were greeted with the ritual and deference due to senior royals, and entered into this jockeying for power and influence at the court of the twelve-year-old boy king. It must have been an extraordinary moment for the young duchess when she made a state entry into London beside her husband, through cheering crowds, with pageants and poems to greet her along the way. At first the parliament was sceptical about the work of the French regency but when they came to understand that John Duke of Bedford had given selfless service in France, they rewarded him for his loyalty and gave him permission to retire.

At first it looked as if he might accept. The couple stayed in England for more than a year, and John Duke of Bedford was granted the wonderful Penshurst Place in Kent. Built in the previous century as an H-shaped medieval manor, Penshurst Place was originally designed as a show house by a wealthy London merchant. It featured a great central hall with a tiled floor and octagonal central hearth, faced by a raised dais for the dining table of the lord and his lady. Behind the dais rose a broad stair to the solar – the private rooms – with windows on three sides over the gardens, which were enclosed by a square of walls with towers at each corner. Bedford built a new wing, now called the Buckingham Building, and put his emblems – the falcon and the ibex – on the gables of the buildings to the west of the hall. He probably added the deep window splays, based on those he had admired at the papal palace at Avignon.

While they were in England – Bedford battling with his rivals on the royal council, and Jacquetta enjoying life at court and overseeing the building of their new English home – she received a message from Luxembourg. Her father had died, probably of the Black Death, a form of bubonic plague. He was only forty-three years old, and had been Count of Luxembourg for only three years.

The Black Death overshadowed Europe in this period, spreading along trade routes, killing more than a third, perhaps more than half, of the population of the continent. Every family lost a cousin, a brother, a daughter, a parent. Everyone paid the price of missing a family member who was earning money, planning the future, or embodying hope. From the poor, who could not get in the harvest or manage the animals, to the rich, who closed their castles in terror of the disease – and still died – the sickness swept through all Europe, destroying the culture with the people.

The death of Jacquetta's father shows why the disease was so feared: neither rank nor the privileges of wealth could protect someone from a disease that was a mystery to doctors. The disease probably started from the bite of an infected flea that, in turn, infected the lymph glands, which swelled to form hard boils called buboes. A high fever and aches and pains were often followed by death within the week. At a time when no one understood how disease was transmitted, the deaths seemed to occur at random. The name 'the Black Death' came not only from the darkened swellings on the patient, but also the intense dark despair throughout Europe in plague years, as the dead could not be buried, the crops could not be got in from the fields, and ordinary life broke down. A city such as Luxembourg, at a centre of trade routes, on pilgrimage paths, and with a number of public hospitals, was particularly vulnerable to the disease.

In July 1434 John Duke of Bedford decided that, despite his weariness and deteriorating health, he had to return to France. The commune of Paris begged for his help as law and order collapsed inside the city, and convoys of food could not get past the marauding soldiers of the French king. Accompanied by Jacquetta, he made the journey back to France, and returned to Paris for the feast of Christmas. Jacquetta's uncle, Louis of Luxembourg, was relieved to restore the power of acting governor to his master. Paris was practically besieged by lawless gangs of soldiers from both sides, and it was dangerous to go outside the city walls.

The fortunes of war were beginning to turn against the English and their allies, with advancing French troops and constant uprisings from the French peasantry. In spring 1435 Bedford and Jacquetta left for the safer city of English-held Rouen, and the duke struggled to keep the supply routes to Paris open from Normandy, though his health was failing as news arrived of new peace negotiations to be held at Arras.

The young French king, crowned by Joan of Arc, and now widely recognised as Charles VII of France, had consolidated the early gains and was now the rising power in the country. The quarrel between John Duke of Bedford and the Duke of Burgundy over Jacquetta was now proving very costly. The Duke of Burgundy abandoned his traditional alliance with

England, probably calculating that he could be more influential with the French king than the English one. The Treaty of Arras would mark his joining with France and the isolation of England. Without their powerful ally, the English were fatally weakened. John Duke of Bedford struggled to maintain English territories from his sickbed in his castle at Rouen.

He tried to fortify the Calais garrison by putting in a new lieutenant. He appointed Sir Richard Woodville, a thirty-year-old soldier who had made his reputation in the English army in Normandy, following his father into royal military service. As the Duke of Bedford's health failed, and he made his will, the young duchess and the young captain of the Calais garrison, Sir Richard Woodville, grew close. John Duke of Bedford, still working for his country, died on 14 September 1435. He was buried, at his request, in the English-held city of Rouen that he loved so well. There can have been no quarrel between him and his young wife for he made her his sole heir in his generous will which left her all his lands for life (excepting one estate) and also gave her his famous and treasured library including the romances of Camelot.

Jacquetta, now aged about nineteen, suddenly a wealthy widow, was still not free to do as she pleased. As a duchess of England her marriage was in the gift of the King of England, and Henry VI sent for her to return. She was granted her dower – a widow's pension – in February 1436 on condition that she did not marry without royal permission, so she can have been in no doubt that a marriage would be arranged by the king's council for her in the future. But Jacquetta was in love, and young, and determined.

Her lover Sir Richard Woodville held the garrison of Calais against an attack by Duke Philip the Good of Burgundy, who was now England's declared enemy. Woodville led the garrison through the siege and threw back the forces of Burgundy, but must have been deeply shocked, as was Jacquetta, when the English-held capital of Paris fell to the French.

SECOND MARRIAGE: LADY OF THE MANOR

There is no record of their wedding, but Sir Richard and the wealthy young widow travelled to England and confessed to their marriage in 1436 or early 1437. Indeed, they may even have been lovers earlier and only married when Jacquetta found she was pregnant. Jacquetta was ordered to pay a huge fine of £1,000; but she was forgiven by the king, and the young couple were officially pardoned in October 1437 in time for the birth of their first child, a girl. They called her Elizabeth and she was born sometime in the winter of 1437 or in 1438.

Jacquetta and her new husband Sir Richard probably divided their time between court and their country house, at Grafton, Northamptonshire. Richard Woodville's father already owned houses and land in Grafton and neighbouring parishes, and it is likely that the young couple set up home near him. The Woodville (or Wydeville) family had been living in the area since the early thirteenth century, probably as farming tenants of the wealthy de la Pole family, who owned the manor of Grafton. The Woodvilles would have regarded themselves as tenants and retainers of the de la Pole family: owing their lord their support in any disputes, bound to him by an almost feudal loyalty. Although they were not vassals in any legal sense, there still survived a system of patronage and protection in return for loyalty and support. Sir Richard also owed a sense of chivalric loyalty to Edmund Beaufort, the Duke of Somerset, who had earlier been his commander in Normandy, and appointed him as his deputy to the Calais garrison. William de la Pole Earl of Suffolk would owe the Woodville's 'good lordship': a share in his good fortune, and his protection. In 1440 William de la Pole sold the manor of Grafton to the young Sir Richard – a favour to the young couple – and made it possible for them to set themselves up as lords of their own manor.

With ownership of the manor and land came responsibility. Jacquetta would now find herself as a lady of the manor, partly responsible for farming the lands, supervising the tenants, maintaining law and order, paying taxes and collecting tolls, dispensing charity and supporting the Church. Jacquetta and Sir Richard would also have been responsible for the maintenance of local roads, and the honesty of local markets. When called upon by their lord they would be expected to recruit soldiers and go to war. When Sir Richard was absent, Jacquetta, like other medieval wives, would take on his duties, running the estate, managing the money, and commanding the workers.

As courtiers they played their role in the life of the court, taking part in its leisure, cultural and religious life, and serving as advisers and assistants to the king. In or around 1438 their first son was born. They named him Lewis, perhaps as a tribute to Jacquetta's illustrious Luxembourg uncle; but the little boy, like many medieval babies, did not survive. The infant mortality rate was more than 30 per cent. The loss of a child, though it may well have been deeply painful, could not have been unexpected. Jacquetta was a fertile woman and raised thirteen children to adulthood, but births were not always noted in this period, and the records are not clear as to the exact date of their births, nor of the siblings who did not survive.

Jacquetta's husband continued to serve as deputy commander of Calais, recruiting men and leading them in forays against France, which continued despite the treaty and other attempts at peace. He was away from home on military service in 1439 when Jacquetta went into confinement and gave birth to her second daughter, Anne, and then the young couple were reunited on his return.

News came from Europe. Jacquetta's brother, Louis, the new Count of Luxembourg, had married his uncle's stepdaughter, Jeanne de Bar, who had tried to defend Joan of Arc. Now Jacquetta's brother was turning his back on his family's traditional loyalty to England. Around 1440, perhaps to ensure that he received his inheritance of Luxembourg and Ligny from the French king, he joined Charles VII of France and later fought alongside him, against the English. This might have caused Jacquetta some embarrassment, but the long wars in France were teaching the gentry of England a hard lesson that they would soon learn: loyalty could not be taken for granted.

WITCHCRAFT

In 1441 the country was convulsed by a scandal that had particular resonance for Jacquetta. She still held the title of Dowager Duchess of Bedford, and would have known the only other royal duchess: Eleanor Cobham. Eleanor had met Humphrey Duke of Gloucester when he was a new husband, married recklessly for love to a foreign countess, Jacqueline of Hainault, who was in dispute with her family and her former husband, and locked in a war for her lands. Duke Humphrey was said to be equally in love with the Countess Jacqueline and with her lands in Hainault; but when Jacqueline came under siege from a coalition of her uncle and former husband, Humphrey Duke of Gloucester abandoned his wife, her lands and her cause, and went home to England with her lady-in-waiting, Eleanor.

In a dramatic act of faithlessness he had his marriage to Jacqueline declared invalid, and married Eleanor, leaving English foreign alliances in ruins, and his former wife Jacqueline without help. It was the scandal of Europe. As she had risen from such modest beginnings Eleanor, the new Duchess of Gloucester, attracted much criticism for her pride. When the king's mother died, and Jacquetta lost status by marrying Sir Richard, a simple knight, Eleanor became the first lady of England, her husband the king's only surviving uncle, and so first in line for the throne of England.

Duke Humphrey opposed the policy of his uncle Cardinal Henry Beaufort, who advised the king against military advances in France. Duke Humphrey claimed to rule England as regent during the minority of his nephew; but the cardinal was determined to reduce the duke's influence on his nephew the king, and set about undermining his reputation. The duke was a known scholar and practitioner of alchemy. But it was the easier target – an unpopular woman, his duchess – who came under attack.

Eleanor was accused of commissioning a horoscope that predicted ill health for the king. This alone was an act of treason, punishable by death; and worse was to follow. Her associate Roger Bolingbroke, a well-known astronomer and scholar, was probably tortured and pleaded guilty to the crime of sorcery, which he said he had undertaken at her command. He did penance before the court at matins 'placed upon a scaffold before the cross of St Paul, in a chair curiously painted, which was supposed to be one of his implements of necromancy and dressed in mystical attire'.

The scholar was exhibited, surrounded by the tools of his trade: equipment for divining, and an effigy. The effigy was said to be a wax model made in the shape of the king that would cause the king to waste away as it was slowly melted.

Another man, Thomas Southwell, Eleanor Cobham's personal physician, was found guilty of saying mass unlawfully – presumably as a spell rather than a religious service – with the aim of destroying the king. A woman known as 'The Witch of Eye', Margery Jourdemayne – a herbalist and wise woman consulted by many of the court – was accused of working with Eleanor and making a wax image of the king which was designed to cause his ill health and perhaps death.

The twenty-year-old king was deeply distressed by this attack on him by his own aunt, and the council was alarmed at evidence of active witchcraft in such high places. Their extreme concern has to be understood in the context of the times. Most people believed that such rituals were effective. What if there were many practising witches at court? What if Eleanor's spells were making the king ill? Alternative horoscopes were drawn up to show the king was well and strong, and all the conspirators were questioned; the men were probably tortured to confess.

Bolingbroke pleaded guilty and was hanged, drawn and quartered. Thomas Southwell was said to have died of sorrow in the Tower the night before his execution – he probably found some way to commit suicide. Margery Jourdemayne, lacking the friends or the influence to bring poison for a less agonising death, was burned as a witch at Smithfield, the meat market in London.

Eleanor confessed only to commissioning her own horoscope, and claimed that she had met with Margery

Jourdemayne for her own fertility treatment. But the king's council had no need to examine conflicting evidence to find a verdict. Eleanor did not receive a fair trial by her peers – indeed she was not tried at all. She was found guilty of treason by royal decree: a decree issued by the king, her young nephew. It was a verdict without a trial; as a woman accused of witchcraft, Eleanor could not hope for justice.

The problem of how to punish her was a difficult one for the royal council. In the end, they set her a penance of parading around the bounds of the City, wearing only her linen shift and carrying a lighted taper, a punishment more often used against women found guilty of sexual promiscuity. Sending her out before the citizens of London barefoot in her underwear, the council intended to publicly shame her. The council then ordered that she be imprisoned in the charge of Sir Thomas Stanley. Her husband, Humphrey Duke of Gloucester, declared that his marriage to her had been brought about by her seduction and sorcery; and the marriage was rendered null and void.

> Stand forth, Dame Eleanor Cobham, Gloucester's wife:
> In sight of God and us, your guilt is great:
> Receive the sentence of the law for sins
> Such as by God's book are adjudged to death.
> You four, from hence to prison back again;
> From thence unto the place of execution:
> The witch in Smithfield shall be burn'd to ashes,
> And you three shall be strangled on the gallows.
> You, madam, for you are more nobly born,
> Despoiled of your honour in your life,
> Shall, after three days' open penance done,
> Live in your country here in banishment,
> With Sir John Stanley, in the Isle of Man.

Eleanor lost her liberty, her husband, and her position at court on the basis of an allegation without evidence, without a trial, and died in prison aged about fifty-two in 1452 after ten long years of imprisonment, constantly watched to prevent her killing herself. Most of her final years were in Peel Castle on the Isle of Man, where even today there is a legend that the unhappy duchess haunts the stairs in the shape of a black dog.

The fate of the Duchess of Gloucester would have served as a stern warning to any woman; but especially to the only other royal duchess, Jacquetta. England, and indeed all of Europe, was a deeply superstitious and religious society, at this time on the brink of one of the panics about witchcraft and sorcery that periodically swept through Europe before the age of enlightenment in the eighteenth century. For people who suffered from natural disasters without under-standing the causes, who faced terrible diseases without effective medicine, the only explanation for catastrophic events was the supernatural. People hoping for good and bad outcomes invoked both religion and magic, sometimes inter-changeably. A miracle might save a sick child, a saint's help could be summoned by the right prayers, a young man might fall in love with the right spell, the plague might be called down on an enemy. The supernatural was daily observed in everyday life: when a blaspheming man fell from his horse, or milk refused to churn into butter, or a priest blessed a sickly child who then grew strong. People who had no understand-ing of science or medicine had to depend on magical explanations, or prayer or casting spells to try to control events. There were no clear distinctions between science, magic and religion. Witchcraft trials would dramatically increase throughout Europe in the next fifty years as the Pope's instructions in the form of papal bulls were issued against 'magicians, and diviners practising witchcraft'.

In another ominous change, suspicion was focused on women. In the two decades before Eleanor Cobham's trial twice as many women had been executed in Europe for witchcraft as men – 110 of them. It is easy now to see why women would come under suspicion. Any woman who was skilled in healing, or who was believed to be able to foretell the future, or ill-wish a victim – thus any woman who served as a midwife, a herbalist, a layer-out of the dead, a fortune teller or an adviser, or any woman who lived on the fringe of society, on the edge of the village, or who seemed to be outside convention or control – would be in danger of an accusation of witchcraft when the levels of public anxiety rose. Women, whose fertility was still a mystery to physicians, whose temperament was said to be changeable under the influence of the moon, easily tempted and easily led astray like Eve, were particularly vulnerable to accusations of meddling with magic, especially in pursuit of power denied to them by the laws of the land and Church. Deep fears about female sexuality and female ambition contributed to the climate of suspicion about women.

Superstition was part of everyday life in the castles as well as in the cottages. Noble women came under suspicion just like the women of the poor. Jacquetta knew that her behaviour would be scrutinised just like the other royal duchess's, and there were some disturbing similarities in their stories. Jacquetta, just like Eleanor, had been the surprising choice of a royal duke who appeared to have been 'enchanted' by her and married her against his best interests. Jacquetta's ancestor was known to be a water goddess: Melusina, who had also tempted a man into marriage against his mortal interests, and who had continued to commune with water throughout her marriage. Jacquetta's family's association with the spirit world was known to everyone: the goddess was named as the founder of her house, appearing on her family tree and in her family crest. In the small world of the royal court, Jacquetta would have known Eleanor Cobham's associates and might have been seen talking with them: Bolingbroke was a scholar in Eleanor's household; he may well have known Jacquetta's first husband, who had been a student of alchemy just like Eleanor's husband. Southwell was a priest at St Stephen's Chapel in Westminster, where Jacquetta may have attended the services. Margery Jourdemayne was a wise woman and herbalist who had many patrons at the Westminster court; she might even have advised Jacquetta among her other clients. If a witch-hunt were to start at court, Jacquetta would be one of the first suspects.

Perhaps Jacquetta thought that the charges were part of a plot against Eleanor and her husband: an attempt to destroy their influence on the young king. Jacquetta would have known that once sorcery or witchcraft was invoked, a woman could be slandered and destroyed with the most flimsy evidence. Dealing in magic was a charge almost impossible to disprove, since a denial, even a denial on sacred oath, was typical of a witch and evidence of guilt. On the other hand, no proof was necessary to support the charge: a single accusation by any man of importance – a priest or a lord – served as evidence of guilt. The case against Eleanor Duchess of Gloucester showed that the highest status in England was not enough to save a woman once she was named as a witch.

COUNTRY AND COURT

Jacquetta and her husband may have been glad to spend time in the country in 1441. Away from the dangerous and anxious court the young couple inherited more land at Grafton, including another house called 'The Bury', on the death of Richard Woodville's father. They conceived their first surviving son, Anthony Woodville, who was probably born in 1442, perhaps followed by two sisters, Mary and Jacquetta, in the two following years. Part of Jacquetta's story is of physical strength: she gave birth to fourteen children, perhaps more. She often had a new baby every year; there was no reliable contraception, which was, in any case, regarded as a sin. She may have completed her family after her last baby, Katherine Woodville in 1458, as a result of menopause, which could well have occurred for her at around forty years old.

Bad news came from Europe. Jacquetta's family's patron, Philip III Duke of Burgundy, captured the castle and the duchy of Luxembourg in 1443. The final heir to the imperial line of the Luxembourg family, Elizabeth of Gorlitz Duchess of Luxembourg, had made an agreement with him that he should have the duchy on her death, but the powerful Duke Philip decided not to wait. The members of the wider Luxembourg family were furious at this theft; but there was little they could do to defend their title against such a wealthy and powerful lord.

Jacquetta was pregnant again in 1444 with her son John when the peace treaty between France and England was sealed with the betrothal of a French princess to the young King of England. Charles VII of France did not betroth any of his own daughters to his traditional enemy, but offered the daughter of one of his vassals. The fourteen-year-old Princess Margaret of Anjou was accepted, and a party of English nobility set out from England to escort the young princess to her new country. They were led by the Woodvilles' landlord and patron William de la Pole, and his wife Alice – granddaughter of the poet Geoffrey Chaucer. With them went the senior courtiers to honour the princess, among them Jacquetta and her husband Sir Richard.

Jacquetta's younger sister Isabelle de St Pol had recently married Charles du Maine, Margaret of Anjou's uncle, so Jacquetta was able to greet the new Queen of England as a kinswoman, and the two young women became friends, sharing the experience of being foreign girls married into the English royal family. Margaret of Anjou chose Jacquetta to be one of her chief ladies-in-waiting, and the regular New Year gifts throughout her reign show the warmth and constancy of their relationship. It was Margaret's habit to pay the servants of her favourites a cash gift of 66/8d. each year, and Jacquetta's servants regularly received this from the queen. Based on her gift records, her two greatest favourites were the two women who greeted her when she was a young royal bride in France: Alice, wife of William de la Pole; and Jacquetta Woodville, the Dowager Duchess of Bedford.

The fifteen-year-old princess arrived in England to meet her sensitive husband, a young man raised as a scholar, inclined to a life of prayer, dominated by his advisers. The two most prominent of these were now his great-uncle Cardinal Beaufort, and the king's cousin, the 38-year-old Edmund Beaufort. The king's uncle Humphrey Duke of Gloucester, still under the shadow of suspicion, was increasingly marginalised. A new man of increasing importance in the king's council was the Woodvilles' lord William de la Pole, now Marquis of Suffolk. Margaret came to like and trust William de la Pole during their slow progress through France to England, and became close friends with his wife Alice. It became clear that he and Edmund Beaufort, the handsome but penniless Earl of Somerset, were working together to command the royal councils, excluding the good advice of other noblemen such as Richard Duke of York, a royal cousin whose long service and military success in France should have guaranteed him the respect of the court. However, since Richard Duke of York was the wealthiest nobleman in the country and an heir with royal blood, there were many who feared his power and influence, and were glad when de la Pole and Beaufort conspired to send him overseas to serve in Calais, and later to Ireland.

Margaret was determined to serve her French kinsman and king, Charles VII of France, and to see her father restored to his hereditary lands in Anjou that had been captured by the English. It did not take long before the English court and subjects started to murmur that she and William de la Pole were serving the cause of France and not of England. Jacquetta, as a lady at the queen's court, would have observed the growing friendship between the queen and William de la Pole, and would also have heard the ugly rumours which suggested a love affair between the fifteen-year-old bride and the 47-year-old courtier. This was the first gossip against Margaret that linked her supposed disloyalty as a queen of England to her alleged infidelity as a wife. Rumours like this were to spoil her relationship with the people of her new country. Jacquetta almost certainly would have warned Margaret that a prominent woman's reputation must be above slander; but the young queen was passionate in her loyalty to her friends and both she and her husband often chose badly. Jacquetta would have taken leave from court in 1445 for the birth of her son John, and the next year to give birth to Richard.

Meanwhile the rivalry between the king's advisers came to a head when the young king, warned by the rising man at court William de la Pole, became convinced that his uncle Humphrey Duke of Gloucester was planning to usurp his throne and assassinate him. In 1447 a parliament was summoned at Bury St Edmunds. When Humphrey of Gloucester arrived, he was put under arrest in his lodgings A few days later he was found dead.

It may well have been a heart attack but there were many who believed that he had been murdered. By the time the gossips got to work on the story, the 'good duke' Humphrey had been assassinated by a combination of plotters: William de la Pole, Queen Margaret, and – absurdly – Cardinal Beaufort, who was actually dying of old age, in his own bed, at the time.

The young King Henry VI was deeply in debt and yet still he recklessly distributed honours and favours, carving into Crown lands and giving away important posts with huge fees attached. His projects – King's College at Cambridge University, and Eton College near Windsor – were more costly than he could afford. William de la Pole was promoted again, from marquis to duke, and the favourite Edmund Beaufort Duke of Somerset was showered with gifts in an attempt to make his fortune rival that of the wealthiest man in England: Richard Duke of York.

The Woodville family benefited too. Sir Richard Woodville was offered promotion to the title of baron in May 1448 and had to choose his new family name. He took the name of 'Rivers' perhaps as a reference to the Redvers family whose griffin sergeant he added to his own coat of arms, or perhaps he was laying claim to the disused title of de Ripariis of Aungre. Perhaps it was a tribute to his wife's watery ancestry of Melusina. Either way, in the next reign it was the source of a great joke against the social climbing of the family, as Edward IV's official court fool declared that he could not walk dry-shod anywhere in England as the Rivers had 'been so high that I could hardly scrape through them'.

A mistimed, misguided, misdirected attack on Fougères in Brittany by the court favourite Edmund Beaufort Duke of

Somerset in 1449 broke the temporary peace between England and France and led to a counter-attack from the French. The English were miserably defeated and the country was appalled as the soldiers and refugees came streaming home. Hungry, defeated, unpaid and without compensation, bitterly critical of the government which had lost their lands, these refugees disrupted the country and blamed the king's council for the worst failure in the long years of warfare. Everything that the king's father, the heroic Henry V, had won, now seemed to be lost, and the young Queen Margaret was regarded as the child of the enemy and widely suspected of secretly working for them.

Her reputation was damaged again when her own father, René of Anjou, a vassal of France, marched against her subjects, laid siege to the great English capital of Rouen, and captured it from the English. For Jacquetta this must have been a particularly painful defeat. Rouen had been the jewel in the crown of the English possessions in France, and her first husband John Duke of Bedford had chosen to be buried in the cathedral there that he had richly endowed. Now his very grave and monument were in the hands of his lifelong enemy, and everything he had fought for was lost to the father of the young Queen of England.

Outraged by English defeats, the parliament charged William de la Pole with treason in 1450, accusing him of planning to marry his young son to his wealthy ward, the Lancastrian heiress Margaret Beaufort, and to seize the throne in their name. William de la Pole was indeed planning for the children's marriage, and a form of betrothal had already taken place; but he proudly denied the charges of a coup, and King Henry, prompted by Queen Margaret, over-ruled his own parliament, and allowed the royal favourite to flee the country for what they planned would be only a brief exile. But as the young royals celebrated their triumph over the parliament, the duke's ship was overtaken at sea by a mystery vessel, the duke kidnapped and cruelly beheaded with a rusty sword on a rocking boat. His body was thrown down on the sands of Dover beach, his head set on a stake. His wife Alice had to tell the queen of his death and young Margaret took to her rooms in the palace of Westminster, crying unstoppably for three days.

The fury and distress of the young royal couple at the murder of their friend and mentor led them to swear vengeance against the whole county of Kent. The sheriff of Kent, William Crowmer, and his father-in-law, the king's treasurer Lord Say, threatened to empty the county of people and turn it into 'a deer park'. But the declaration of vengeance only inspired a rebel who rose up in Kent and called for the reformation of the king's council. He was Jack Cade, also using the names Jack Amend-All and John Mortimer in a compliment to the family name of the absent and disregarded Richard Duke of York. He petitioned that the king should reclaim the royal lands that he had so readily given away; he should punish the kinsmen of William de la Pole for his crimes; he should take new councillors from among the traditional lords, especially the Duke of York; he should bring the alleged murderers of his uncle Humphrey Duke of Gloucester to trial (by which he meant Edmund Beaufort); he should punish those responsible for losing the lands in France (Edmund Beaufort again); he should end unfair taxation and dismiss corrupt officers of his household (probably Edmund Beaufort again) and dismiss those who were unjust or corrupt in the county of Kent. An army gathered around Cade, whose military skill and experience – perhaps learned as an English soldier in France – was powerfully demonstrated as he marched his men, including yeomen and gentry of the county, to face the royal army south of London.

Jacquetta and the queen probably watched King Henry put on his battle armour, and ride out of London at the head of a royal army to command the rebels to go home. The rebels retreated south into Kent pursued by a small detachment of the royal force, including Jacquetta's husband Lord Rivers and a young man, nineteen-year-old John Grey of Groby Hall. A skilled feint from Cade's army led the royal army into a trap and Cade won the first battle, killing two royal commanders and putting the troops to flight. Rivers and his young recruit Grey were lucky to get away with their lives. It was a dramatic defeat for royal power. Many soldiers of the king's army immediately deserted and joined Jack Cade, and more rebel volunteers came in from all the southern counties of England as the news of his victory spread. The men of Kent had started a popular uprising against royal tyranny.

After hesitating for a couple of days, Henry and the queen ignored the pleas of the Mayor of London, and abandoned the city to fend for itself, dashing a hundred miles north, to the fortified castle of Kenilworth, one of the safe royalist Lancaster-owned properties. The lords and nobility in fear of their lives, most probably with Jacquetta and her husband among them, piled into the most defensible place – the Tower of London – and prepared for a siege.

The rebels entered the city in triumph, Cade striking the London stone, a monument traditionally regarded as the heart of the city, and thus claiming ownership of the capital of England. The Mayor of London gave him the keys to the city and hosted a dinner for him. For a heady two days it looked like a victorious popular revolution. Cade, dressed in stolen armour and wearing the dead royal commander's spurs, demanded that the men who had sworn to destroy Kent be released to him, and the lords in the Tower meekly sent Lord Say and the sheriff of Kent out to certain death. Cade held a mock court and ordered their execution. Their severed heads were paraded on pikes in a triumphant march.

The city had so far supported the rebels; but when Cade's men started looting houses and businesses, the London merchants and apprentices counter-attacked; the royalist forces in the Tower, Sir Richard Woodville probably among them, came out and together they drove the rebels out of the city, over the bridge to the south of the river. There, they were issued with royal pardons in a transparent attempt to persuade them to go home. These pardons were not all honoured: Cade took his pardon in the name of Mortimer but was hunted down as Jack Cade and killed. The king returned from the country and personally supervised the trials and execution of more than thirty of the rebels: an inglorious end to his inglorious debut in arms.

THE COUSINS IN CONFLICT

Jack Cade was dead – betrayed by a king who did not keep his word – but Jack Cade's cause was not forgotten. Richard Duke of York used the rebellion as an instance of the failure of the king's council to keep the peace, adopted Cade's manifesto as his own programme of reform, and demanded admission to the king's council, and the arrest of Edmund

Beaufort Duke of Somerset. The queen personally defended the royal favourite and blocked his arrest. Now the two royal kinsmen – Edmund Beaufort Duke of Somerset of the House of Lancaster, and Richard Plantagenet Duke of York – were locked in a bitter rivalry to influence the king. The opposing cousins in the war that would be named after them – 'the cousins' war' – were identified. Later historians would give the battles the name of 'the Wars of the Roses' as York used a white rose as its emblem and Lancaster sometimes showed a red rose among its badges; but at the time, the people who marched in the ranks, and were summoned by their lords, called this 'the cousins' war': an argument inside a family, with all the bitterness of a family feud.

Matters came to a head when York landed from his post in Ireland, marched on London and walked, unannounced and uninvited, into the king's own rooms. His first demands were that his service to his country be recognised, and that he be consulted as to the governing of the country. Later he was to demand reforms, justice, and the impeachment of Edmund Beaufort Duke of Somerset for losing the lands in France and for failing in his duty to give good advice. But first York assured the king of his personal loyalty. There was no question yet of him wanting to be named as heir to the still-childless king.

It was a dramatic intervention; but it had almost no effect on the king and queen, so Richard Duke of York took his complaints to the parliament and started slowly to build up support as a reformer, calling for the impeachment of the royal favourite Edmund Beaufort Duke of Somerset, for his loss of English Normandy.

JACQUETTA POSTED TO PLYMOUTH

This victory of the French army against the English in Normandy meant that the French were now free to turn their attention to the rich lands of Gascony around Bordeaux, which the English had held for generations. This was the dowry of Eleanor of Aquitaine, the English heartland in France: everyone was clear that it must be defended. King Henry appointed Jacquetta's husband, Richard Woodville Lord Rivers, as seneschal of Gascony, and Jacquetta probably went with him to Plymouth as he mustered an army and the ships to transport it to Bordeaux. They would have planned to reinforce the English settlers in Bordeaux; they would have expected to live there as Lord and Lady of Gascony. In a life that had already had many changes, Jacquetta, who gave birth to Martha in 1450, must have prepared herself for new lands and a new position.

A fleet of eighty-six ships was commandeered, and an army of 4,000 men recruited that summer. But there were no funds to pay them. Richard Woodville Lord Rivers struggled to keep his fleet and his force together through the winter, receiving small payments from the king, who was forced to raise money from the clergy of Canterbury and the London customs, seize cargoes from the Genoese merchants and even sell jewels and plate to raise funds.

Lord Rivers struggled to keep his unpaid and unhappy force together and ready to embark. For a whole year, as his men stole and begged in Cornwall and Devon, Jacquetta's husband negotiated to hold his fleet and army together, and Jacquetta waited for the date of sailing. But in July 1451 the town of Bordeaux surrendered before the expedition to save it had even cast a rope or set a sail. For Richard Woodville and Jacquetta, whose early lives had been devoted to the holding of English lands in France, it must have been a bitter year of failure. They had waited at the dockside with their expeditionary force doing nothing, while the brave English citizens of Bordeaux had gone down fighting.

There was no time for regrets. The court's attention nervously shifted to the defence of English Calais, the last great English stronghold left in France, and Richard Woodville Lord Rivers was commanded to forget all about Bordeaux and his vigil in Plymouth, and instead go to Calais with a crack division of sixty lances and 530 archers. He was ordered to serve under the favourite Edmund Beaufort Duke of Somerset, trusted with the defence of England's last key possession in north France. Jacquetta, once again pregnant, must have feared for him as he set sail.

Though Henry VI of Lancaster was clearly unable to either maintain peace in England or guard English lands in France, this does not seem to have shaken the loyalty of Jacquetta and her husband to the Lancaster king and queen. They had seen at first hand his inability to raise funds or get things done, but – whatever criticisms they may have had of the king's rule in private – Jacquetta and her husband were still unswervingly faithful to him and to his House in public. This was the way of the medieval lords, who were just moving from a feudal society into one where loyalties could be negotiated. Both Jacquetta and Richard had been raised to respect the ruling House of Lancaster. Their landlord, William de la Pole Duke of Suffolk, had died in its service, Jacquetta had been married to one of the great men of the House, and Sir Richard had been born and bred to serve it. The couple were leaders at the court of the Lancaster king and queen, and had been well rewarded. They may have been devoted to the House of Lancaster without a moment of doubt; they may even have been on the defensive, believing, as the royal couple warned, that the Duke of York's call for reform was nothing more than cover for a treasonous plot against the rightful king.

THE MARRIAGE OF ELIZABETH

Certainly Jacquetta planned to keep her oldest daughter inside the House of Lancaster. In about 1452, the Rivers arranged the marriage of their oldest daughter Elizabeth – and they chose a Lancaster supporter for her husband. The match was made with Sir John Grey, the oldest son of Sir Edward Grey and his wife Lady Elizabeth Ferrers, who lived at Groby Hall, Leicestershire, and owned other houses and lands in the area. The Ferrers were great local landowners and the Greys could trace their line back to the Norman conquest. Their loyalty to the king and the House of Lancaster was proven. It was the young Sir John who had ridden out with Richard Woodville in the unsuccessful pursuit of Jack Cade in Kent. One of the Grey kinsman, Lord Grey of Ruthin, had murdered no less a person than the Speaker of Parliament as he was marching to support Richard Duke of York, the year before. This was an alliance between two staunch Lancastrian families. Elizabeth was aged fifteen, and her new husband was twenty. It was a good marriage for Jacquetta's daughter, putting her among the established aristocracy of England with a fortune safely based on widespread lands in their neighbouring county.

Leabharlanna Poiblí Chathair Bhaile Átha Cliath
Dublin City Public Libraries

Jacquetta and Richard had eight other children to dispose of, including a new-born girl Eleanor: it must have been a relief to know that the oldest was settled.

A SORT OF PEACE

Perhaps the country might be at peace, too? In February of this year Richard Duke of York had marched an army to the very gates of London and found the city barred to him on the orders of the king. He had hoped to propose himself as the king's heir, and to block the favourite Edmund Beaufort from the position; but he was unable to recruit support among the nobility. Instead, in a humiliating ceremony at St Paul's, Richard Duke of York was forced to repeat his oath of loyalty to the king, and promise never to raise an army against him again. In return the forgiving king issued a general pardon for all rebels.

Perhaps Henry's mildness could command England? Perhaps Henry could even conquer France. In the garrison town of Calais, Jacquetta's husband Richard Woodville Lord Rivers received orders to requisition all the ships and bring them to Sandwich to ferry an invading force over the sea to France, that was to be led by the king himself. Henry VI had decided that he was going to follow in his father's footsteps and invade France to reclaim the English lands around Calais. It would be typical of Richard Woodville Lord Rivers to put his fleet together in readiness for the king. At any rate we know that – typically of the king – the planned invasion never happened.

Instead Henry VI undertook another of his journeys around his kingdom, overseeing the trials of rebels against his rule. Kings of England traditionally lived in a travelling court, moving from one house to another to allow for cleaning, and to spread the burden of housing and feeding the court. In summer most kings travelled for the pleasure of hunting new areas, and to visit distant parts of the kingdom, demonstrating the majesty of the Crown. Henry VI used these progresses to enforce the law and to punish rebels. These tours of punishment, organised by the Duke of Somerset, were so successful in executing traitors that they were called the 'harvest of heads'. This tour, from spring to autumn 1452, took the court westwards, into Richard Duke of York's heartlands.

Travelling with the queen and the favourite Edmund Beaufort Duke of Somerset, the king personally supervised the trials and sentencing of men who lived in the areas loyal to Richard Duke of York and were accused of treason to the king. It was a strong implied criticism of the Duke of York, whose job it was to maintain the law in his domain. The king and court even stayed at Ludlow – Richard Duke of York's principal town – but snubbed him and his family by not visiting Ludlow Castle.

That year, 1452, the court celebrated Christmas at Greenwich near London, and Jacquetta and her husband were probably reunited as Sir Richard came home for the festivities in which the king's half-brothers Edmund and Jasper Tudor were knighted and made Earls of Richmond and Pembroke. These young men had emerged as the sons of a secret marriage made by the king's mother, Catherine of Valois, in the years of her widowhood after the death of Henry V. Jasper Tudor, the new Earl of Pembroke, received lands that had been confiscated from a York supporter; his brother, the new Earl of Richmond, would later be given the wardship of the fabulously wealthy Margaret Beaufort, with a view to marrying her and gaining her fortune. It must have seemed that the reign was finally becoming established. Treason had been rooted out over the previous summer, the rebels had been defeated, Richard Duke of York had been quiet under the snub to him and his house – and finally there was to be a new expedition against France, to regain the lands around Bordeaux, led by the veteran John Talbot Earl of Shrewsbury.

Better still, the court was delighted and relieved to learn in the spring of 1453 that at last Queen Margaret was pregnant, after seven years of barren marriage. Jacquetta, as one of the queen's ladies, would have been among the first to know the news; the king, one of the last. Usually a queen would tell her husband the good news in private, and then he would announce it to the wider world. Margaret of Anjou sent a formal message to Henry VI by his chamberlain and he replied with a gift to her and rewarded the messenger as well.

Jacquetta too was expecting another baby; this was probably the year that she gave birth to Lionel, perhaps joining the court on another summer progress to the troubled regions, trying rebels and enforcing the king's rule. But when they arrived at the royal hunting lodge in Wiltshire, they received terrible news from France. The veteran general John Talbot Earl of Shrewsbury, riding out for England at the age of sixty-five, had been wounded at Castillon outside Bordeaux and then cut to pieces by a battle axe; his son Lord Lisle died at his side. Talbot had fought for Henry VI's heroic father, he had fought alongside Jacquetta's husband the Duke of Bedford, he had been captured and released on parole by the French. The terms of his freedom were that he would not bear arms against the French again. Obedient to the rules of chivalry, which held that a knight's word of honour could not be broken, he had led the English troops into battle without carrying any weapon to defend himself. His death and the final, irretrievable loss of all the English lands around Bordeaux were a dreadful reflection on Henry VI, the defeated heir to the previous, more heroic, generation. The records say that the king took 'a sudden and thoughtless fright', complained of feeling sleepy, and went to bed early. In the morning he did not stir; he slipped into a catatonic state, and the court simply could not wake him.

THE FISHER KING

Margaret, seven months pregnant, and still only twenty-three years old, took the extraordinarily bold decision to conceal the fact that the King of England was incapable of speech, thought or even movement. Jacquetta would have been party to the secret as they moved the king from Wiltshire to Westminster and kept him in his rooms. He was passive and silent even when the queen and her advisers shouted at him and then tortured him with medieval cures. Doctors were called in secret and he was leeched, purged, sweated and chilled, but he showed no signs of recovery.

What was wrong with the king? Modern opinion suggests that he may have had some form of stroke from the shock of the news of Talbot's death and the defeat of England, or he may have inherited madness through his Valois mother, perhaps schizophrenic catatonia. Medieval medicine, based on the theory of 'humours', could offer no useful diagnosis or treatment. All they could do was to try to change his 'cold' and 'moist' temperament by heating him up through purging, bleeding, blistering and medicating. Queen Margaret personally hired alchemists, physicians and herbalists to try to restore him to full health.

Once the news leaked out from the small court circle, there was a storm of gossip and a whirlwind of claims that the king was sick as a result of magic and enchantment. On 12 July 1453, one man accused a group of Bristol merchants of bringing about the king's collapse by sorcery. Another man confessed to casting a spell over the king's cloak. Magical, mystical and metaphysical explanations were offered. The metaphor of a sick king became widespread in the culture. People referred to the myth of the Fisher King – a king whose weakness and sickness bled the kingdom of vigour, and who must be replaced by a healthy young champion who alone could heal the malaise of the kingdom. The Fisher King was a king so wounded that he was all-but dead, but he would not die and leave an heir. In the story, all he can do is go fishing, waiting for a saviour to arrive. This story was painfully close to the reality of the sleeping king and his unborn child and when disseminated in ballads, art and story-telling it would do much to encourage the House of York when the healthy and energetic Richard Duke of York was compared with the enfeebled king. Alchemical theories that spoke of the inevitable collapse of the old and the rise of the new were applied to the decline of Henry and the rise of his rival.

Margaret first took her all-but unconscious husband to Westminster Palace but soon realised that he had to be kept away from the noise of the city, and out of sight of gossips, and so moved him to Windsor Castle. She had to leave him there, in the hands of his physicians, to go into her confinement at Westminster. She was supported by her women, including Jacquetta, when she went into the shaded enclosed rooms at Westminster Palace that were traditional for the six-week royal confinement. During this time she could see no men, she had to be attended exclusively by women; even the visiting priest had to celebrate Mass behind a screen. In effect, the country was without any ruler as the king was asleep and the queen in confinement.

It must have been a long anxious wait: childbirth and the related infections and complications were a life-threatening experience, and this was Margaret's first pregnancy. No male physicians were allowed to examine the queen, whose body was almost sacred; but anyway male physicians had little knowledge. The midwives would have been experienced; but there was no science of gynaecology or paediatrics, and no awareness of hygiene or the transmission of infection. Jacquetta's own eleven births must have made her a leader among the women as they waited for the baby to come and prayed that the queen would survive and the king recover.

Though formally in seclusion Margaret knew that in the outside world the jockeying for position was still going on. In the absence of the king, Edmund Beaufort Duke of Somerset was dominating the councils of the lords, and excluding his rival Richard Duke of York. Richard in turn was still threatening to accuse Edmund of treason for the loss of the English lands in France. Even worse for the queen was her knowledge that, outside the hushed confinement chamber, her husband was slipping deeper and deeper into a death-like state. On 13 October 1453 she gave birth to the long-awaited son and heir and named him Edward. She must have wondered what his future would be.

To be established as a son and heir to the King of England, the baby had to be recognised by the king before a great council. Somerset called the lords together for the event; excluding the Duke of York. Though the queen was still in confinement, recovering from childbirth, the Duke of York's

89

wife, the redoubtable Cecily Neville, came into the confinement chamber to appeal to the queen for her husband's right to attend. The duchess's intrusion paid off, and her husband Richard Duke of York was present when the baby was taken up the river from Westminster to Windsor Castle to be presented to the king. It was a ceremony that must have given the ambitious duke yet more hope. The council travelled by barges upriver to the king's apartments at Windsor Castle and watched as the baby was placed in his arms – the king responded not at all.

To some people this suggested that the king was not the true father. They claimed that a true father would have woken at the sight of his new-born child. More seriously, it indicated that the baby could not be christened as Prince of Wales since he had not received the king's formal recognition as his son and heir. Usually, the king would recognise his son, present him to the nobility, and then the boy baby could go on to his christening and recognition as heir to the throne. In this situation, there was no constitutional precedent; nobody knew quite what should be done.

Despite all this, the queen boldly pressed ahead with the christening of her son, and nobody had the political force or the will to refuse her. Prince Edward was baptised in Westminster Abbey by the king's own confessor, Bishop William Waynflete. One of his godfathers, defiantly chosen by the queen herself, was Edmund Beaufort Duke of Somerset, fuelling gossip that suggested that the controversial court favourite might even be the baby's true father. Richard Neville, the Earl of Warwick, ally to Richard Duke of York, said in public that the baby was a bastard, palmed off on a torpid cuckold.

In November, Jacquetta was with the queen as she emerged for the great ceremony of 'churching': the new mother's purification and return to the outside world. Margaret came out of her confinement chamber to find York increasingly powerful in the Privy Council; so much so that he had gained a majority and was at last able formally to accuse Edmund Beaufort Duke of Somerset of treason. The lords who came to arrest Beaufort found him with the queen in her private rooms, seized him despite her protests, and took him to the Tower.

The king's illness could not be ignored for ever; the lords who were already in dispute about lands and power took the opportunity to pursue their quarrels without fear of royal intervention. The royal council still tried to behave as if it was reporting to the king, but now issued petitions in its own name. Christmas came and went and there was no king leading the festivities at court. In effect, England was without a king, and had been so for the best part of half a year, though nobody dared ask what was to be done.

Margaret, in defence of her little son and his father's throne, proposed herself as regent, demanding the power, privileges and income of the king. She had been raised by the mighty Yolande of Aragon and had seen the great women of her childhood running their countries when the lords were away. She thought that such an arrangement could be made in England. But, beyond the circle of her friends in the established court party, she gained very little support for the idea. Neither the country nor the parliament could forgive her French background, few people trusted her, and almost nobody wanted a woman running England. They can have been in no doubt that to make Margaret regent would be to release Edmund Beaufort from the Tower and to restore the full power of the Lancastrian party. In an atmosphere of gathering tension, with the lords bringing their private armies into the city and Edmund Beaufort Duke of Somerset ordering his friends and affinity to rent rooms around his prison in the Tower, presumably in preparation for a break-out, the death of the king's chancellor Cardinal Kemp in March 1454 meant that a new chancellor had to be appointed and new seals made. Only the king could make such an appointment. The king simply had to wake up and name a new chancellor.

Once again a delegation from the council went on the cold journey upriver to Windsor Castle to ask the mute king to nominate a new chancellor. Three times they asked him for a response – but, once again, he heard and said nothing.

YORK TAKES COMMAND

It was enough for everyone but the stubborn queen. Three days later, on 27 March 1454, the council admitted that they had to have a leader. Richard Duke of York was appointed protector and defender of the kingdom until the recovery of the king or the inheritance – fourteen long years ahead – of his baby son. One of York's first acts was to send the queen to Windsor Castle to join her husband and son, and suggest that they all stay there. The royal family was under house arrest, their favourite Somerset – charged with treason – was still imprisoned in the Tower, their adherents quietly removed from office: the Yorks were in power and they were ruling without a king.

For Jacquetta this was an uncomfortable and dangerous time. She was pregnant again this year with the baby she named Margaret, perhaps as a tribute towards her beleagured queen: the two women were all-but imprisoned together in Windsor Castle with a comatose king, a small prince and a diminished court. Jacquetta was parted from her husband: he was isolated overseas, left in command of Calais, still at his post throughout these changes, defending the greatest, indeed the last, English garrison in France. Richard Woodville Lord Rivers had been appointed by the king and Edmund Beaufort; and now the king was asleep and Edmund Beaufort imprisoned.

His situation grew even more perilous when Richard Duke of York appointed himself as Captain of Calais, in place of the imprisoned Edmund Beaufort Duke of Somerset, bringing the drama of the command of Calais to an absolute crisis point. As if this were not bad enough, parliament had once again failed to grant adequate funds to the garrison. Once again Richard Woodville was in command of unpaid soldiers and once again he had to cope with mutiny and rebellion. This time however, he had no superior officer, he had no king to invoke. The soldiers seized the goods and wool sacks of the English merchants and Richard Duke of York could do nothing from London. Richard Woodville had to allow the mutinous soldiers to sell their stolen goods and keep the profits of mutiny and theft. Indeed he may have done more. He may have encouraged, or even ordered, the mutiny in order to keep the garrison in the hands of the Lancastrian party, and to maintain his own independence from York. If he held the garrison in the name of the king he was obeying his duty to the king, and providing a valuable base for any counter-attack on York.

Viscount Bourchier, a York kinsman, had to resolve the stand-off by bringing the unpaid wages from London, with new orders that Rivers and his fellow-commander Lord Welles should remain in command of Calais, under the suspicious glare of the new Protector of England. The veiled enmity between the garrison and the man who now ruled England came to crisis point when York decided to enter his town of Calais and sailed from England. The garrison, commanded by

Jacquetta's husband, raised the chain across the harbour and prevented York from entering, as if he were an enemy vessel. In effect, they prepared the garrison for siege against its own official commander. It was a tremendous insult, it was open defiance; and it probably signalled the start of a secret campaign in support of the imprisoned Duke of Somerset. Richard Woodville may have been preparing an expedition to free his commander from the Tower of London. Certainly, Richard Duke of York must have feared that the Calais garrison, having resisted his arrival, might mount an invading force against England, release their commander Somerset from the Tower, free the queen and the prince, and make war on him.

But then, in December 1454, after nearly a year and a half of illness, to the ecstatic joy of the court party – the king recovered.

With the recovery of their king, the see-saw of politics threw the Lancastrian party as high as they had ever been. Richard Duke of York resigned his office, and his friends and kinsmen lost their posts as the king and queen returned their friends and favourites to power. Edmund Beaufort Duke of Somerset emerged triumphant from the Tower of London; the king declared him a loyal servant, and presented him with the keys to Calais in March 1455. For Jacquetta and her husband it must have been a great moment. Richard Woodville's command of his men and the famous Calais garrison's *esprit de corps* had held the town against the Yorkists, so that it could be returned in triumph to Edmund Beaufort and the Lancastrian party.

Richard Woodville probably came home from Calais for a visit to the triumphant court and conceived a new baby, born this year: Edward. The king confirmed Richard Woodville's captaincy of Calais, for later that year he returned to his post, once more holding the garrison town for his lord Somerset.

It must have been a great celebration for them all. Within two or three months the king and the queen had restored all their favourites and the old sense of uneasiness that the king was badly advised was justified once again by the new carving-up of the Yorkist lands and posts. Wavering supporters who had admired the good judgement and rule of Richard Duke of York, who had benefited under the protector's order, justice and peace, were alienated by this wholesale return of the House of Lancaster. These were men who were by nature royalists; but in the face of this wilful provocation they would feel driven to become the reluctant allies of Richard Duke of York.

THE COUSINS AT WAR

The king and queen announced that they were calling a great council to meet in the queen's favoured town of Leicester, in the heartlands of Lancastrian power – it was significant that they felt safer in the Midlands than in their own capital city of London. Pointedly, the Yorkist house and supporters were excluded from the council, and not invited to the meeting. Richard Duke of York, who had served so well as protector, resigning his power as agreed, was not even to be admitted to offer his advice in the royal council. York and his allies, suspecting that they were to be publicly humiliated again or worse, broke their oaths of loyalty to the king, and mustered their followers. The king's party demanded they lay down their arms; the Yorkists refused to do so unless they too were invited to the council. Jacquetta and the queen stayed in

Westminster as the king moved out of London and went slowly north, recruiting forces on his way to the council meeting at Leicester. York came south faster than anyone had expected and took up battle-ready positions around St Albans, a small town twenty-five miles north of London. Messages went to and fro and King Henry raised his banner, as if to prepare for battle, in the centre of the town.

It was all over within half an hour. Richard Duke of York led his men in a frontal assault against the royal army barriers which tried to hold him out of the town, while the forces of his ally, Richard Neville Earl of Warwick, fought from street to street, coming into the town by little lanes and through the gardens, surprising the royal army, who were not ready for battle, not yet armed as Warwick's men entered the town. The Earl of Warwick may have deliberately targeted Edmund Beaufort Duke of Somerset. The favoured duke was killed, trying to fight his way out of an inn where he had taken refuge. Shockingly, the king himself was abandoned by his personal guard and wounded by an arrow in his neck. Richard Duke of York found the royal banner propped against a wall and the wounded king in a tanner's shop having his neck bandaged. The Duke of York knelt, in a show of fealty, before the wounded king.

On hearing the alarming news of the defeat, the queen took her two-year-old son and, probably attended by Jacquetta, fled into the Tower of London and prepared for a siege. She was deeply distressed by the death of her dear friend Edmund Beaufort Duke of Somerset, and appalled at the thought that the Duke of York and his allies would now take control of the kingdom. She was right to fear them. They escorted the king to London, Richard Duke of York on his right hand, Richard Neville Earl of Salisbury on his left, Neville's son, the 27-year-old Richard Earl of Warwick, proudly leading the way, holding the king's sword. When they reached London everything was turned upside down again. Richard Duke of York seized the post of Constable of England, and Richard Neville, the Earl of Warwick, named himself as captain of the castle at Calais, where the garrison, still under the command of Richard Woodville Lord Rivers, promptly and courageously refused to admit him.

Jacquetta probably stayed with the queen when she came out of the Tower of London and had to obey the orders of Richard Duke of York. He sent her first to Windsor Castle, and then even further afield: twenty miles north of London, to Hertford Castle, with her son, Prince Edward, and the king. They would have observed that the king was shocked by his first violent taste of warfare and was becoming ill again. Three doctors attended him and he signed over his beloved colleges, Eton and King's Cambridge, as if he feared he could not continue to oversee them. The king attended the summer parliaments, though York suggested that the queen should stay out of London. She obeyed him and went to Greenwich Palace. Sometime this year Jacquetta probably left the troubled court to stay with her daughter Elizabeth as she gave birth to her first child, a boy: Thomas Grey. Jacquetta herself also had a baby boy this year – Edward Woodville – while her husband, far away over the narrow seas (the English Channel) still held the garrison of Calais for the defeated king, with little prospect of relief and no opportunity to come home. These must have been dark and frightening times for Jacquetta.

By November of 1455 the king was clearly once again too ill to govern and York was invited to be protector by a parliament that preferred a strong regent to a weak king in uncertain health, and was afraid of popular unrest in the country generally, and specifically riots in the West Country.

The queen requested that her husband be sent to her at Greenwich, and cared for him there, while creating a court party around herself and her son.

The king now experienced periods of good health interspersed with mental illness. He did not fall asleep again but he was depressed and quiet. He recovered enough in the spring of 1456 to end the protectorate but this time he did not replace the Duke of York's appointees with those of his own choosing, instead leaving them in place. Jacquetta's husband, Richard Woodville Lord Rivers, was finally released from his command of Calais when the king commanded that Warwick should be admitted as Captain of Calais, and those mutinous soldiers who had seized the merchants' stocks of wool and closed the door to the Yorkist lords should be pardoned. Apparently, the king had decided to rule alongside Richard Duke of York, and when a Scottish invasion threatened, it was Richard Duke of York who mustered arms and rode north as Henry's champion.

In the summer of 1456 the king and queen made a progress around the most staunchly loyal area of the country, the Midlands, and Jacquetta was among the ladies in attendance when they entered Coventry. Her husband, Sir Richard, safely returned from Calais, was probably with her, in attendance on the king. The queen requested that the city show her the honours due to a reigning king, and not those appropriate for a queen and consort. This was an extraordinary demand; and later historians would regard it as Margaret seeking inappropriate power and behaving in an 'unwomanly' manner. But at the time her favourite city did not refuse her, acknowledging her power and giving her a state entry suitable for a king. Jacquetta, in the train of her friend and queen, would have witnessed the extra honour that Margaret was now claiming as her due.

Coventry, the third city of England, was to become the new centre of government for a king who now spent much of his time on retreat in religious houses, and a queen who was openly disliked by the increasingly unruly capital city of London. No parliament was called in this period, and so no parliamentary taxes were levied; the royal household fell deeper into debt. Yorkist appointments were quietly replaced with the friends and supporters of the queen, and the king was widely regarded in the country as being 'simple-minded': under the control of his wife.

Matters deteriorated further in 1457 with the queen creating a network of adherents across the country, and putting her supporters into local-government posts while London suffered riots, pirates raided shipping in the Channel, and the French forayed into Kent under the leadership of the glamorous Pierre de Brézé, a known friend of the queen's. To add a sarcastic insult to injury the French force under de Brézé first plundered and burned the town of Sandwich and then played a game of tennis among the smouldering ruins before sailing for home. The king appeared powerless to defend his coast; indeed many people believed that the queen had summoned the raid. Those losing faith in the monarchy looked instead for protection to the Yorkist lord the Earl of Warwick to defend the English coast with his formidable fleet from his base at Calais.

JACQUETTA POSTED TO ROCHESTER

Richard Woodville Lord Rivers was among the noblemen summoned by the queen to defend the vulnerable south coast: he was made constable of Rochester Castle on the River Medway in November 1457, and Jacquetta went with him to live in the great Norman castle. It would have quickly become apparent to the couple that they were not there to defend the coast from attacks by the French, but to prepare to repel an invasion from Calais, from their fellow country-men led by the Yorkist commander the Earl of Warwick, who dominated the narrow seas, using the powerful base of Richard Woodville's former command: the fortress of Calais.

The king himself tried to end this stand-off, calling a great council which met in the tense city of London, ringed with 13,000 archers, in January 1458. His intention was to resolve the demands for vengeance by the young heirs of the Lancastrian lords killed at St Albans. They were so insistent that the Yorkist lords be held to account for the deaths of their fathers that there was a real danger that a series of blood feuds might develop. The lords called to account – the Duke of York, the Earl of Salisbury and the Earl of Warwick – came to London heavily armed and deeply suspicious. The Mayor and sheriffs of London armed themselves and patrolled the streets, trying to keep the angry retinues apart. Some believed that matters were so far gone that violence would break out when the two sides met at the council meeting.

Extraordinarily, the king – whose idea this was, whose sweetness of temper it reflected, whose trust in the funda-mental goodness of mankind was its inspiration – stayed away from the seething city until March, hoping that the council would meet and determine for itself what should be done. No friendly resolution emerged from this meeting of enemies until finally the king broke his self-imposed silence and proposed a financial settlement for those heirs who had lost their fathers, and a bond for the Yorkist lords to bind them over to keep the peace. York, Warwick and his father the Earl of Salisbury were also to pay for a chantry in memory of the dead of St Albans. The king then declared a 'Loveday' when there was to be a solemn procession to the cathedral of St Paul's with the warring cousins parading, arm in arm.

The young Duke of Somerset, injured at the first battle of St Albans, where his glamorous father Edmund Beaufort had been killed, walked hand in hand with the Earl of Salisbury. Behind them came the notoriously vindictive Duke of Exeter, hand in hand with the Earl of Warwick, the young commander at the battle whose guerrilla tactics had won the day and whose piracy still dominated the seas and Calais. Then came the king alone, crowned and robed, probably the only man with any genuine faith in the ceremony. Behind him came the queen, hand in hand with the man she now regarded as her bitter enemy: Richard Plantagenet Duke of York. Behind them came the courtiers, among them Jacquetta, probably pregnant with her last baby, Katherine. She walked beside her husband Lord Rivers, with as much faith in the parade as they could muster.

The symbolism of the procession is interesting. The king walked alone, above controversy, as he should always be. Next came the queen. Traditionally, she should have appeared walking alone, like the king, superior to faction. Alternatively she could have been shown walking at his side or just behind him, representing mercy: the queen's traditional role. But in this procession Margaret was not shown as acting like a queen; neither as an intercessor for pardon, nor as the neutral wife of the king, far above petty politics. Instead, she was shown as one of the combatants. She was publicly walking on the Lancastrian side. Though she was ostentatiously hand-fast with the Duke of York, symbolising their new-found friendship, her position publicly identified the two of them as former enemies. The procession was designed to show reconciliation and unity; but in fact it revealed some dangerous truths: that everyone knew exactly which side they were on, that they were prepared to line up to show it, and that the queen was on the side of Lancaster.

Within a few months she would demonstrate this. She accused Warwick of using the base of Calais as a home for piracy, especially against the German merchants of the Hanseatic League, who should have been protected by a treaty with England. She summoned the earl to London to stand trial. Warwick arrived with 600 retainers, all fully armed, and complained after only one day that the inquiry was inspired by the malice of the queen. A riot broke out in the London streets and the queen herself ordered pikemen into the city to restore order, which they did by attacking aldermen and citizens of London. A few months later, in the autumn, Warwick, walking through the royal kitchens, was accidentally stabbed by the end of a spit. A fight broke out in the grounds of the royal palace, between the royal household and Warwick's men, and the queen demanded that the council try him for treason and strip him of the captaincy of Calais. A kitchen boy was publicly accused of attempted murder, but then privately smuggled away, probably by agents of the queen. Jacquetta witnessed the queen descend from her role, which should have been far above faction, to become a participant in a brawl.

Boldly, Warwick refused to be dismissed from Calais by the royal council and instead demanded a ruling from the parliament that had appointed him to the captaincy. As he left the council chamber he was attacked by men in the liveries of the Duke of Somerset and the Earl of Wiltshire – a genuine assassination attempt this time, almost certainly ordered by the queen. Warwick fought his way out and withdrew to Calais to prepare to defend himself by arms if necessary, and the queen, probably accompanied by Jacquetta, left London to build up her support in the Lancastrian heartlands of the Midlands.

The Loveday would prove to be a tragic landmark. It was the last time the king commanded all his nobles to act in concert. The following year saw him either in retreat at abbeys, or under the influence of the queen, keeping a distance from London. The queen's enmity to the lords who had affiliated with Richard Duke of York was now explicit.

Margaret created a livery for her son the prince – the swan's badge, the traditional insignia for the House of Lancaster. It was based on the mythical story of a magical woman who marries a man and gives him beautiful sons who each wear a collar of gold around their throats. Her spiteful mother-in-law replaces the children with dogs and the husband blames his wife for losing the children; but in fact she has changed them for their own safety into swans who can be identified from the wild flock by their gold collars. At the end of the story all their sons return to them but for one prince who stays as a gold-collared swan. The legend was rewritten as the story of the Swan Knight in the Camelot legends. Margaret was invoking ancient myth as part of building loyalty to her son. At a metaphorical level perhaps she was also seeing herself as the mysterious woman (like Melusina) who comes into the world of men, and whose son is in danger and whose place in the world is challenged.

She took this promotion of her son to the extreme when she publicly suggested that he should be made king, and his father, Henry VI, abdicate. Although some lords supported this suggestion the king refused to abdicate his throne; but other than this defence of his position, he took very little part in the deteriorating circumstances, spending much of the autumn on religious retreat. In his absence, the queen maintained her own household, and Jacquetta would have served her through the anxious days of the spring of 1459. Some historians describe a queen intent on seizing power; Jacquetta may have seen a woman quite alone, not yet thirty, struggling to rule over a divided country, with no authority and little support, trying to preserve the safety and inheritance of her son, with a husband increasingly absent in mind and sometimes in body.

BLORE HEATH AND LUDLOW: DEFEAT AND VICTORY

Margaret summoned the gentry of England, in the name of the king, to arm and meet in Coventry in June 1459. The queen brought the five-year-old Prince Edward to the meeting as an emblem of the future, and accused the absent Yorkist lords of treason. The Yorkist allies, hearing this, agreed that they must arm to defend themselves. Richard Neville Earl of Warwick crossed the narrow seas from Calais, his father the Earl of Salisbury marched south with his army from the family castle at Middleham, planning to meet Richard Plantagenet Duke of York at his home at Ludlow Castle in the west of England. The queen, probably with Jacquetta in attendance, was staying at Eccleshall Castle, with her own army. She ordered James Touchet Lord Audley to command the royal army in the name of Prince Edward and to intercept the Earl of Salisbury as he marched south-west towards York's castle at Ludlow. Lord Thomas Stanley volunteered to lead the Lancastrian army but was ordered to join Lord Audley's force. Instead he sent promises – this was not the last time that

Stanley would prefer being on standby to being in action – but his brother William Stanley actually joined the other side, the Yorkists, serving with the Earl of Salisbury.

Jacquetta and the queen watched the Lancastrian Lord Audley's force – of about 10,000 men, including powerful cavalry – march out to catch the Earl of Salisbury's men as they emerged from thick woodland near the village of Blore Heath on 23 September 1459 just after midday. It is likely that Jacquetta's husband Richard Woodville was among them, drawn up on the heath, waiting for the far smaller force to emerge from the woods. The Yorkist soldiers must have been appalled when they saw the force waiting before them: they were outnumbered by two or three to one. The legend says that they kissed the ground as their deathbed and formed a line on a hill behind a little brook. It was an inadequate defence but they were able to use their archery against the Lancastrian cavalry, who had to cross the water and ride uphill into the withering fire of experienced archers. The fighting lasted for about four hours, until dusk; amazingly it went the way of the Yorkist force. About 3,000 men were killed, perhaps as many as 2,000 Lancastrian soldiers, including their commander Lord Audley. The battle ended as the Lancastrians fled from the field. The queen, perhaps with Jacquetta in attendance, is said to have climbed the spire at Mucklestone church to watch the defeat, and – again according to local legend – was so frightened that she paid the village blacksmith to reverse the shoes on her horse so that the Earl of Salisbury could not order scouts to track and capture her as she fled from the scene.

Lucky once more, Lord Rivers probably with his son-in-law John Grey and his son Anthony survived the battle; but they must have been shaken by the defeat. The victorious Earl of Salisbury marched on to meet with his son Richard Neville Earl of Warwick, and his brother-in-law Richard Duke of

York, at Worcester. They were now convinced of the enmity of the queen and the court party, and agreed that they must free the king from his aggressive advisers. In public statements they blamed the Earls of Shrewsbury and Wiltshire, and Viscount Beaumont, avoiding any direct attack on the king or queen. The Yorkist lords met at Worcester and swore loyalty to each other and to their king in a solemn mass in the cathedral; a copy of their written oath of brotherhood to each other and loyalty to the king was taken to Henry VI by the prior of the cathedral. When no reply came from the king, they believed that they had no choice but to defend themselves with arms and they withdrew to the fortified headquarters of the Duke of York, his principal home, Ludlow Castle.

The royal army pursued them, headed by the king and queen, to Ludlow, where battle lines were drawn up on either side of the River Teme, which curls like a protective moat around the town. The king flew his royal standard outside the Duke of York's town, and offered a pardon to any man deserting the Yorkist lords. It was too tempting an offer for the 600 soldiers from Calais who had served under Richard Woodville and the late Duke of Somerset of the House of Lancaster; they had followed their new garrison commander so far, but had not expected to make war on the king himself. With their commander Sir Andrew Trollope, they deserted to the Lancastrian side and took the Yorkist battle plans with them. Trollope's former captain Richard Woodville would have welcomed him to the king's army.

Once again, the Yorkist lords faced a battlefield where they would be heavily outnumbered – historians think the royal army was more than 40,000-strong; the Yorkists had probably no more than 20,000 – but this time they avoided battle. The three lords slipped away overnight: the Earls of Warwick and Salisbury went to their safe haven of Calais, taking the

Duke of York's young son Edward Earl of March with them. They were ferried across the narrow seas by Sir John Dynham, a Devon man who would serve the Yorkist cause again. Richard Duke of York slipped away to his post in Ireland, abandoning his men, his town and even his wife and younger children, who were left to face the royal army as it poured into the town, ready to loot, drink and run riot.

According to the tradition, Cecily Neville Duchess of York had to wait for the enemy at the centre of the town, under the market cross, with her children: thirteen-year-old Margaret, eleven-year-old George, and seven-year-old Richard. It must have been a terrifying experience for the children, as the ill-disciplined royal army burst into the town and set about looting goods and raping women. This was the first sight of war for the seven-year-old Richard, who would go on to command two pitched battles in this war but never again experience defeat until he went down into the mud of Bosworth.

The battle had been won by the king and queen; but in allowing Richard Duke of York to escape to Ireland, and the Earls of Warwick and Salisbury and the young Edward Earl of March to get to Calais, they had left England in danger of attack both from the south across the English Channel and from the west across the Irish Sea. Their next urgent task must be to dislodge Warwick from Calais and defend the south coast.

JACQUETTA KIDNAPPED

The young Duke of Somerset was sent to Calais to expel Warwick, which he failed to do; the garrison was now loyal to its new commander and supporting the cause of the Yorkists. Instead Somerset occupied the nearby castle of Guisnes. Lord Rivers with his wife Jacquetta and their seventeen-year-old son Anthony Woodville were sent to reinforce the port of Sandwich and raise an expedition to support Somerset in the recapture of their old garrison. Rivers set about the task of repairing the defences of Sandwich and raising men. But in a cold January dawn, Warwick's captain Sir John Dynham, who could handle a ship in winter seas, came out of the darkness with a raiding force of 800 men, landed at Sandwich and marched into the town. The alarm was sounded and Richard and Jacquetta abruptly woken. Richard came dashing out of his house, his breastplate under his arm, and was captured by the Yorkist soldiers. Jacquetta was taken too, and their son Anthony Woodville – riding to his parents' help from the nearby castle of Richborough – was seized, and the three of them were bundled on board ship and taken back to Calais in triumph. The Yorkists regarded the capture as a good joke: 'Rivers was commanded to have landed at Calais by the king, but he was brought there sooner than he liked . . .'

They were held outside the town until evening, so that the citizens and soldiers of Calais should not protest against the capture of their former commander, and when night fell they were taken, under cover of darkness, into the great hall of Calais Castle to stand before the Earls of Warwick and Salisbury and the young Edward Earl of March. It seems as if Jacquetta's husband protested fiercely at their capture, accusing the Yorkist lords of treason, and the Yorkist lords were angry in reply:

My Lord Rivers was brought to Calais, and before the lords with eight score torches, and there my lord of Salisbury rated him, calling him knave's son that he should be so rude to call him and these other lords traitors, for they shall be found the King's true liege men when he should be found a traitor, etc. And my lord of Warwick rated him and said that his father was but a squire and brought up with King Henry the Vth and sees himself made by marriage and also made lord, and that it was not his part to have such language of lords being of the King's blood. And my lord of March rated him in like wise.

What Jacquetta, a dowager duchess of England, must have felt, as she and her seventeen-year-old son listened to her husband being abused for social climbing by marriage to her, can perhaps be imagined. To be insulted by Edward Earl of March, a young man only the same age as their son, must have been particularly galling. However, the Rivers were lucky to escape with nothing worse than insults. A later raid on Sandwich in June saw the Captain of Sandwich kidnapped to the Rysbank Tower in Calais, and beheaded.

Unlike him, the Rivers were spared. Jacquetta was sent home to England within a few weeks, but Lord Rivers and his son Anthony were held as prisoners in the castle he used to command for six long months, until the invasion of England by the Yorkist lords in June 1460, when they were released.

Meanwhile in England, the royal court, fortifying Kenilworth with cannon recklessly stripped from the Tower of London, and calling up reserves, could not inspire a disaffected country to resist the Yorkist invasion. The Kentish towns opened their gates to the Earl of Warwick's small force of about 2,000 men, and some of the royal party changed their allegiance as the earl started a triumphant recruiting march on London. The city gates were thrown open to him; only the Tower held out under a Lancastrian commander, and there were Londoners who remarked that they would have preferred not to experience this troublesome token of support from the Lancastrians. The Earl of Salisbury stayed in London to lay siege to the Tower while the Earl of Warwick and Edward Earl of March went directly north to meet the king, recruiting as they went, publicly declaring that they only wanted to set their grievances before the king, invoking the help of the Church and Commons, and naming the king's bad advisers. Probably, they had agreed to capture the king and separate him from his wife and court, thinking that they could rule England through him. Perhaps they even considered putting Richard Duke of York on the throne in his place.

The royal army, of about 10–15,000 men, dug in before the River Nene, outside the Abbey of Delapré, Northampton, just eight miles from the Rivers' home at Grafton. It was a well-fortified position with a water-filled ditch protected with sharpened staves before them, and field artillery drawn up to protect the men-at-arms. They were commanded by the Duke of Buckingham, the king was nearby, and the queen and the prince were in Eccleshall Castle once more, awaiting results. Jacquetta was probably with them. It would have been an anxious time for her; she probably did not know if her husband and son were alive or dead, or still imprisoned at Calais.

As soon as the Yorkist force, now an impressive 20,000-plus, came up, the Earl of Warwick sent two messages to the king, asking for parley. The Duke of Buckingham blocked these, so that no concessions could be made by the merciful king. Forced into fighting, without a chance to negotiate, the earl ordered his forces into three contingents or 'battles', put himself in the centre, and – with eighteen-year-old Edward Earl of March and Lord Fauconberg on either side – prepared to advance and sent the dramatic message: 'At 2 o'clock I will speak with the King or I will die.'

Steady rain had turned the water-meadows into sodden ground, and soaked the powder of the Lancaster cannon, rendering them useless. The Lancastrian opening volleys of arrows caused no damage, and the Yorkists trudged through the mud to engage in hand-to-hand fighting, which made almost no progress until Lord Grey of Ruthin, the kinsman of Elizabeth Woodville's husband Sir John Grey, suddenly turned traitor against his king. He heaved the young Earl of March over the barrier, commanded his men that they were now fighting for York, and the two troops, working together, fought their way inside the Lancastrian defences. The battle was over in an hour, with no prisoners taken and no ransoms offered – a new standard of ruthlessness for these battles, which now departed from any pretence to the ideals of chivalry. About 400 men were killed, including four Lancastrian lords who may have died trying to help the king escape. They died in vain: the king was found by a Yorkist archer, praying in his tent, and the three Yorkist lords once again knelt to him in their victory and did him homage; and then took him with them to London.

As soon as the queen had news of the catastrophic defeat she took her son and rode to the protection of Jasper Tudor in Wales. Quite unprotected on her journey, she was robbed by her own attendants on the way; but after days of travel she got behind the grey stone walls of Denbigh Castle, and planned her escape to Scotland, seeking the help of the widow of James II of Scotland, Margaret of Gueldres. Jacquetta almost certainly made her own way to her nearby home and prayed for the safe return of her husband and son. When Sir Richard and Anthony finally arrived, they probably thought it best to stay quietly at their home at Grafton. Their queen and prince were plotting in Scotland, their king was held by the Yorkist lords, and the Duke of York was on the march, coming from Ireland. Even the city of London was a dangerous place: the Lancastrian lords still held out in the

Tower, bombarding their fellow citizens, and irritating them so much that most Londoners wished a speedy victory to the Yorkists laying siege to the Tower. Finally, the Lancastrian defence collapsed and they fled, their commander Lord Scales among them, to be killed by Londoners.

A purge of Lancastrian officials followed the victory of the Yorkist commanders. Lancastrian supporters were dismissed from the king's service and replaced by men loyal to York. The Duke of Somerset surrendered the castle of Guisnes outside Calais. The king himself went on pilgrimage to Canterbury in August, and when in London seems to have lived quietly under the control of the Earl of Warwick; a contemporary observer described him as 'more timorous than a woman, utterly devoid of wit or spirit'.

There is no record of the Rivers family in October 1460 when Richard Duke of York, arriving from Ireland, astounded everyone by entering London to the sound of his own trumpets, his sword carried before him, claimed the throne of England as his own, by descent from Edward III through his third son Lionel Duke of Clarence, and went to the royal palace of Westminster and occupied the royal apartments. Perhaps we can speculate that the Rivers were at home in Grafton, appalled by events, keeping their heads down and wondering how to serve a king who was in the keeping of his treasonous kinsman, and a queen who was far away.

King Henry nervously stayed in the rooms traditionally allotted to the queen and avoided his self-aggrandising cousin whenever they might have met in the labyrinthine corridors of Westminster. If Jacquetta and her husband were at Grafton they would have heard of the astounding settlement that York reached with the lords and with King Henry in October. After weeks of investigation into his claim to be the true heir to the throne, an agreement was made: York was to serve as protector of the realm as he had done during the king's illness, and he was to be heir to the throne, succeeding on the death of the king. In the meantime he could collect fees on the assets of the heir to the throne, as if he were Prince of Wales, Duke of Cornwall and Earl of Chester; and all royal officials were to obey him as if he were king. Fundamentally, it was a total coup. Richard Duke of York would be served as the king and would be regarded as prince and heir.

For the Woodville family, as for the rest of the kingdom, this must have been unthinkable. The kingship of England was not elective, it was hereditary – though sometimes won by force of arms. Richard Duke of York's claim to the throne might be as strong as that of his cousin Henry of Lancaster, but he had never promoted it before, and indeed he had sworn fealty more than once to Henry as King of England. In these new circumstances what was to happen to the queen? Was she to be deposed on the death of her husband? And who could doubt for a moment that she would fight to defend the inheritance of her son?

Jacquetta, who knew Margaret so intimately after fifteen years of friendship and service, would have foreseen that the queen would do anything to defend her own power and her only son's inheritance. His very title was threatened by the settlement: was young Edward not to be called Prince of Wales any more? Jacquetta, waiting in Grafton, must have predicted with some confidence what would happen next.

Margaret made reckless agreements with the Scots, which included the surrender of Berwick-upon-Tweed, and the betrothal of her son the prince to one of the Scots princesses, in return for military support; then she marched in December at the head of this new army, south to meet the

Lancastrian lords of Somerset and Devon and the commander from Calais, Sir Andrew Trollope, at Hull. Sir Richard Woodville Lord Rivers and his son Anthony almost certainly joined their peers at Hull in the queen's army. Jacquetta probably went too, to serve the queen as she returned to England. At the city of York, Margaret declared her defiance to Richard Duke of York, and challenged him to settle the succession by force of arms. Replying to the challenge, Richard Duke of York and the Earl of Salisbury left Salisbury's son the Earl of Warwick to guard London, and marched north, as representatives of the new royal power, to confront the queen's army, as soon as Christmas was over.

The Duke of York had planned to spend the time of Christmas truce in his castle at Sandal, but came out to confront the strong Lancastrian force and joined battle. Some accounts suggest he was lured from his stronghold by a mock attack and retreat, others that his men were ill-disciplined and away from the castle when it was attacked, or a truce may have been in force which the Lancastrians dishonoured. In any case, it was a grave error for the duke and it brought a punishing defeat. York was killed in the battle, as was his second son Edmund of Rutland – his favourite son, whom he had kept at his side through the difficult months. Salisbury's own fourth son, Sir Thomas Neville, died on the field, and Salisbury himself was killed the next day at Pontefract: 'The common people of the country, which loved him not, took him out of the castle by violence and smote off his head.'

York's corpse was beheaded, and the head, crowned with paper, was spiked beside his son Edmund's severed head, over the Micklegate Bar at York: a traitor's end and a paper crown for a man who had been a king only on paper. York's eldest son and heir, Edward Earl of March, learned of the death of his father as he was marching on the town of Shrewsbury, intending to prevent the Lancastrian forces led by the loyal Jasper Tudor from joining the queen. It must have been a very daunting moment for the eighteen-year-old. His father's death made him Duke of York and the head of the family at war with the rightful king after a major defeat that surely must signal the end of the entire campaign. But Edward pressed on. With an army of about 3,000 he faced the Lancastrian force of about the same size led by the experienced soldiers Tudor father and son: Owen and Jasper. As the young York lord prepared for battle near Mortimer's Cross on 2 February 1461 he saw something that his troops regarded as a miracle: a parhelion appeared in the sky above his army, a phenomenon caused by ice crystals sparkling in

A parhelion, the origin of the 'sun in splendour'

the atmosphere that created the illusion of three suns in the sky over Edward.

It was a deeply impressive sight to the superstitious armies of both sides. To Edward it was the blessing of God – the Father, Son and Holy Ghost – and he was quick-witted enough to reassure his army that it foretold their victory. Other commentators would see the three suns prefiguring the three sons of York who would fight side by side and found a new royal family: Edward and his brothers George and Richard. The sight of the three suns meant so much to Edward that he incorporated them into a personal badge: 'the sun in splendour'.

A contemporary stained-glass window showing the sun in splendour

Edward held a strong position on the crossroads at the entrance to Worcester with the River Lugg at his back. The Lancastrian forces had to make a frontal attack and though they broke the Yorkist right they were thrown back from the

centre of the line, commanded by Edward. The final charge
of the Lancastrian forces broke and fled from the field.
Edward captured Owen Tudor and executed him at
Hereford, ending the life of a man who had risen very high:
from service in the royal household to a secret marriage with
the Dowager Queen of England, Catherine of Valois, to
found the Tudor line. Jasper Tudor escaped the Yorkist
pursuit, abandoned his nephew, the young Henry Tudor,
at Pembroke Castle – where he became the ward of the
new overlord of Wales, William Herbert – and took a ship
from Tenby to exile overseas. He would be gone for nine
years.

Meanwhile, with contrasting fortunes, the victorious
Lancastrian army, with Queen Margaret at their head, started
to move south, pillaging and destroying firstly the lands of the
Yorkist lords, and then of everyone else. It is hard for us now
to imagine the terror felt by people living in the Midlands and
the south as the northern hordes approached. Religious
houses buried their treasure, and monks and nuns went into
hiding; great landowners fortified their walls and took up
their drawbridges; the poorer people braced themselves for
rape, theft and destruction. The Scots recruits had been
promised plunder instead of pay and they took everything
they felt was owed to them. The prospect of the arrival of the
queen and the northern men – widely regarded as savages –
threw the south and the city of London into a state of utter
terror.

Jacquetta's husband Richard Woodville was trying to lead
this undisciplined marauding force; probably their son
Anthony was serving, too. Richard Woodville persuaded his
friend Sir Henry Lovelace to join the queen's army and abandon his loyalty to York. Lovelace kept this new allegiance
secret and marched with the Yorkist army for the time being.

Also serving the queen was the Rivers' son-in-law Sir John Grey, Elizabeth's husband, who commanded the queen's cavalry. Both Lord Rivers and his son-in-law may have found it almost impossible to impose discipline on their troops. Most of the army were northerners, disinclined to march very far south away from home; there was no pay to reward them, and they had been licensed to steal. Rivers, trained in France by the Duke of Bedford, who had urged that enemy lands be treated well – for fear of creating more enemies – must have found himself trying to limit the brutality at every halt.

The Earl of Warwick was the only Yorkist commander available to resist the steady advance of the Lancastrians, and so, taking the king with him as a hostage, he marched out of London by the Great North Road and on 17 February 1461 met the queen's forces at St Albans.

Warwick must have remembered his previous triumph at St Albans, and positioned his archers – who had been so powerful before – in the town. But the queen's prize captain Sir Andrew Trollope led an advance guard around the Yorkist barricades in a lightning night march, arrived unexpectedly, and drove the Yorkist archers out of the town. York regrouped and deployed cannon and a new style of handgun. But as snow fell the powder became damp and the weapons exploded in the hands of the gunners. The arrows of the Yorkist archers, fired against the wind, could not reach the advancing Lancastrian army; and when Lovelace, Richard Woodville's recruit, abandoned his pretended allegiance to York and joined Lancaster, he left a disastrous gap in the line, which broke under a cavalry charge, probably led by Sir John Grey, Elizabeth Woodville's husband. Grey, just twenty-nine years old, died in this battle, perhaps giving his life at this moment of triumph.

The left wing of the Yorkist army fled from the field, and Warwick was forced to sound the retreat. Holding his surviving army together he marched away into the darkness, abandoning the king, who had been guarded throughout the battle by the Yorkist lords Lord Bonville and Sir Thomas Kyriell. They stayed with him, seated under an oak tree, and handed him over, unhurt, to the victorious Lancastrian lords to be reunited with his wife Queen Margaret and his son Prince Edward.

The king knighted the prince, who then had the power to create other knights as a reward for their courage on the battlefield. Then the Yorkist lords Lord Bonville and Sir Thomas Kyriell, who had guarded the king's safety, were brought before the royal party. According to some accounts the queen asked her young son what death the two lords should die and the seven-year-old boy chose that they should be beheaded: a shocking exchange even for violent times, a shocking precocity even for an age when men grew up young.

The royal party, Jacquetta among them, stayed at the Abbey of St Albans, and the royal army pillaged for food and goods in the surrounding areas, to the horror of the people. Terror spread to London and the Lord Mayor's carts, carrying supplies out from the city for the Lancastrian army, were seized by the mob to prevent them supporting the Lancastrians. They saw the royal army as their enemy, and prayed to be rescued by the armies of Edward the new Duke of York and his friend and ally the Earl of Warwick. Edward's mother Cecily Neville, the widow of Richard Duke of York, living in London, who had surrendered to the royal army at Ludlow, sent her sons George and Richard overseas to the court of the Duke of Burgundy for their safety. She must have feared that the army of northern men, under the command of the queen, would be even worse than the royal army at Ludlow.

The Lord Mayor chose Jacquetta, Anne Neville Duchess of Buckingham, the widowed Lady Scales and some clergymen to represent the city, asking the three noble – and popular – ladies to negotiate with the queen and get an assurance that the marauding northerners would not be allowed to loot the city.

It was not an easy task for Jacquetta. The aldermen and councillors of London were prepared to admit the king and the queen but only on condition that they would guarantee the safety of the city. However, the merchants, tradesmen and citizens of London had heard terrifying stories of the rape and looting by the army of the north, ever since they crossed the Trent. It was generally known that Margaret allowed her soldiers to steal in lieu of their pay, and the people of London did not want an army of thieves and rapists inside the city walls. Worse, they did not trust the word of the queen that they would be safe.

Jacquetta, the Duchess of Buckingham and Lady Scales negotiated with the citizens of London and then reported back to the queen at Barnet. When she heard of the city's reluctance, she sent the ladies back again to London to demand that the city proclaim Edward of York as a traitor, and open the gates to her. But even as Jacquetta tried to persuade the Londoners, the queen confirmed everyone's worst fears by secretly dispatching two bands of soldiers, one up the river to Westminster, where they were driven away by the city militia, and the other to Aldgate, where they tried to force open the city gate.

Infuriated by this double-dealing the Londoners barred the gates, and Jacquetta and the two ladies had to leave the city and report to the queen that London would not declare for her – even worse, that now it was raising money to support the Yorkist armies. Since Edward and Warwick were approaching, the queen took her army to Dunstable, nearly forty miles away, as the Yorkist army marched into London to a heroes' welcome. The people proclaimed Edward as the rightful king, and a council of lords invited him to take the throne, and then presented him with the crown and sceptre in a hasty ceremony at Westminster Abbey. Edward took the crown and promised that he would have a formal coronation when Henry VI and the queen were either dead or in exile. The time for any sort of agreement or compromise was over. There were now two crowned kings in England. It was going to be a fight to the death.

The queen abandoned her hopes of London and led her army back north. They regrouped at York, pursued by Edward and the Earl of Warwick. A detachment of the royal army, commanded by Jacquetta's husband Richard Woodville with the young Duke of Somerset, held the crossing of the River Aire at Ferrybridge in Yorkshire, and Edward sent a vanguard force ahead to attack them and open his road to the king and queen, who were staying at York. Lord Clifford, for Lancaster, ambushed the Yorkist troops, before they even got to Lord Rivers's troop, killing most of the Yorkists and wounding the Earl of Warwick. The Yorkists were halted, and then a message arrived from King Henry asking for a truce: it was Palm Sunday, the Sunday before Easter Day, 1461.

Edward resisted the temptation to pause, broke the tradition of peace on a Sunday, and pushed on to Ferrybridge, fighting on foot himself and forcing Lord Rivers's men back off the bridge. Rather than lose the bridge, Rivers and Somerset destroyed it. The Yorkist forces built a raft to get across, and the two armies fought for control of the raft. The Rivers troop won that skirmish; but then the Yorkists broke off from that battle, went further upstream and crossed the river at Castleford.

Fighting halted for the night, and overnight it started snowing, unseasonal spring snow which made the prospect of a battle in the early-morning light even worse. The Lancastrian army had the advantage of higher ground above the village of Towton as the Yorkists came up from the south; on one side of the battleground was a steeply banked river – the Cock Beck – on the other was the River Wharfe. Both rivers were running fast and in flood with melt-water and spring rains. The Lancastrian archers were blinded by the snow blowing into their faces and the wind was against their volleys. Yorkist archers were far more accurate, even though shooting uphill, since they were shooting with the support of the wind, arrows scything into the Lancastrian ranks from an enemy that they could hardly see. The Lancastrians charged down the hill and the battle swayed one way and then another for three hours. Perhaps as many as 50,000 men were fighting, led by three-quarters of the peerage.

Only the surprise late arrival of the men from the eastern counties, under the command of the Duke of Norfolk, fighting for York, broke the Lancastrian left flank and brought an end to the battle. The Lancastrian army fled as the Yorkist lords mounted up and pursued them down the river bank to the Cock Beck, where the bridge gave way under the weight of men struggling to flee, drowning them in waters which were already flowing red with blood.

It was one of the most lethal battles in British history: almost every great northern family lost a son; the Lancastrian forces lost most of their best captains. It was said that all the fields from Tadcaster to Towton, a distance of more than two miles, were filled with the bodies of dead men. Amazingly, Jacquetta's husband and her son Anthony survived. Once again they experienced the bitterness of defeat. But this time there was no marching away and regrouping. They had to surrender their swords to the young man that they would have to learn to call King Edward.

The defeated Queen Margaret and the young prince fled from York, getting away just before the enemy arrived at the city gates, and headed north for Scotland and ten long years of exile, the king with them. Edward marched into the city and ordered the heads of his father and brother taken down from the spikes on the city walls. Jacquetta, her husband and her son probably left at once, back the way they had come, riding south, nearly 140 miles to their home at Grafton. They may have stayed there until the new King Edward was formally crowned on Sunday 28 June 1461. He issued full pardons to Lord Rivers and his son Anthony Woodville in July. Edward IV, as he now was known, would prove to be a pragmatic king and his pardon of the Rivers family was part of his policy of trying to befriend and reunite the divided nobility.

Perhaps they all felt that life must go on. Anthony was nineteen and ready to marry. Jacquetta organised the marriage of her oldest son to Elizabeth de Scales, the daughter of the Lancastrian commander who had held the Tower of London during the Jack Cade rebellion, and again when the Yorkists invaded, breaking out only to be killed by Thames watermen. It may have been a marriage of affection as well as arrangement. The Woodvilles knew Lord Scales when he commanded the Tower against Jack Cade, and Anthony would have met his daughter Elizabeth. On the death of her father she inherited the title of Baroness Scales and, as her husband, Anthony took the title, and entered the Yorkist parliament as Lord Scales.

Meanwhile, Jacquetta's oldest daughter Elizabeth was

struggling to stay in her dead husband's home at Groby Hall. She was entitled to receive an income from three Grey family manors held in trust for her, but her mother-in-law, Lady Ferrers, had no intention of allowing her to live off them indefinitely. Such a drain on the estate could go on till Elizabeth's death. Lady Ferrers disputed the purpose of the trust, and Elizabeth went home to her parents at Grafton while she applied to senior members of the family to argue the case for her and for her two young sons.

In this new world the Rivers family no longer had the access to court, nor to the power that they used to exert. They could not make Lady Ferrers honour her word. Their king was an exile, sometimes in Scotland, sometimes hiding in the north-east of England, a hunted man; their queen and her son were in France with a few banished English lords, trying to persuade the rulers of Europe to support the defeated House of Lancaster. The Rivers themselves were newcomers to the Yorkist councils, regarded with some suspicion: they had no influence.

But the Rivers had their pardon, and could rise again. In 1463 Sir Richard Lord Rivers and his son Anthony, now Lord Scales, were summoned to the king's council to advise King Edward, and started the process of climbing into the monarch's confidence and trust. All three men must have had to make an effort to forget the night in Calais when the young rebel had scolded Lord Rivers for rising through marriage, and the several times when they had been on opposite sides of the battlefield; but all three seem to have managed it.

A year later, in early summer, that most seductive season in England, when the may is as white as snow in the hedges, and every bird is singing, King Edward, on his way north, recruiting men to fight against a Lancastrian army at Hexham, stopped at Grafton and was greeted by the Rivers' widowed daughter Elizabeth, who appealed to him to support the claim for her dowry lands. The leading Yorkist lord, William Lord Hastings, made an agreement to share her inheritance if his influence won it for her, but – as it turned out – Elizabeth did not need his help. She did not even need her dower. The attraction between the outstandingly beautiful 27-year-old widow and the 22-year-old king must have been mutual and instant: they were married in secret within weeks of first meeting.

Once again, the shadow of witchcraft falls over the reputation of Jacquetta and, from this moment, her daughter too. The marriage was said to have taken place on 1 May, the greatest festival in the witch calendar, known as Beltane. For pagans and witches this date celebrates fertility and love at the start of summer, when the otherworld grows close. The wedding of the young king and Elizabeth Grey took place in secret and exhausted the young king, who was said to have returned to his camp and slept all day. Most ominously of all, later witnesses said that they found two lead images of a man and a woman, bound together with threads of gold, which they said had been used to charm the king and the widow into love with each other.

Jacquetta may perhaps have made lead images. She may have recited spells. She would certainly have used herbs and believed in the power of invocation, blessings, curses and prayer. She had been raised in a world where such things were done, perhaps by many people, with the expectation of success. Certainly, she was the most senior witness at a phenomenally important secret wedding which was to have such explosive political implications for the king, his kingdom and his Council; and she may have kept it a secret from two of his councillors: her husband and her son. Without a doubt, having spent her life so close to the centre of power, she knew exactly what she was doing when she allowed her daughter to wed and bed the young man who had claimed the throne of England. Elizabeth may have been blinded by love; Jacquetta would have been well aware that the marriage would make a Rivers grandson the King of England. She may have tried magic, or she may have used the quiet skills of a covert politician, adept in the art of women's power and seduction; but she and her daughter changed history that night in May 1464.

For Edward it was a marriage of irresistible desire, and he may have hoped that he would be able to conceal it, or even deny it. Indeed, it may be true that he had previously promised marriage to Lady Eleanor Butler and then denied the promise; an unscrupulous womaniser, he may have thought he might play that trick again. But the wedding that Jacquetta witnessed and perhaps planned had to be revealed in September 1464, when the royal councillors meeting Edward at Reading urged him to confirm his intention of marrying the sister-in-law of the King of France, Princess Bona of Savoy. Edward decided to admit that he was already married, and to a woman formerly of the House of Lancaster, a woman of no fortune, and a woman who was not a virgin; but on the contrary had two strapping sons from a former marriage.

The uproar that ensued was the major step in the gradual alienation of Richard Neville, the Earl of Warwick, from his young cousin and protégé. Edward turned more and more to his new in-laws as his advisers, and Jacquetta's husband Richard Woodville became Earl Rivers in 1466 and was appointed to the prime post of Constable of England. Jacquetta made sure that all the Woodville children made superb marriages, mopping up all the eligible heirs and heiresses, and leaving Edward's former great friend and supporter with two daughters on the shelf. Even Elizabeth's son from her first marriage, Thomas Grey, married an heiress, the little daughter of the Duke of Exeter. All this caused yet more concern to the established aristocracy, especially the Earl of Warwick.

For Jacquetta, the rise of her daughter meant her own restoration to the place of a leading lady in England and Europe. Jacquetta's younger brother Jacques of Luxembourg came to Elizabeth's grand coronation on 26 May 1465, representing his lord, the Duke of Burgundy, and demonstrating to the English snobs that the new queen had noble relations on her mother's side, even if her father had been nothing more than a knight. At the same time, Jacquetta's oldest brother, and the head of her house, Louis, the Count of Luxembourg, was playing European politics and had turned against Louis XI of France to take the side of his brother Charles Duke of Berry. The gamble paid off for the moment: in the settlement which followed, Jacquetta's brother Louis was appointed Constable of France and took, as his second wife, Maria of Savoy, the sister of the Queen of France.

Jacquetta was first lady at the English court once again, related to European royalty, her husband a royal kinsman just as when she was a young woman. It must have struck her powerfully that although she was fully restored – and even grander than before – the house that she had served for so long had utterly fallen. In July 1465 her former king, Henry VI, was brought into London with his feet tied to his horse's stirrups, a prisoner, captured near Brungerley in Lancashire. He was held in the Tower of London; he may have slipped into mental illness once again. Jacquetta's own grandson, Thomas Grey, was among the five members of the royal household appointed to wait on her former king.

Jacquetta and her family would seem to be established for life, until the man who had been nicknamed 'the

Kingmaker' – the Earl of Warwick – defied Edward IV and married his daughter Isabel to the king's younger brother, George Duke of Clarence. Based in the formidable fortress of Calais, Warwick once again stirred up unrest in Yorkshire, complaining about the influence of royal favourites – 'certain seditious persons' – this time meaning Jacquetta and her family; and in July 1469, Warwick, his brother-in-law the Earl of Oxford and his son-in-law George Duke of Clarence invaded England, once again from Calais.

Edward was waiting in Nottingham for reinforcements, before making his march on the rebels. Elizabeth his wife was in the city of Norwich, continuing with a planned royal progress. Richard Woodville Earl Rivers and his sons were with the king, and Jacquetta was at the family home at Grafton when the royal reinforcements, marching on their way to join King Edward, crossed the path of the Yorkshire rebels marching south to meet the Earl of Warwick. A muddle or disagreement between the royal commanders, the Earls of Pembroke and Devon, led to the victory of the rebel forces at Edgecote near Banbury and to Edward's first defeat.

Edward, understanding very well that his wife's family were in mortal danger from the victorious rebels, whose complaints included the bad influence of the Woodville family, sent his father-in-law Sir Richard Woodville Earl Rivers with his son John Woodville away from the conflict. Father and son went back to their home at Grafton and then started to make their way into the safety of Wales. Jacquetta may have seen them leave the family home that she had shared with her husband for thirty years. It would be the last time she would see the man she had married for love, and the son she had managed to wed to a duchess.

Father and son were captured by the Earl of Warwick's men and taken to Coventry. Sir Richard Woodville, that faithful knight who had survived so many battles, was beheaded with his 24-year-old son John at his side on the orders of the Earl of Warwick and George Duke of Clarence. There was no charge and there was no trial – indeed there could be none – for the 64-year-old Richard Woodville and his son were fighting for their anointed king against rebels. Their heads were struck from their bodies and put on the walls of Coventry, like traitors. The king himself was captured by Warwick and taken to the Warwicks' family seat of Middleham Castle in Wensleydale.

Warwick sent an armed guard to the Woodville home at Grafton and had Jacquetta snatched from her home by a squire named Thomas Wake, with the intention of trying her as a witch. The punishment for witchcraft was death – perhaps Warwick's hope was that if he killed the key Woodville family members, especially the queen's parents, he would regain his dominance over the young man he had raised to be king.

There was a formal trial for the duchess accused of witchcraft. Jacquetta was arraigned and witnesses were called. A small model was produced: 'an image of lead made like a man of arms of the length of a man's finger, broken in the middle, and made fast with a wire'. The court was told that it had been made by Jacquetta to perform witchcraft and sorcery.

Another witness was called: John Daunger, the parish clerk of Stoke Bruerne, Northamptonshire, who lived just two miles from Jacquetta's home at Grafton. He said that there were two other images made by Jacquetta: one to symbolise the king and one for the queen.

This evidence alone was enough to justify a death sentence for Jacquetta. Warwick had already executed her husband and son without trial; he may have been planning to punish the entire family for their seduction of the king. He may also have genuinely believed that Jacquetta was a practising witch – this was a time of increased fear and suspicion about witchcraft that would culminate in 1484 with a papal bull calling for the pursuit and arrest of witches.

Jacquetta, newly widowed and mourning the loss of her son, must have been very afraid. She would remember the three women that she had known personally who had suffered under the same accusation, and she would have heard of many others. Her own first husband had ordered the death of Joan of Arc, burned for witchcraft, and she had been present at the trial that led to the burning of Margery Jourdemayne and the miserable and long punishment of Eleanor Cobham, another royal duchess.

But amazingly, Warwick failed to conclude the trial with a sentence and an execution. Perhaps, when he actually faced Jacquetta, he did not dare to send such a powerfully well-connected and formidable woman to her death. Although he was clearly preparing the court for a death sentence, something made him change his mind, and he released Jacquetta.

What can have persuaded Warwick against sentence and execution, even though he had such compelling evidence to hand, and witnesses who swore to Jacquetta's guilt? Although the witnesses later recanted and quarrelled among themselves, there was more than enough evidence to justify a sentence of guilty and an execution as a witch. Perhaps he feared Jacquetta's powers, perhaps he feared the influence of her family, her long friendship with Margaret of Anjou or the devotion of her daughter the queen, and the other surviving Woodville children, all of them highly placed thanks to their mother's marriage arrangements. At any rate, he released her and she went to join her daughter Elizabeth, who was holding the Tower of London ready for a siege. A little later, Warwick also failed to hold Edward the king, who defied his imprisonment by behaving like a monarch on an extended house visit, summoning his councillors, and enjoying the amenities. Warwick could not manage the country without a king, especially when there was a new outbreak of unrest. Edward took his freedom and rejoined his wife.

Jacquetta's grief for the loss of her husband and son must have been intense. But at least her daughter was safe and restored to her position by the return of her husband and a compromise agreement patched up between Warwick and Edward IV. Warwick's nephew was named as Duke of Bedford – it must have irritated Jacquetta to see her first husband's title given away – and the young boy was betrothed to the young York princess, Elizabeth. Jacquetta appealed to the great council before the king and the Archbishops of Canterbury and York to clear her name of the slur of witchcraft.

It is this complaint, recorded in the Calendar of Patent Rolls, that describes Jacquetta's accusation and trial by Warwick. Confronted by Jacquetta's son-in-law the King of England, and the lords of the land both temporal and spiritual, the witnesses dissolved into mutual recriminations and withdrew their accusations. Warwick himself was present when Jacquetta's name was officially cleared; but the slur of witchcraft, of course, remained. Indeed, it remains to this day.

The accord between the king, his brother George and his former mentor Warwick was to be short-lived. In a second attempt on England, Warwick, with the king's brother George Duke of Clarence, now in alliance with the former queen Margaret of Anjou, invaded in September 1470 and caught Edward unawares. Jacquetta had to see her oldest son

Anthony and the king flee for their lives into exile as they escaped dramatically, in a small boat across the sea to the Low Countries. In Flanders, they found safety with Jacquetta's kinsman the Duke of Burgundy. Jacquetta herself, her pregnant daughter Elizabeth the queen, and the three York princesses – Elizabeth (four), Mary (three) and Cecily (just one year old) – fled into the safety of sanctuary in Westminster Abbey, in the crypt of a church in St Margaret's churchyard. It was there, with Jacquetta assisting, that the new baby was born. In a stroke of fantastic luck, that Edward so often enjoyed, the baby was a boy, an heir for the House of York and a powerful symbol for their future. They called him Edward.

The convention of 'sanctuary' – the immunity of criminals from arrest if they stayed on hallowed ground – guaranteed the safety of the little family only while they stayed within the confines of the sanctuary house of the abbey, so Jacquetta, her daughter and grandchildren were in effect under house arrest in a basement, with no prospect of release other than a counter-coup. Henry VI was taken out of his imprisonment in the Tower of London, and paraded through the city for an official crown-wearing ceremony, to symbolically re-establish his rule. True power was in the hands of Warwick and his son-in-law George Duke of Clarence; but it may have been the king who insisted that sanctuary was respected and that Jacquetta and her daughter and grandchildren were not arrested.

However, George Duke of Clarence had been secretly turned against his ally the Earl of Warwick. In a conspiracy of women, George's mother and sister had sent a lady-in-waiting over to France to persuade him to ally with his brother Edward. When Edward invaded England, George changed sides, deserted Warwick and joined with his brother to enter

London in triumph and then defeat the Earl of Warwick, fighting through thick mist at the battle of Barnet on 14 April 1471. The weather was so disadvantageous to Warwick and his army that there were people at the time who thought that, once again, Edward had been assisted by witchcraft.

Jacquetta was liberated with her daughter Elizabeth, the baby prince and the three princesses, and went to the Tower for safety while Edward led his army straight from victory at Barnet to face the invasion of Margaret of Anjou with her seventeen-year-old son Edward. It must have been painful for Jacquetta to know that her son-in-law was facing her friend and former queen at the battle of Tewkesbury, and she must have been grieved when she learned that the young Prince Edward had been killed and his mother Margaret of Anjou captured. She had little time to worry about her former friends for the Tower of London now came under siege from Lancaster supporters and Jacquetta and her daughter Elizabeth the queen had to endure an attack on the Tower; it was defended by Jacquetta's son, Anthony Woodville, who had returned from the battle of Tewkesbury to protect them. When Anthony Woodville led the counter-attack and the Lancastrian forces were defeated, Jacquetta was there to greet her royal son-in-law's victorious progress into the city with the defeated queen, Margaret of Anjou, brought in as a captive in a triumphant parade.

That night, the royal House of Lancaster was ended with the murder of Henry VI, either committed by Edward himself, his brothers, or by his friends or servants; certainly on his orders. Margaret of Anjou was held as a prisoner in England, firstly at the Tower and then at the home of her old friend Alice de la Pole, the Dowager Duchess of Suffolk, who had been her lady-in-waiting alongside Jacquetta when Margaret first came to England. Finally, in 1475, Margaret was released to her cousin Louis XI of France and returned to her home in Anjou.

Jacquetta saw her son-in-law proclaimed king once more, and her daughter restored to her throne. She died the following year in 1472, at the age of fifty-six, a good age for a medieval woman, and a remarkable age for a woman who had survived two husbands, fourteen or more childbirths, and two wars. She had lived to see her daughter's triumphant return to the throne, and she must have been confident that the safety of her daughter and grandchildren was assured, and the House of York firmly established as the royal family of England.

She left an interesting legacy. Her love of books and learning was passed down to her son Anthony and to her daughter Elizabeth and they inherited the impressive library that her first husband, the Duke of Bedford, had willed to her. This was before the age of printing. These books would be hand-copied and, often, illustrated or illuminated manuscripts. Each one was a small work of art, and Jacquetta treasured them and passed them on to her children.

Anthony may have loaned the precious volumes from this library to Sir Thomas Malory, a knight and an adventurer who used them to write his *Morte d'Arthur*, the first version written in English of the tales of Arthur and the Round Table. Malory was probably imprisoned, both by the Lancastrian court and then by the Yorkists, and his characters, though based on the traditional tale, may have been inspired by Jacquetta's family and the optimism and glamour of the early years of the York–Woodville court that he briefly served.

Anthony's education, inspired and perhaps instructed by his mother, made him one of the first Renaissance men in Europe. He met William Caxton, who was pioneering the process of printing in Bruges, and invited him to England.

A stained-glass window of c. 1475 of William Caxton presenting his first printed page to King Edward IV and his queen, Elizabeth Woodville

Anthony Woodville sponsored the first ever published book in England, Chaucer's *Canterbury Tales*, and in 1477 Caxton published Anthony Woodville's own translation *Dictes or Sayengis of the Philosophres* (Sayings of the Philosophers). Caxton is said to have been surprised that Anthony did not include the traditional misogynistic complaints about women in the collection; perhaps we may see the influence of his redoubtable mother here also. Books from the Caxton press, including the *Dictes*, may have been given to the Prince of Wales, Edward, whose education was supervised by Anthony Woodville. Jacquetta's daughter Elizabeth read the book in its early stages and suggested some editorial changes, and she may have been a patron of Caxton, commissioning him to translate *The Book of the Knight of the Tower*.

> This book has come into my hands at the request and desire of a noble lady who has brought forth many noble and fair daughters who have been raised and taught virtuously. Because of the great love she has always had for her fair children and still has, she wants them to know more about moral behaviour so that they may always be virtuous themselves. To this end, she has asked me to translate this book out of French into our common English so it may be better understood by all who shall read it or hear it read. Therefore at the lady's request and according to the small skill that God has sent me, I have endeavoured to obey her admirable wish.

Perhaps the Woodville love of books and study can be traced down the generations to Henry VIII and his scholarly daughter Elizabeth I.

Jacquetta had another darker legacy: the accusation of witchcraft that was first made explicit when the Earl of Warwick changed sides in 1469 and plotted to execute her. Rumours against the foreign-born descendant of the water goddess almost certainly preceded this accusation; but it was Warwick who openly accused her of witchcraft, and Warwick who ordered the trial at which the prosecution produced the little images of lead and witnesses who swore that she was a witch. Jacquetta escaped the normal punishment of death by strangling or burning, and cleared her name when Edward returned to the throne. But the accusation was repeated after Edward's death by his youngest brother. Richard III set aside the York children's claim to the throne which he usurped, on the basis that the marriage of their parents – Edward IV and Elizabeth Woodville – was not legitimate, and that it had been brought about by magic. Though the marriage had been accepted by everyone for nearly twenty years, Richard accused his dead brother Edward of bigamously marrying Elizabeth in a false ceremony while he was already married to Lady Eleanor Butler. Richard's claim was supported by Robert Stillington Bishop of Bath and Wells, but Lady Eleanor was, by then, dead. Richard also made the potent allegation that the marriage had been brought about by the magical craft of the witch Jacquetta and her daughter Elizabeth.

It was too good a story not to be repeated, and Jacquetta's and Elizabeth's reputations as seducers, social climbers and witches endure to this day. Like her mother, Elizabeth Woodville was slandered with accusations of magic, and linked to the legend of Melusina, the founder of the family of St Pol.

In conclusion, I have to wonder why the story of Jacquetta is so little known. I suppose that much of the history of this period is filtered through the pro-Tudor historians and their great playwright William Shakespeare. For them, the founding mother of the family had to be Margaret Beaufort, Henry VII's mother, and not his mother-in-law Elizabeth Woodville. The histories of Elizabeth Woodville and her mother Jacquetta were neglected in favour of the more conventional founding mother: Margaret Beaufort, whose courage and determination put her son on the throne and whose political astuteness led her to manage the writing of their history, and the exclusion of the rival family.

I think also that the lives of Jacquetta and her daughter make uncomfortable reading for historians who find accounts of female power, female sexuality and female magic disturbing. The bland, censored and very conventional accounts of Lady Margaret Beaufort are a more acceptable view of medieval women than the history of these adventurous, sexually active, ambitious women. And so it gives me pleasure to offer this brief essay as a reference point for readers who have met and loved Jacquetta in my novel *The Lady of the Rivers* and also as a starting point for the historical studies of Jacquetta Duchess of Bedford that I hope will follow.

Jacquetta's signature

NOTES AND SOURCES

The famous call to arms is from Shakespeare, *Henry V*, Act 3, Scene i. Joan's threat to Bedford is cited in Warner, M. *Joan of Arc: the image of female heroism*, London: Weidenfeld & Nicolson, 1981.

The Glendower and Hotspur conversation is in Shakespeare, *Henry IV, Part I*, Act 3, Scene i. I am indebted to the owner of Penshurst, Viscount de L'Isle, for information about the building.

Jacquetta's children are difficult to establish. I would suggest that she had fourteen pregnancies, of which thirteen children grew to adulthood. After lengthy discussions with David Baldwin in which we agreed principally that there is no definitive list (!) I would suggest this: Elizabeth, b. 1437, (Lewis, b. 1438, d. in infancy), Anne, b. 1439, Anthony, b. 1442, Mary, b. 1443, Jacquetta, b. 1444, John, b. 1445, Richard, b. 1446, Martha, b. 1450, Eleanor, b. 1452, Lionel, b. 1453, Margaret, b. 1454, Edward. b. 1455, Katherine (or Catherine) b. 1458.

The description of the trial of Eleanor Cobham and her associates is mostly drawn from Godwin, W. *Lives of the necromancers: or, An account of the most eminent persons in successive ages, who have claimed for themselves, or to whom has been imputed by others, the exercise of magical power*, London: F.J. Mason, 1834, and the very clear account by Jessica Freeman, 'Sorcery at court and manor: Margery Jourdemayne, the witch of Eye next

Westminster', *Journal of Medieval History*, 30 (2004), 343–57. Shakespeare has a judgement scene with the king, Henry VI, taking part, though in fact he kept well away from proceedings: *Henry VI, Part II*, Act 2, Scene iii. Shakespeare thought it was Thomas Stanley, but it was, in fact, John.

The legend of the black dog which haunts Peel Castle and also Leeds Castle, where she was imprisoned, is still told: http://www.mysteriousbritain.co.uk/england/isle-of-man/legends/peel-castle.html. Margaret of Anjou's gift records are interestingly analysed by Helen E. Maurer: *Margaret of Anjou: Queenship and Power in Late Medieval England*, Woodbridge: The Boydell Press, 2003.

The celebrated joke against the rising Rivers is cited in *The Paston Letters, AD 1422–1509*, ed. J. Gairdner, 6 vols, iii (1904), 204, William Paston to his brother John, 28 January 1460; the joke against the Rivers arriving in Calais is in Gregory's chronicle, cited Griffiths, R.A. *The Reign of King Henry VI*, Stroud: Sutton, 1998. The account of the abuse of the Rivers family by the Yorkist lords was told in the Paston letters; quoted here is the modernised spelling version from Griffiths, R.A. *The Reign of King Henry VI*, Stroud: Sutton, 1998.

The description of Henry VI under the control of the Earl of Warwick as more timorous than a woman comes from the contemporary observer Francesco Coppini CMiLP, 1 61 cited in Griffiths *as above*. The death of the Earl of Salisbury is quoted by Wolffe, B.P. *Henry VI*, London: Eyre Methuen, 1981.

The details of Jacquetta's trial for witchcraft are recorded by the court that cleared her, in the Calendar of Patent Rolls 1467–77. A new edition of *The Knight of the Tower*, the book requested by Elizabeth Woodville, has been published: Barnhouse, R. *The Book of the Knight of the Tower: Manners for Young Medieval Women*, Palgrave Macmillan, 2006.

BIBLIOGRAPHY

Amt, E. *Women's Lives in Medieval Europe*, New York: Routledge, 1993

Baldwin, D. *Elizabeth Woodville: Mother of the Princes in the Tower*, Stroud: Sutton Publishing, 2002

Barnhouse, R. *The Book of the Knight of the Tower: Manners for Young Medieval Women*, Palgrave Macmillan, 2006

Bramley, P. *The Wars of the Roses: A Field Guide and Companion*, Stroud: Sutton Publishing, 2007

Castor, H. *Blood & Roses: The Paston Family and the Wars of the Roses*, London: Faber, 2004

Cheetham, A. *The Life and Times of Richard III*, London: Weidenfeld & Nicolson, 1972

Chrimes, S.B. *Lancastrians, Yorkists, and Henry VII*, London: Macmillan, 1964

Cooper, C.H. *Memoir of Margaret: Countess of Richmond and Derby*, Cambridge: Cambridge University Press, 1874

Duggan, A.J. *Queens and Queenship in Medieval Europe*, Woodbridge: The Boydell Press, 1997

Field, P.J.C. *The Life and Times of Sir Thomas Malory*, Cambridge: D.S. Brewer, 1993

Freeman, J. 'Sorcery at court and manor: Margery Jourdemayne, the witch of Eye next Westminster', *Journal of Medieval History*, 30: 343–57, 2004

Godwin, W. *Lives of the necromancers: or, An account of the most eminent persons in successive ages, who have claimed for themselves, or to whom has been imputed by others, the exercise of magical power*, London: F.J. Mason, 1834

Goodman, A. *The Wars of the Roses: Military Activity and English Society, 1452–97*, London: Routledge & Kegan Paul, 1981

Goodman, A. *The Wars of the Roses: The Soldiers' Experience*, Stroud: Tempus, 2006

Griffiths, R.A. *The Reign of King Henry VI*, Stroud: Sutton, 1998

Grummitt, D. *The Calais Garrison, War and Military Service in England, 1436–1558*, Woodbridge: The Boydell Press, 2008

Haswell, J. *The Ardent Queen: Margaret of Anjou and the Lancastrian Heritage*, London: Peter Davies, 1976

Hicks, M. *Warwick the Kingmaker*, London: Blackwell Publishing, 1998

Hipshon, D. *Richard III and the Death of Chivalry*, Stroud: The History Press, 2009

Hughes, J. *Arthurian Myths and Alchemy: The Kingship of Edward IV*, Stroud: Sutton Publishing, 2002

Jones, M.K., and Underwood, M.G. *The King's Mother: Lady Margaret Beaufort, Countess of Richmond and Derby*, Cambridge: Cambridge University Press, 1992

Karras, R.M. *Sexuality in Medieval Europe: Doing unto Others*, New York: Routledge, 2005

Laynesmith, J.L. *The Last Medieval Queens: English Queenship 1445–1503*, Oxford: Oxford University Press, 2004

Levine, N. 'The Case of Eleanor Cobham: Authorizing History in 2 Henry VI', *Shakespeare Studies* 22: 104–21, 1994

Lewis, K., Menuge, N.J., and Phillips, K.M. *Young Medieval Women*, Stroud: Sutton Publishing, 1999

MacGibbon, D. *Elizabeth Woodville 1437–1492: Her Life and Times*, London: Arthur Baker, 1938

Martin, S. *Alchemy and the Alchemists*, London: Pocket Essentials, 2006

Maurer, E. *Margaret of Anjou: Queenship and Power in Late Medieval England*, Woodbridge: The Boydell Press, 2003

Neillands, R. *The Wars of the Roses*, London: Cassell, 1992

Newcomer, J. *The Grand Duchy of Luxembourg: The Evolution of Nationhood*, Luxembourg: Editions Emile Borschette, 1995

Péporté, P. *Constructing the Middle Ages. Historiography, Collective Memory and Nation Building in Luxembourg*, Leiden and Boston: Brill, 2011

Phillips, K.M. *Medieval Maidens: Young women and gender in England, 1270–1540*, Manchester University Press, 2003

Prestwich, M. *Plantagenet England 1225–1360*, Oxford: Clarendon Press, 2005

Ross, C.D. *Edward IV*, London: Eyre Methuen, 1974

Rubin, M. *The Hollow Crown: A History of Britain in the Late Middle Ages*, London: Allen Lane, 2005

Seward, D. *A Brief History of The Hundred Years War*, London: Constable, 1973

Simon, L. *Of Virtue Rare: Margaret Beaufort, Matriarch of the House of Tudor*, Boston: Houghton Mifflin, 1982

Storey, R.L. *The End of the House of Lancaster*, Stroud: Sutton Publishing, 1999

Thomas, K. *Religion and the Decline of Magic*, New York: Weidenfeld & Nicolson, 1971

Vergil, Polydore, and Ellis, Henry *Three Books of Polydore Vergil's English History Comprising the Reigns of Henry VI, Edward IV and Richard III*, Kessinger Publishing Legacy Reprint, 1971

Ward, J. *Women in Medieval Europe 1200–1500*, Essex: Pearson Education, 2002

Warner, M. *Joan of Arc: the image of female heroism*, London: Weidenfeld & Nicolson, 1981

Weinberg, S.C. 'Caxton, Anthony Woodville and the Prologue to the "MorteDarthur"', *Studies in Philology*, Vol. 102, No. 1: 45–65, 2005

Weir, A. *Lancaster & York: The Wars of the Roses*, London: Cape, 1995

Williams, E.C. *My Lord of Bedford, 1389–1435: being a life of John of Lancaster, first Duke of Bedford, brother of Henry V and Regent of France*, London: Longmans, 1963

Wilson-Smith, T. *Joan of Arc: Maid, Myth and History*, Stroud: Sutton Publishing

Wolffe, B.P. *Henry VI*, London: Eyre Methuen, 1981, 2006

ELIZABETH WOODVILLE

1437/38–1492

David Baldwin

❧ THE CHILDREN OF ELIZABETH WOODVILLE ❧

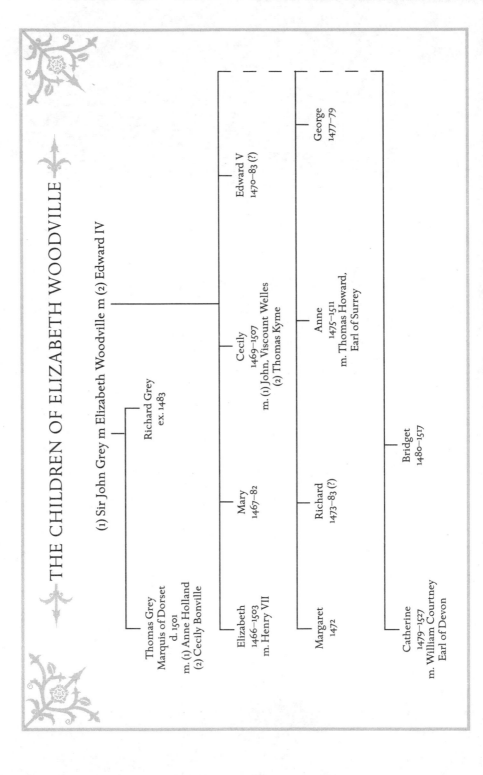

(1) Sir John Grey m Elizabeth Woodville m (2) Edward IV

Richard Grey
ex. 1483

Thomas Grey
Marquis of Dorset
d. 1501
m. (1) Anne Holland
(2) Cecily Bonville

Elizabeth
1466–1503
m. Henry VII

Mary
1467–82

Cecily
1469–1507
m. (1) John, Viscount Welles
(2) Thomas Kyme

Edward V
1470–83 (?)

Margaret
1472

Richard
1473–83 (?)

Anne
1475–1511
m. Thomas Howard,
Earl of Surrey

George
1477–79

Catherine
1479–1527
m. William Courtney
Earl of Devon

Bridget
1480–1517

ELIZABETH'S EARLY LIFE

Elizabeth Woodville, the future 'White Queen', was probably born at Grafton in Northamptonshire in 1437 or early in 1438. We cannot be more precise because her parents' whereabouts at the time of her birth are uncertain, and estimates of her age are based on a note added to a later portrait indicating that she was twenty-six when the original was painted in 1464. She was therefore almost certainly the eldest of the estimated fourteen children born to Sir Richard Woodville of Grafton and his wife, Jacquetta, Dowager Duchess of Bedford, a couple whose secret marriage in 1436 had surprised contemporaries almost as much as their daughter's would outrage public opinion years later. Jacquetta, who had been married to John of Bedford, Henry V's brother, and who ranked as England's third lady after Henry IV's second wife and Henry V's widow, had been expected to give her hand to a great nobleman; and her choice of Sir Richard, a county knight with limited prospects, raised eyebrows in a society which thought that everyone should know his or her place.

Sir Richard was not without merit, however. His reputation as a soldier and jouster grew steadily in the early 1440s, and it would be unfair to assume that Jacquetta's influence with Henry VI's wife, Margaret of Anjou, was entirely responsible for his elevation to the peerage as Baron Rivers in 1448. The young couple could now enter fully into English noble society, but Jacquetta's dower (her life interest in a third of her late first husband's wealth) was steadily eroded by the loss of English-held lands in France at the end of the Hundred Years' War and by the inability of the royal treasury to meet all the demands made upon it. Keeping up appearances and providing for a growing family on a reduced income was as problematic then as at any other time, and the young Elizabeth would have learned that money had to be spent carefully. Her surviving accounts indicate that she knew how to manage her finances, and her expenditure did not exceed her income even when queen.

What was life like for a young girl of good family growing up in the Northamptonshire countryside in the middle of the fifteenth century? Like most children, she probably found the regular religious services and polite formality tiresome (particularly when her parents were in attendance), but they were all part of learning how to conduct herself in a 'proper' manner. She would have been taught to ride and hunt – hunting was always a favourite pastime of the aristocracy – and her gentler accomplishments would have included needlework, dancing and perhaps singing. Medieval girls were not always well educated – the Paston Letters indicate that some young gentlewomen could barely sign their names – but Jacquetta was noted for her love of literature and her daughters may have fared rather well in this respect.

Long before Elizabeth reached marriageable age her parents would have concerned themselves with the question of whom she would marry. Local alliances were often forged in this manner, and it was agreed that she would wed John, son of Sir Edward Grey and his wife Elizabeth Lady Ferrers, a youth about five years her senior. She would not have been asked if she would like to marry John – her duty to her family came before her own personal feelings – and she was probably sent to live with her future husband and in-laws at Groby in Leicestershire some time before the wedding. The Tudor writer Thomas More thought that she was placed in service to Queen Margaret either now or later, but his 'Elizabeth Grey' was probably another lady with the same name. He may have confused Elizabeth with Margaret's lady Isabella Grey (who was much older), or with an Elizabeth, the widow of Ralph Grey of Heaton, who was serving the queen in 1445.

We do not know when Elizabeth and John Grey were married, and references to the age of their eldest son, Thomas, are not very helpful. He is said to have been thirty-seven in 1492 in one document or thirteen in 1464 in another, and was therefore born either in 1455 or in 1451, when his mother would have been only thirteen or fourteen herself. This may seem unlikely, but Margaret Beaufort was only thirteen when she gave birth to her son, the future King Henry VII, and it may be another case of a marriage being consummated as early as possible. The Church held that a union was invalid unless both partners consented to it, and allowed children to opt out of whatever arrangements their parents had made for them when they reached puberty. Few did so in practice, but consummation effectively closed the window of opportunity and made the contract between the families secure.

The decade that Elizabeth spent as a young wife is all but lost to us, but her everyday life would not have been unlike that of other girls who found themselves in a similar situation. It is probable that she and John made their home on one of the Grey family's subsidiary manors – perhaps Astley in Warwickshire or Bradgate in Leicestershire – and it was there that a second son, Richard, was born to them a few years later. Elizabeth would soon have become accustomed to giving instructions to servants and farm workers, and to planning ahead to ensure that her family was fed and clothed in all seasons. Most importantly of all, she would have taken John's place when he was away on business or royal service, and dealt with disputes or anything that affected their joint interests. Such marriages may not have been founded on love – at least not to begin with – but they could be companionate and agreeable all the same.

These were some of the most peaceful – and perhaps also the happiest – years of Elizabeth's life, but from time to time she would hear that there was trouble in high places and that the great men of the kingdom had come to blows. The first battle of the Wars of the Roses – at St Albans in 1455 – did not involve her husband, father or brothers directly, but they were almost bound to be drawn into the conflict as the situation worsened. We have already seen how, in January 1460, Lord Rivers, Jacquetta and their eldest son Sir Anthony were captured by the Earl of Warwick's men at Sandwich, taken to Calais, and there given a thorough dressing-down by Warwick, the future Kingmaker, his father the Earl of Salisbury, and the Duke of York's son, Edward Earl of March. Elizabeth would have been mortified when she learned of what had happened, but she could do nothing except hope that her parents' and brother's enemies would not harm them physically, and wonder whom she might ask to intercede for them. Warwick had given her cause to both fear and dislike him, and there would be other occasions as the years passed.

Elizabeth's father had been a member of the peerage for twelve years by this time, a year longer than Warwick, and Anthony was shortly to marry the heiress to the barony of Scales. But the abuse hurled at them at Calais turned on the notion that they were upstarts who lacked the older, more dignified, nobility of their critics rather than on their 'misguided' loyalty to Henry VI. This was, of course, a year before this same Edward Earl of March was proclaimed king as Edward

Garter Stall Plate of Richard Woodville, first Earl Rivers, Elizabeth's father. St George's Chapel, Windsor

IV and four years before he married Elizabeth Woodville and became Lord Rivers's son-in-law. It would be interesting to know if they ever reminded one another of the occasion, and smiled grimly at the irony of it.

Elizabeth was undoubtedly relieved when her parents and brother were released unhurt a little before or after the Yorkist victory at the battle of Northampton on 10 July, but worse was to follow. Her husband, Sir John Grey, was killed at the second battle of St Albans on 17 February 1461, and she found herself a widow with two young sons. John had led his servants and tenants to join Queen Margaret's Lancastrian army as it moved southwards after its victory over the Yorkists at Wakefield in Yorkshire on 30 December, and it was almost certainly one of these men, breathless and dust-stained, who brought her the terrible news. The Earl of Warwick had deployed the southern Yorkist forces at St Albans, twenty miles from London, expecting an attack from the north, but Margaret and her commanders had surprised him by advancing from the north-west through Dunstable. Desertions had added to Warwick's difficulties and he had been driven back and forced to abandon the battlefield, although not without a struggle that cost the lives of many loyal Lancastrians. John's body would have been brought home and buried in the Grey family mausoleum at Astley, but no monument survives today.

We may suppose that Elizabeth tried to appear outwardly calm as the tired rider blurted out his story, but her thoughts would have been in turmoil. Life was bound to become more difficult, and her troubles multiplied when her mother-in-law, Lady Ferrers, attempted to recover three Grey family manors which her own late husband had settled on John and Elizabeth in 1456. Lady Ferrers feared that the properties would be all but lost to her if her daughter-in-law lived to a ripe old age or remarried; and although Elizabeth was able to establish her right to them it was unlikely to be the end of the matter. Disappointed litigants often resorted to threats and violence when the law ruled against them, and Lady Ferrers had greatly strengthened her hand by marrying Sir John Bourchier, a son of the Earl of Essex and King Edward's aunt Isabel. There was a very real possibility that she would make the dispute an excuse to settle her family lands on her new husband and any children she might have by him (giving them priority over John and Elizabeth's offspring), and Elizabeth turned to William Lord Hastings, King Edward's viceroy in the Midlands, for help. On 13 April 1464 they signed an agreement by which Hastings promised to do what he could to ensure that her son Thomas's right to inherit the estates was not frustrated, on condition that Elizabeth shared the profits with him and Thomas married his (as yet unborn) daughter. He drove what one historian has described as a 'very hard bargain'; but his good offices were no longer needed when she married his royal master only eighteen days later on 1 May.

It would be fascinating to know when and where Edward and Elizabeth first met, and how long they had been romantically involved with each other. Stories of a handsome young king's liaison with a beautiful, older widow were bound to grow with the telling, and we will probably never know if the 'Queen's Oak' ever spread its branches over them, or if they really were married on May Day. What is clear, however, is that the speed of events must have surprised even Elizabeth, since she would not have sought Hastings's assistance (or anyone else's for that matter), if she had known she was about to become Queen of England. She may have felt that she could not abruptly terminate her negotiations with him without arousing suspicion: but the indications are that this was the briefest of courtships; in one author's words, 'the impulsive love match of an impetuous young man'.

Lord Rivers had been forgiven his allegiance to Lancaster and had become a member of the Yorkist royal council, so it is likely that King Edward would have visited Grafton when, from time to time, he journeyed northwards to mop up pockets of resistance. Elizabeth had returned to her family home after her husband's death, and would have been able to speak to him on one of these occasions without having to waylay him in a forest. Edward always had a roving eye for a pretty girl, and probably assumed that if he spoke kindly to her she would become his mistress. Any rejection of his advances would have only increased his determination to have her, and Jacquetta, wise woman that she was, would have readily appreciated how the royal passion could be turned to her daughter's – and indeed, her whole family's – advantage. The chroniclers record that she was the only family member present when they were secretly married at Grafton, and that she brought Elizabeth to Edward's bed (without, apparently, even her husband knowing of it), whenever he happened to be in the vicinity. Concealment was dangerous in that the validity of a private, clandestine wedding could always be challenged later, but it was a risk she had to take.

The king's choice of bride – a widow with two sons whose family had fought against him – would have raised a few eyebrows even in the twenty-first century, but to contemporaries it was both startling and illogical. A ruler could have affairs with attractive ladies who took his fancy, but his marriage was an entirely different matter. A foreign-born queen would bring with her a large dowry and the expectation of an alliance with her native country, advantages that would both be lost if the king defied convention by marrying one of his own subjects. Edward's councillors reasoned that he would not have put his private feelings before his duty to his country unless his normally good judgement had been affected by witchcraft or another malign influence. It was a slur that would haunt Elizabeth for the rest of her days.

ELIZABETH AND THE KINGMAKER

Edward kept his marriage secret for as long as he could, only revealing it to his startled courtiers after five months of subterfuge. When the council met at Reading Abbey in September 1464, he was asked to confirm that he would marry a high-born French lady, and had to admit that he was married already. No chronicler described the scene – perhaps the anger was too palpable – but however much the assembled nobles and prelates disliked the arrangement they could do nothing about it. The king was not obliged to marry in public or give his advisers prior notice of his intentions; and Warwick's close associate John Lord Wenlock spoke for many when he remarked 'we must be patient despite ourselves'.

These men might look down on Elizabeth and bemoan missed opportunities, but Edward's choice was not entirely without merit. Her ability to fulfil her new role would only become apparent later, but no one could deny that she was beautiful (in an age when beauty was associated with goodness), or that she was likely to give her new husband an heir. Her father's comparatively humble origins were, arguably, compensated by her mother's descent from the House of Luxembourg, and her Lancastrian antecedents sent a clear message to Henry VI's supporters that they too had a place in the new Yorkist England. Edward had broken with convention because he loved Elizabeth, but perhaps he was not as heedless of the consequences as some thought.

A more serious disadvantage was that, by marrying Elizabeth, Edward had effectively made himself responsible for her large family. No self-respecting king could allow his wife's relatives to live in genteel poverty, and many of her five surviving brothers, seven sisters, and the two sons of her first marriage had to be promoted or found marriage partners of appropriate status. Margaret, who is sometimes described as her eldest sister, was married to Thomas Lord Maltravers, the Earl of Arundel's heir, in October 1464, and their siblings

Anne, Joan, Jacquetta and Mary were all wed or betrothed to the sons of senior noblemen within the next two years. Her father Lord Rivers was appointed to the lucrative office of Treasurer before being created an earl, and in October 1466 Elizabeth bought the marriage of the heiress of the Duke of Exeter for her eldest son Thomas. Anthony, her eldest brother, was given the lordship of the Isle of Wight, while Lionel, one of the younger members of the brood, was fast-tracked to high office in the Church.

The problem, of course, was that lords who had hoped to secure these and other positions and marriages for their own sons and daughters were disappointed, and some were positively outraged when King Edward allowed Elizabeth's brother John, who was aged about twenty, to marry the sixty-something Dowager Duchess of Norfolk. This was an age in which impoverished young men often made their fortunes by marrying rich widows, but the arrangement so offended contemporary sensibilities that the chronicler was moved to describe it as a *maritagium diabolicum* (no translation needed!). In the event, John was executed in 1469, and so the already thrice-married duchess outlived him too.

The Dowager Duchess of Norfolk was the Earl of Warwick's aunt, and Warwick had every reason to feel aggrieved at the way in which Edward and Elizabeth's schemes had affected his plans for his own family. He had hoped to secure the Exeter heiress for his nephew (he had no son), and was further disappointed when the young Duke of Buckingham, whom he regarded as a potential husband for his elder daughter, Isabel, was married to Elizabeth's sister Katherine. Matters were not improved when King Edward refused to allow Isabel to marry his own brother and heir apparent George Duke of Clarence and then rubbed salt in the wound by depriving Warwick's brother George Archbishop of York of the chancellorship.

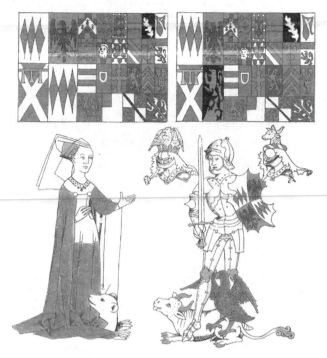

Richard Neville, Earl of Warwick, the 'Kingmaker', and his wife Anne Beauchamp, from *The Rous Roll*

Warwick had always favoured a French alliance, and Edward's decision to wed his sister Margaret to Charles Duke of Burgundy (the King of France's enemy and Elizabeth's continental relatives' overlord), was, in the opinion of the well-informed Croyland chronicler, the last straw.

Edward had been a mere nineteen-year-old stripling when Warwick had promoted his successful bid for the throne in 1461, and was bound to become increasingly his own man as he grew in confidence. It was almost inevitable that monarch and minister would sometimes favour different policies, but what irked Warwick was the fact that he had made Edward king while the upstart Woodvilles – who now enjoyed his favour – had been fighting for Lancaster. Elizabeth was only indirectly responsible for her husband's decisions and could not be blamed for being part of such a large family, but the fact remained that if she had not married Edward few, if any, of these things would have happened. The king's fool might jest that the Rivers had become so high that he could not 'scrape' through them, but Warwick would not have been amused.

Warwick swallowed hard, even helping to escort Edward's sister Margaret to Margate, from where she was to embark for her marriage to Charles of Burgundy, but he had probably already decided to bring his royal master to heel. The Middle Ages had no concept of what we today call 'loyal opposition' – no permitted mechanism by which a subject could seek to frustrate royal or 'government' policy – and so he had to tread carefully, working through proxies he could disown in the event of failure. The popular uprising known as Robin of Redesdale's rebellion, which broke out in Yorkshire in June 1469, was led by men loyal to the Nevilles, and seemed initially to accomplish its purpose. Warwick seized the opportunity to marry his daughter Isabel to George of Clarence, and Edward, who was then at Nottingham, told Elizabeth's father and brothers to make a run for it shortly before the main royal army was defeated at Edgecote, near Banbury. He knew only too well that the Woodvilles would bear the brunt of the rebels' anger, and would have been more saddened than surprised when he learned that Earl Rivers and his son John had been hunted down and executed on Warwick's orders. No legal process is recorded, presumably because capital charges could not be brought against them when they were loyal to a king whom Warwick himself still recognised. It was an act of private vengeance on the earl's part.

Elizabeth was at Norwich when she heard that King Edward had been taken into 'protective custody' by

Archbishop George Neville at Olney in ┊
and learned of the deaths of her father and br┊
had again turned her life upside down, and the┊
doubt that henceforward she regarded Warwick┊
son-in-law George of Clarence (her own brothe┊
her mortal enemies. She would have spent man┊   ┊ss
nights wondering what the future held for her family – what
would happen to them if, in the worst-case scenario, her husband was forced to reject her as the price of keeping his
throne – but found that she had less to fear than she expected.
Warwick soon realised that he could not rule through
Edward – few would accept orders that did not come from
the king personally – but he was not held to account when he
released him and allowed him to return to his capital. On the
contrary, Edward was at pains to placate the Nevilles, even
betrothing his eldest daughter to Warwick's nephew, and
Elizabeth would have been obliged to receive them at court
and smile as though nothing had happened. Her private feelings would have all but overwhelmed her, but public duty
came first.

Warwick had eliminated some of his rivals, but found that
the episode had not improved his ability to change the king's
policies or influence his choice of ministers. His thoughts
began to turn towards replacing Edward with George, and in
March 1470 he stirred another uprising, this time in
Lincolnshire. Edward did not immediately suspect treason
and even asked Warwick and George to raise troops to help
deal with the trouble; but they could not deny their involvement after the leaders of the Lincolnshire men were routed at
'Losecote Field' – so called because the rebels discarded their
heavy padded jackets as they ran for safety – and confessed
that the earl and his son in-law were the 'partners and chief
provokers of all their treasons'. The scheming pair accepted

that they had lost this round of the contest, but rebuffed King Edward's offers of pardon. They fled to France, leaving Elizabeth with the satisfaction of knowing that her husband would not readily trust them again.

The king and queen hoped that the troublemakers' departure signalled an end to their problems, but they were soon to be disillusioned. In France, Warwick and George were reconciled with the exiled Lancastrian queen, Margaret of Anjou, and agreed to help her restore her imprisoned husband, King Henry, to the throne. King Edward was away in the north when the rebel lords returned to England on 13 September, and found that he had no answer to their popularity. Warwick was able to pose as a 'leader of the opposition' to a government that had spent nearly a decade disappointing its subjects, and the desertion of his brother John Neville (whom the king had continued to trust) proved devastating. Edward and a few loyal friends made a dash across Lincolnshire, narrowly escaping drowning in the Wash before commandeering several fishing boats they found at Lynn. Their little flotilla was chased by hostile ships but managed to reach the friendly coast of Holland where the king, who had no money with him, rewarded the master of his vessel with a fine furred gown. Warwick took charge of the government, and the hapless Henry VI was brought out of the Tower of London to resume his long-interrupted 'reign'.

When news of Warwick's return reached Elizabeth in London, she began to provision the Tower to withstand a siege, but abandoned the stronghold when it became apparent that the situation was hopeless. She was eight months pregnant and afraid that Warwick's men would force the Westminster sanctuary where she took refuge with her mother and three young daughters; but the Kingmaker ordered that all such places were to be respected and her first

son by Edward was safely delivered there on or shortly after
1 November. In normal circumstances, a person claiming
sanctuary had forty days to surrender to the authorities or
leave England, but no pressure seems to have been brought
to bear on Elizabeth. She was allowed to receive gifts of food
and other essentials from the abbot and from sympathetic
Londoners; the new government paid Elizabeth Lady Scrope
£10 to 'attend' (presumably to supervise) her; and she could
anticipate an occasional, smuggled, letter from her husband.
Boredom would have been her worst enemy, but she was with
her mother and her young children and was not unused to
looking after herself and coping with difficult situations.
Perhaps she found the cramped conditions less irksome than
if she had been a high-born princess.

Elizabeth could not have anticipated how long she would
have to remain in the sanctuary or what might, or might not,
become of her. Her rival, Queen Margaret, had spent many
years as a fugitive and in exile before the opportunity to
reclaim her throne presented itself, and Elizabeth too could do
nothing but wait and hope that somehow her husband would
be able to regain the initiative. King Edward returned to
England with some men and equipment supplied by Duke
Charles, his sister Margaret's husband, on 14 March 1471, and
found that luck, and boldness, favoured him. He gained access
to York by claiming (implausibly) that he had come only to
reclaim his father's duchy, and found that neither of Warwick's
two northern armies seemed inclined to intercept him. Henry
Percy, who commanded one of them and whom Edward had
restored to his forfeited earldom of Northumberland less than
a year earlier, had already been asked to at least remain neutral,
and the uncertainty seems to have affected his supposed ally
John Neville, who decided not to intervene until Percy's
attitude became clearer. Unchallenged, Edward marched

southwards gathering troops as he went, and on 3 April was formally reconciled with his brother George of Clarence. Warwick's new-found commitment to the House of Lancaster had effectively destroyed George's hopes of becoming king himself one day, and the chronicler describes how his mother, sisters, and some leading churchmen joined forces to persuade him that his future lay with his Yorkist brothers. When Edward met him on the Banbury road there was 'right kind and loving language betwixt them' and their two armies became one.

The Earl of Warwick shut himself up in Coventry and refused to fight until reinforcements arrived, so Edward struck out for London, partly to reclaim his capital but also to rescue his wife and new-born son. In the words of the chronicler he

> then went to the Queen and comforted her that had a long time abiden and sojourned at Westminster, assuring her person only by the great franchise of that holy place, in right great trouble, sorrow and heaviness, which she sustained with all manner patience that belonged to any creature, and as constantly as hath been seen at any time any of so high estate to endure; in the which season nevertheless she had brought into this world, to the King's greatest joy, a fair son, a prince, where with she presented him at his coming, to his heart's singular comfort and gladness.

Elizabeth's relief must have been considerable, but next day, Good Friday, the royal couple were informed that Warwick and the hitherto uncertain John Neville were advancing southwards. Leaving his wife in London, Edward drew up his forces at Barnet on the Saturday evening, and next day – Easter Sunday, 14 April – won a stunning victory over his old mentor. A mist that concealed his own movements caused confusion in the ranks of his enemies, and his smaller army overcame the greater numbers ranged against it. Warwick and John Neville were both killed, the former as he tried to escape, and their lifeless bodies were displayed publicly at St Paul's.

The rest of the story can be briefly told. Queen Margaret only landed in England on Easter Sunday, and was devastated when news of Warwick's defeat at Barnet was brought to her. Edward lost no time in setting off in pursuit of the new army her friends were raising in the West Country, and after covering thirty-six miles in one period of twenty-four hours (twice as fast as an army normally marched), cornered her at Tewkesbury on 3 May. Next day he destroyed her forces and killed her son, the Lancastrian Prince Edward, but Elizabeth would have been unaware of this when the 'Bastard of Fauconberg', a natural son of Warwick's late uncle Lord Fauconberg, raised the standard of rebellion in Kent and threatened London. Her brother Anthony (now Earl Rivers) drove Fauconberg's men back from the Tower, where she was living, and held out until reinforcements from the king's army reached the capital, but the danger had been all too real while it lasted. If the counter-attack had faltered she was, in the words of a contemporary, 'likely to stand in the greatest jeopardy that ever she stood'.

Edward's return to London and Henry VI's convenient 'death' a day or so later brought what was undoubtedly the most dramatic and often fearful period of Elizabeth's life to a conclusion. She had no genuinely powerful foreign relatives who would shelter her (another disadvantage of her being her husband's subject), but her apparent stoicism in remaining in England throughout the troubles only added to her growing reputation. The Speaker of Parliament, William Alyngton, 'declared before the King and his noble and sad [serious] council, the intent and desire of his commons, especially in the commendation of the womanly behaviour and the great constancy of the Queen, he being beyond the sea'. There were many who had thought her unsuited to be Edward's wife seven years earlier, but no one, it seems, questioned her fitness now.

ELIZABETH THE QUEEN

Alyngton did not say in so many words what he meant by 'womanly behaviour', but he was almost certainly referring to the birth of the young prince, christened Edward after his father. Elizabeth may have disappointed her husband by giving him only daughters in the early years of their marriage, but she more than made up for it by producing two more sons (as well as four more daughters) in the course of the 1470s and 1480. Neither Margaret (b. 1472) nor George (b. 1477) was destined to live long, and Mary (b. 1467) died aged fourteen; but the seven children who survived their father seemed more than enough to secure the future of the dynasty. They included Henry VII's future queen, Elizabeth of York (b. 1466), and Richard (b. 1473), who would become the younger of the 'Princes in the Tower'.

King Edward had loved Elizabeth as his consort in the early years of their marriage, but after 1471 treated her increasingly as his partner in government. She became the effective head of her son Edward's council when he was created Prince of Wales in June 1471 (the subcommittee managing his day-to-day affairs was charged to act 'with the advice and express consent of the Queen'), a task she fulfilled

A 1410 painting of Melusina

John Duke of Bedford receiving a book from Jean Galoys
in a contemporary painting

Melusina's crest on the heraldry of the Counts of St Pol

Elizabeth Woodville. Panel Portrait. An early sixteenth-century copy
of a now lost original

Elizabeth Woodville (detail) and Edward IV (detail), stained glass, Martyrdom Chapel, Canterbury Cathedral c. 1482

Edward, Prince of Wales, afterwards Edward V (contemporary stained glass at Little Malvern Priory, Worcestershire)

Richard III. The earliest surviving portrait, although an early-sixteenth-century copy

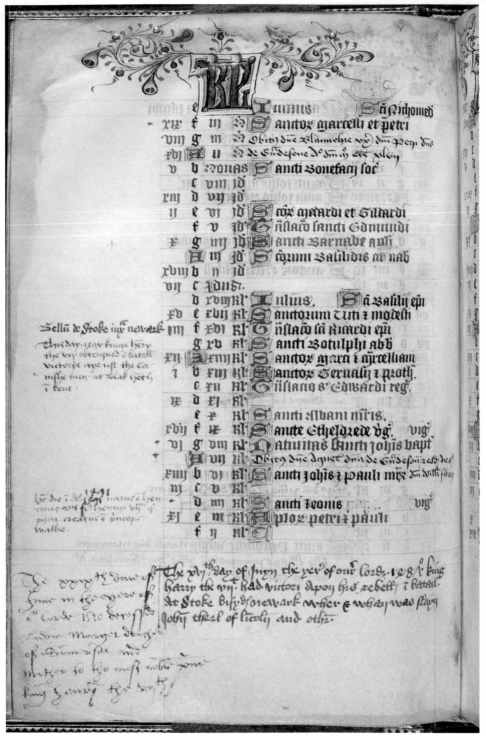

A dynasty triumphant – Margaret Beaufort's book of hours records the birth of her grandson, the future Henry VIII – and victory over her son's enemies at Stoke

This later full-length portrait of Margaret by Rowland Lockey emphasises her piety but – despite its magnificent setting – underplays her political power

The tomb effigy of Margaret at Westminster Abbey shows us a pragamatic and ruthless political survivor

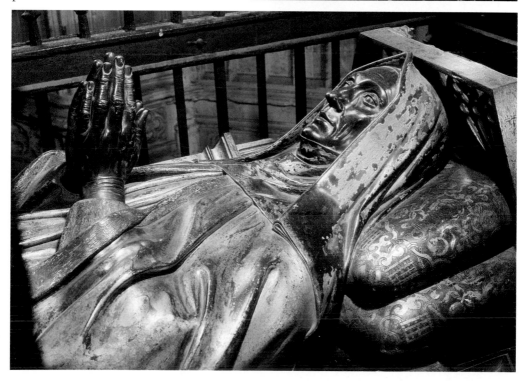

A portrait bust of the first Tudor king, Henry VII, by the Florentine sculptor
Pietro Torrigiano

until the child was given his own household at Ludlow in the Welsh Marches twenty months later. Even then she accompanied him to his new home (where he was to be supervised primarily by her brother Anthony), and became one of the three people entrusted with a key to his coffers. It is also significant that when the king embarked on his abortive invasion of France in 1475 he named her the principal executor of his will if he failed to return. She was to take the leading role in arranging their daughters' marriages, and was given wide-ranging powers to dispose of his goods.

Elizabeth and her brother have been accused of persuading King Edward to allow them to turn Wales into a kind of family fiefdom, but there is no real evidence that this was the case. There were almost bound to be occasions when Anthony issued instructions under his own seal or associated his nephew with them as an afterthought (such actions merely reflected the actuality of the situation), and only a fool would have shunned the opportunity to employ or reward his own followers. The prince's council was not 'packed' with Woodville nominees as some have suggested, and although Elizabeth and Anthony were in a majority among the key-holders there is no indication that they used the boy's money for their own purposes. On the contrary, there were occasions when Anthony paid bills himself.

We have seen how anything that worked to the Woodvilles' advantage was almost certain to be at the expense of others, and Thomas Grey, Elizabeth's eldest son by her first marriage, faced similar criticisms when he was created Marquis of Dorset and given particular responsibilities in the West Country. Thomas seems to have fulfilled his new role adequately – at least there is no hint that the situation there deteriorated during his period of office – but his promotion would have been regarded as yet another example of

Woodville aggrandisement in some quarters. The reality was that Anthony, the future king's uncle, and Thomas, his half-brother, were almost bound to be given senior positions in the world that was a-making, but – again – none of this would have happened if Elizabeth had not become queen.

Thomas Grey's claim to the Exeter estates had lapsed when his first wife had died childless within a year of their marriage, but in 1474 Lord Hastings allowed him to marry his step-daughter Cecily Bonville, heiress to the West Country baronies of Bonville and Harrington. It is likely that Elizabeth had cajoled her husband to persuade Hastings, his great friend, to enter into this agreement with her, and this time there were to be no slip-ups. If Thomas died before the wedding his brother Richard was to marry Cecily to preserve the contract, and Elizabeth was to recoup the £2,500 she undertook to pay Hastings by collecting the revenues of the Bonville and Harrington properties until her daughter-in-law reached the age of sixteen. It is worth noting that ten years had passed since she had last agreed that Thomas should marry into the Hastings family (when, as a frightened widow, she had sought protection shortly before her own wedding to King Edward), and that this time the bride was not to be Hastings's (landless, and then unborn) daughter but his wealthy stepdaughter. She was negotiating from a position of strength.

Elizabeth and the Woodvilles may well have seized every opportunity to promote their own interests, but their machinations hardly compare with those of the king and his two brothers, George of Clarence and Richard of Gloucester. Richard married Anne Neville, Warwick's younger daughter, in 1472, and immediately demanded half the inheritance that George had assumed would fall to him as the husband of her elder sister Isabel. Neither was willing to make concessions, and a further complication was that many of the lands the

Kingmaker had held would only descend to Isabel and Anne in time, if ever. The Beauchamp-Despenser estates of the widowed Countess of Warwick would not pass to her daughters until she herself died, and Warwick had entailed ('settled') his northern Neville lands on George, his brother John's son, the boy who had been betrothed to the king's daughter. Edward finally settled the matter by barring George Neville's claims and by declaring the Countess of Warwick to be *legally* dead – so that her daughters and their acquisitive husbands could inherit her properties without having to wait for her to die naturally! This was manifestly unjust, but there is every indication that the brothers would have resorted to armed conflict if the king had not found a solution that benefited them both.

Elizabeth's next major role, after bearing her husband's children, was to be at his side on great state occasions and participate in the ceremonies in an appropriate manner. Documents describing several of these royal gatherings have survived from the 1470s, and show her fulfilling her duty as impeccably as any woman born into the purple. When Louis de Gruthuyse, who had sheltered King Edward during his exile in Holland, was invited to England and created Earl of Winchester in September 1472, Elizabeth, we are told, 'ordered a great banquet ... with abundant welfare ... in her own chamber'. No expense was spared to make the guest of honour feel welcome and comfortable, and the after-dinner entertainment included dancing by some of the greatest in the land. When all was finished, the king and queen escorted Louis to 'three chambers of pleasance all hanged with white silk', and to a bed 'of as good down as could be thought ... as for his bed sheet and pillows they were of the Queen's own ordinance'. Elizabeth had as much reason to be grateful to him as her husband, and her thoughtful touches complemented the greater honour only Edward could bestow.

Elizabeth Woodville portrayed in her coronation robes as a member of the London Skinners' Company's Fraternity of Our Lady's Assumption, probably c. 1472. The legend reads: 'Oure moost goode and graciouse Quene Elizabeth, Soster unto this oure Fraternite of oure blissed Lady and Moder of Mercy Sanct Mary Virgyn the Moder of God'

In 1476 King Edward decided to rebury the remains of his father, Richard Duke of York, and brother Edmund with greater respect than they had received after their deaths at the battle of Wakefield sixteen years earlier. The bodies were exhumed from their original graves in Pontefract in Yorkshire and brought south to the Yorkist mausoleum at Fotheringhay in Northamptonshire, where elaborate tombs had been prepared for them. Richard Duke of Gloucester headed the cortège accompanied by other peers, bishops and heralds, and ensured that his father and brother were appropriately honoured at each stage of the journey. A lifelike effigy of the duke with a white angel holding a crown behind – or over – his head to symbolise that he had been king as of right, was placed over his black-draped coffin, and the hearses were ceremonially guarded at each place they stopped for the night. When they arrived at Fotheringhay on 29 July they were met by Edward, who respectfully kissed his father's image before it was received into the church by the assembled clergy. The appropriate obsequies were observed, after which Lord Hastings, on behalf of the king, and Lord Dacre of the South, acting for Elizabeth, laid seven and five pieces of cloth of gold over the body in the form of a cross.

Next day the numerous dignitaries attended a mass of requiem at which the duke's regal status was again emphasised. Walter Lord Ferrers of Chartley rode a black-trapped warhorse displaying the royal arms of England to the choir entrance, after which Edward offered his mass-penny and bowed to the catafalque followed by Elizabeth and their two eldest daughters. The queen was dressed all in blue (the royal colour of mourning) 'without a high headdress', and, in the words of a contemporary, 'made a great obeisance and reverence to the said body'. After the burial the royal party repaired to a 'village' of canvas pavilions where they fed a large number of people (our author claims 20,000), and gave alms to all who asked for them. The guests who partook of the royal munificence could not fail to be impressed by the king's generosity and his ability to command.

The third great ceremonial occasion of the decade took place on 15 January 1478 when the king and queen's second son Prince Richard was married to the Lady Anne Mowbray, the late Duke of Norfolk's heir. The bride was conducted from the queen's chamber at Westminster to St Stephen's Chapel by the Earl of Lincoln (King Edward's nephew), Anthony Earl Rivers, 'and many ladies and gentlewomen'. Edward,

Elizabeth, three of their daughters and the king's mother awaited them, seated beneath a canopy of cloth of gold, and listened patiently while a papal bull was read permitting the young couple to marry even though they were related within the prohibited degrees. Afterwards, Richard of Gloucester 'cast gold and silver among the common people', and a great banquet was followed a week later by a tournament in which Anthony, Elizabeth's two sons from her first marriage, and her youngest brother Sir Edward Woodville all participated. It confirmed the strength of the ruling dynasty, and emphasised the prominence of the Woodvilles in its midst.

Prince Richard was only four when he wed his five-year-old bride, and was left a widower less than four years later at the tender age of eight. The aim, of course, had been to secure the Norfolk estates for the royal family, and King Edward had already ensured that they would not revert to Anne Mowbray's own relatives in the event of her death. In a move reminiscent of his deprivation of the Countess of Warwick he arranged for parliament to give his son a life interest in the inheritance which would then pass to any children he might have by another wife. The two co-heirs, John Lord Howard and William Viscount Berkeley, were bound to be disappointed, and although Howard did not protest openly (unlike Berkeley), he must have felt that his many years of service to the House of York had been poorly rewarded. It is hardly surprising that he supported Richard of Gloucester's bid for the throne in 1483.

It would be easy to assume that now Elizabeth was queen she could spend without worrying about where the money came from, but King Edward was determined to restore the Crown's solvency after the extravagances of Henry VI's reign. The lands granted her on her accession yielded approximately £4,500 per annum, and she was almost certainly told that her expenses must not exceed this figure. Only one account survives – for 1466–7 – but her surplus of £200 for that year contrasts strikingly with Margaret of Anjou's 'loss' of £24 (after spending over £7,500), in 1452–3. There were some extravagances – £14 10s. spent on sable furs and £54 on goldsmith's wares, for example – but the overriding impression is that she managed with a smaller staff than her predecessor and reduced fees and household expenses whenever she could.

Some commentators have suggested that Elizabeth was not personally interested in everyday economics, and that her treasurer John Forster was responsible for the careful budgeting that characterised her accounts in 1466–7. Professor Myers thought that 'there is no reason to suppose that she understood finance beyond the usefulness of money for gratifying her desires', but it seems unlikely that senior servants like Dr Roger Radcliff, her chancellor, and John Dyve, her attorney-general, could have had their fees reduced unless the queen had been personally involved in the process. Medieval aristocrats were more inclined to exact the last penny than to be careless of their income and expenditure, and it would not be surprising if Elizabeth checked her accounts in the same way that we know her son-in-law Henry VII checked his. Forster may have been charged with balancing the books on a day-to-day basis, but is unlikely to have done as he wished.

Like other aristocratic ladies, Elizabeth had her own household which was quite separate from that of her husband and which was staffed by her own officers. Her chamberlain was himself a peer, her ladies-in-waiting were usually the wives or relatives of knights and noblemen, and her council included not only her senior employees but also greater men whose influence and advice she valued. Her estates, concentrated as they were in particular regions, meant that she was bound to be regarded as the local 'good lady' in these areas, and expert guidance in matters such as dispensing patronage (minor offices and cash annuities), maintaining values, and settling disputes would have been essential. She could – and did – delegate much of this work to others, but the ultimate responsibility was hers alone.

Intercession had long been a part of medieval queenship, and Elizabeth would have received a stream of petitions from both corporate bodies and individuals who thought that they would gain more by approaching her than by going directly to the king. Queens were traditionally kind-hearted and sympathetic towards their subjects, and were expected to use their influence with their husbands to win concessions or right wrongs that would not have been addressed in other circumstances. The requests she received from corporate bodies included one from the city of Coventry in 1474 and another from the Merchant Adventurers four years later. She and her son the Prince of Wales had been well received in Coventry in April (even though it was a former stronghold of Warwick the Kingmaker), and the citizens appealed to her when one Reginald Buckley, a servant of her husband, caused trouble there a few months later. She told them to imprison Buckley until Edward could deal with him, and assured them that, in the meantime, she would speak to the king personally. No more is heard of the matter, and she was presumably as good as her word.

The Merchant Adventurers found themselves in difficulty when the tonnage and poundage they owed to the Crown fell into arrears and they were ordered to pay £2,000. Attempts to persuade the Exchequer to rescind or defer part of the debt were unsuccessful, and they asked the Marquis of Dorset, Lord Hastings and Elizabeth, for help. Hastings advised them to direct their main suit to Elizabeth (although he would do what he could to assist also), and at a meeting of the company 'court', or assembly, held on 8 January 1479 they were informed that 'it hath pleased the Queen's good grace so to labour and pray for us unto the King's grace that at the instance of her prayer, of the said £2,000 is released 500 marks [£333 6s. 8d.]'. A second 500 marks was cancelled three days later, and they were required to pay only two-thirds of the original sum.

It is not, perhaps, particularly surprising to find powerful interest groups approaching Elizabeth, but ordinary people also sought her assistance when more conventional means of obtaining redress failed. One such petitioner was the Norfolk gentleman Simon Bliaunt who complained to her that Sir John Paston was ignoring his better title to the manor of Hemnals in Cotton and was refusing to surrender it to him. The Earl of Oxford, who was dominant in that part of East Anglia, had promised to appoint arbitrators and to reinstate Bliaunt if they failed to reach a decision by Easter 1467; but Oxford was on good terms with the Pastons and showed no inclination to expel his clients. Elizabeth could have taken the view that Bliaunt was a 'nobody' whose difficulties were beneath her attention, but far from ignoring the matter she wrote to the earl in no uncertain terms telling him she 'marvelled' that he had not honoured his undertaking. 'Wherefore we desire and pray you that you will, at the contemplation of these our letters, show unto the said Simon all the favourable lordship that you goodly may, doing him to be restored and put into his lawful and peaceable possession of the same [manor], as far as reason, equity and good conscience shall require, that he may understand himself to fare the better for our sake, as our very trust is in you.' Again, the end of the story is missing, but Oxford presumably obeyed!

Sir John Paston found himself on the wrong side of the argument on this occasion, but two years later had occasion to seek Elizabeth's assistance on behalf of his own family. His late father had greatly improved their fortunes by persuading the wealthy but childless knight Sir John Fastolf to make a new deathbed will leaving him all his properties, but his gain had made enemies of a number of powerful figures (not least the Dukes of Norfolk and Suffolk), who had themselves expected to share in the inheritance. John's only hope was to find someone as powerful as, or preferably more powerful than, his opponents who would intercede for him, and it was for this reason that 'at the special request of the Queen', he appointed John Yotton, one of her chaplains, to a sinecure at Caister Castle. Elizabeth was one of the few people in England who could stand up to the dukes, but even she did not presume to order them directly. Instead, she wrote to their wives, asking them to speak to their respective husbands and to let them know her mind in the matter. Such a move was unlikely to change attitudes, but it was a way of warning Norfolk and Suffolk that they could not simply do as they pleased.

Elizabeth's ability to intervene successfully in these matters owed a great deal to her personal relationship with her husband. She could only seek favours on behalf of others if she was on good terms with him, and this cannot always have been easy. King Edward was notorious for his voracious sexual appetite, and had affairs both before and during his marriage. Thomas More remarked that 'he was of youth greatly given to fleshly wantonness, from which health of body, in great prosperity and fortune, without a special grace hardly refraineth', while Dominic Mancini's comment that 'he had been most insolent to numerous women after he had seduced them, for, as soon as he grew weary of dalliance, he gave up the ladies much against their will to the other courtiers', implies that he changed little as he grew older. The King of France, Louis XI, once invited him to Paris, and told him jocularly that 'if he would come and divert himself with the ladies, he would assign him the Cardinal of Bourbon for his confessor, who he knew would willingly absolve him ... for he knew the cardinal was a jolly companion'!

Elizabeth must have been aware of these liaisons, but she did not allow them to sour her relationship with her husband. Words there may have been, but she continued to bear him children throughout their life together – Bridget, her last daughter, was born in November 1480 when she was forty-three – and there is no evidence that his trust in her ever diminished. No self-respecting medieval king would admit to changing his attitude or his policies because his wife asked him to, but there are hints that Edward could be far less forgiving on occasions when they were apart and Elizabeth was unable to influence him. He was justifiably angry that a number of nobles and knights – including some he had thought were his friends – fought against him at the battle of Tewkesbury, but to have a dozen of them dragged from the sanctuary of the nearby abbey and beheaded after the merest formality of a trial was as shocking as it was unprecedented. We cannot be sure that he would have behaved differently if Elizabeth had been present and able to calm him; but there is a striking contrast between this and his considered and sometimes markedly affable demeanour on other occasions. It would be fascinating to know how much real power Elizabeth, and other medieval queens, actually wielded behind the scenes.

There is one other aspect of Elizabeth's queenship we have not so far dealt with, namely her obligation to give small sums of money to deserving subjects who found themselves in financial difficulties. All direct evidence that would have allowed us to see her at work in this capacity has long since perished, but it can be glimpsed in a single surviving privy-purse account recording gifts made by her daughter Queen Elizabeth of York. The younger Elizabeth was approached by various individuals who were in some way acquainted with her or who lived near to Richmond Palace, where she was then residing, and who often brought her small presents in anticipation of her willingness to help them. Two poor women who brought gifts of apples and butter to the queen were given twenty and eight pence respectively, and twenty pence was given to 'a poor man in [an] almshouse sometime being a servant of King Edward IV'. Both William Pastone, a page of the queen's beds, and Leonard Twycross, who served the apothecary John Grice, were helped to buy their wedding clothes, while Nicholas Grey, clerk of the works at Richmond Palace, was compensated with sixty shillings when his house caught fire. A friar was given eight shillings 'for the burying of the men that were hanged at Wapping Milne', a girl about to enter a convent was provided with a dowry, and Christopher Plummer was reimbursed twenty-three shillings for 'money by him given in alms for the Queen at divers times in her journeys'. Elizabeth of York would have been regarded as a good and gracious lady by those she assisted, just as her mother would have been blessed by those who approached her and went away happy. In such ways were reputations made.

ELIZABETH THE WOMAN

We have seen something of how Elizabeth responded to the demands and responsibilities of queenship, but can we tell what she was like as a person? Modern historians have alleged that she indulged in feuds, behaved meanly towards those who displeased her, and was careless of others' welfare, but much of their evidence is open to interpretation. One charge that can be dismissed quite easily is that she plotted the execution of the Irish Earl of Desmond who had dared to suggest to King Edward that it was still not too late for him to reject her and marry a well-connected foreigner. This appears to be no more than a 'family tradition' first mentioned by the earl's grandson in Henry VIII's reign, and although Desmond *was* beheaded there were sound political reasons for his downfall. Allegations that Elizabeth persuaded her husband to appoint the Earl of Worcester (who had agreed to avenge her) as his deputy in Ireland and purloined the royal signet ring to validate a 'feigned' letter ordering Desmond's execution are almost certainly tales concocted years later. The Desmonds may have preferred to peddle the story that their ancestor had fallen victim to a spiteful woman rather than admit that he had conspired against the Crown.

Another criticism of Elizabeth is that her new royal status had 'gone to her head' and made her insufferably haughty. No one said this in so many words however, and the idea seems to be based mainly on the observations of some visiting Bohemians who were invited to see her 'churched' (formally received back into society following her period of ritual impurity) after the birth of her eldest daughter, Elizabeth of York, in 1466. One of them, Gabriel Tetzel, described the banquet that followed the service in great detail, noting that

> The Queen sat alone at table on a costly golden chair. The Queen's mother and the King's sister had to stand some distance away. When the Queen spoke with her mother or the King's sister, they knelt down before her until she had drunk

water. Not until the first dish was set before the Queen could the Queen's mother and the King's sister be seated. The ladies and maidens and all who served the Queen at table were all of noble birth and had to kneel so long as the Queen was eating. The meal lasted for three hours. The food which was served to the Queen, the Queen's mother and the King's sister and the others was most costly. Much might be written of it. Everyone was silent and not a word was spoken.

It would be easy to suppose that Elizabeth thoroughly enjoyed making these ladies who had once far outranked her kneel in the rushes, but such a view takes no account of the strict rules governing English court protocol. The great respect shown her was as traditional as the silence that so impressed Tetzel, and would probably not have attracted comment if she had been a high-born princess. Elizabeth did not personally insist on any of these things, nor could she dispense with or modify them. She was an English queen, and did as English queens did.

A more substantial charge is that Elizabeth and other members of her family were at odds with Sir Thomas Cook, a former Mayor of London, supposedly because he had refused to sell her mother Jacquetta a particular tapestry 'at her pleasure and price'. Cook's troubles began in 1467 or 1468 when he was approached by a Lancastrian agent named John Hawkins who asked him to lend the exiled Queen Margaret some money. He declined, but at the same time decided not to report the incident to the authorities; and was accused of 'misprison of treason' (i.e. being aware that a crime was being committed but failing to reveal it), after Hawkins was arrested and forced to reveal the names of his contacts. The chronicler Robert Fabyan reported that some members of the queen's family ransacked Cook's London house in the hope of finding evidence against him, while others took possession of his country estate in Essex. Fabyan, who was apprenticed to Cook, may not have been an entirely disinterested observer, but there is no reason to doubt that the Woodvilles' men 'made such havoc of such wine as was left that what they might not drink and give away they let run in the cellar' in London, or 'destroyed his deer in his park and spoiled his house without pity' in Essex.

Fabyan was in no doubt that these attacks had been instigated by Elizabeth's parents, Earl Rivers and Jacquetta, but the queen herself became implicated when she demanded £800, an extra 10 per cent added to Cook's huge fine of £8,000, under the ancient right of 'Queen's Gold'. This was usually levied only on voluntary fines, those paid for a licence or pardon, for example, so Cook's representatives approached her solicitor and, as a result, he 'had his end, how well there was none open speech of it after'. The precise meaning of this is uncertain, but it appears that some – or perhaps all – of the claim was rescinded, and that he was far from ruined. According to Fabyan, he 'builded and purchased as he did before'.

It seems possible that Elizabeth had been told, perhaps by family members who disliked Cook, that here was an opportunity to obtain a substantial sum to which she was properly entitled, but that her attitude changed when the 'mistake' was pointed out to her. Later writers who took the view that no Woodville ever did anything good found it easy to misconstrue the situation however, and the same is true of her decision to place a daughter of Sir William Stonor in the household of her sister-in-law Elizabeth Duchess of Suffolk, at some time between 1470 and 1473. The girl was unhappy there and asked her parents if she could return home; but her mother, who had been reluctant to sanction the arrangement in the first place, told her in no uncertain terms that she could do so only with the queen's permission. Her best course of action was to ask the duchess to release her 'so that my husband or I may have writing from the Queen with her own hand, or else he nor I neither dare nor will take upon us to receive you, seeing the Queen's displeasure afore'.

It would be easy to suppose that Elizabeth was not particularly interested in the girl's welfare, but her own view would have been that she had given someone from a less exalted background an unrivalled opportunity to mix and mingle with the best in society. Children 'placed' in other households were often homesick, but it was all part of the process of gaining self-confidence and learning what others expected of them. We do not know how, or if, this particular difficulty was resolved, but some years later (it could have been as long as a decade), Sir William again found himself in correspondence with Elizabeth and again potentially on the wrong side of the argument. The reason this time was that Elizabeth had heard that he had been hunting deer in her 'forest and chase' of Barnwood and Eggshill (Glos.), and was sceptical of his claim that he was acting under a commission 'to take the view and rule of our game' granted him by her husband. Her terse, no-nonsense letter required him to 'show unto us or our council your said commission, if any such ye have, and in the mean season [time] spare of [desist from] hunting within our said forest or chase *as ye will answer at your peril*' (my italics). She was not a lady to be trifled with!

Elizabeth would have had little direct contact with men like Cook and Stonor, and their differences were probably isolated incidents; but her sometimes difficult relationship with William Lord Hastings, her husband's close friend and chamberlain, was an altogether different matter. She may have never quite forgiven Hastings for the hard bargain he struck when she sought his help before her royal marriage, and undoubtedly held him responsible for her husband's licentious behaviour. No one who was 'secretly familiar with the King in wanton company', to quote Thomas More, could seriously expect the queen to look kindly upon him, and the fact that Hastings was twelve years older than her husband made it easier to blame him for leading Edward astray. Hastings himself seems to have been likeable enough – 'a good knight and a gentle . . . very faithful . . . a loving man and passing well beloved', according to More – but Elizabeth probably treated him coolly and wished that her husband favoured him less than he did.

The situation was not helped by the friction that also existed between Hastings and Elizabeth's brother Anthony Earl Rivers, and between Hastings and the elder son of her first marriage, Thomas Grey Marquis of Dorset. Hastings replaced Anthony as Captain of Calais soon after King Edward's restoration in 1471, and although Anthony was subsequently honoured – by being given prime responsibility for Prince Edward, for example – the loss of Calais still rankled. Rumours began to circulate that the doggedly loyal Hastings was planning to betray the stronghold to the French, and – according to More – 'was far fallen into the king's indignation and stood in great fear of himself'. King Edward would never have thought this of his trusted friend in other circumstances, and it is tempting to conclude that Elizabeth was working against him behind the scenes. The storm passed and Hastings kept his position; but his relations with the Woodvilles would not have been improved.

Hastings and Anthony were very different personalities, the former affable and libidinous, the latter serious and noted for his asceticism and literary interests as well as for his ability as a jouster. They had probably never been friends, but neither had Hastings and the Marquis of Dorset, who both found the hedonistic Yorkist court to their liking. Dominic Mancini says they quarrelled over 'the mistresses whom they had abducted or attempted to entice from one another', and it is likely that both resented the other's influence with King Edward. By the 1470s Hastings was in his forties while Dorset was more than twenty years younger; and it would not be surprising if Hastings feared that his more energetic, perhaps more attractive, rival would soon replace him in the royal affections. Elizabeth would have wanted to diminish Hastings's hold over her husband by any means possible, and may have seen Edward's fondness for her son as a new opportunity after the allegation that Hastings intended to betray Calais failed.

Historical evidence cannot always be taken at face value, however, and it is possible to argue that Elizabeth and Hastings were really on good terms for much of this period. Hastings not only agreed to allow Dorset to marry his step-daughter, Cecily Bonville, in 1474, but nominated both the Marquis and his younger brother Richard for membership of the Order of the Garter two years later. Elizabeth, for her part, gave Hastings's sister, Elizabeth Donne, and his sister-in-law Anne, his brother Ralph's wife, places among her ladies; but were these merely gestures designed to hide their true feelings and foster the illusion that the Yorkist court was united? It is hard to dismiss the 'deadly feud' mentioned by Mancini as being no more than hearsay, and the Croyland writer surely spoke from personal knowledge when he remarked that 'there had long existed extreme ill-will between the said Lord Hastings and them'.

So what do these relationships and incidents tell us about Elizabeth as a person? She has been much criticised for promoting her family's interests, and there were undoubtedly some people whom she liked more than others; but how many of us would reject an opportunity that would benefit those closest to us, and how many find some working relationships 'difficult'? Elizabeth was probably no better – or worse – than most human beings, and her actions must be viewed in the context of her own era. The fifteenth century was a hard and sometimes unprincipled world in which life was cheap and kindness seldom a priority. A man (or woman) who lacked the ability or strength of character to keep what he had would soon lose it, and appeals to law were useless unless he happened to be wealthier or enjoyed greater influence than his opponent. The Woodvilles' treatment of Sir Thomas Cook – perhaps the most outrageous incident described above – does not seem to have shocked contemporaries, who probably thought he had been adequately compensated when he was allowed to deduct the cost of the damage done to his properties from his fine! Elizabeth herself behaved no less imperiously towards the Stonors, but she was the queen and no one questioned her right to act as she did.

Some insight into a person's character can also be gained from their interests, and we have a little knowledge of how Elizabeth chose to pass her leisure hours and of her concern for both learning and matters of religion. When Louis de Gruthuyse visited England in 1472, King Edward took him to Elizabeth's private chamber, 'where she sat playing with her ladies at the morteaulx [a game resembling bowls]', while others played 'closheys [closh, or ninepins] and divers other games' or danced. She may have shown him her books, a collection which came to include a devotional *Hours of the Guardian Angel* (most people of wealth possessed and used such volumes), and three others which she either owned or which had been presented to her children and were essentially for entertainment. They included stories of the Trojan

War, the legend of Jason's search for the Golden Fleece, and a collection of Arthurian romances, all of which passed for history at the time. It is unclear if she read them herself, read them to her offspring, or had them read to her, but she had clearly inherited her mother's love of literature and wanted her own children to do the same.

Elizabeth's interest in learning first became evident when, at the beginning of her reign, she intervened to save both Queens' College, Cambridge, and Eton College from dereliction. The Queen's College of St Margaret and St Bernard that Margaret of Anjou had founded in 1448 had fallen on hard times after the Yorkist triumph, but in 1465 King Edward gave the members a licence to hold property to the value of £200 annually. He informed them that they now had a new patron in Elizabeth, and when statutes regulating the institution were issued ten years later, she was described as *vera fundatrix* (true foundress), and her arms replaced Margaret's on the college seal. The president and twelve fellows were enjoined to study theology rather than law, a decision that may not be unconnected with the fact that many worldly popes had been canon lawyers rather than theologians. Elizabeth was said to be 'specially solicitous concerning those matters whereby the safety of souls and the public good are promoted, and poor scholars, desirous of advancing themselves in the knowledge of letters, are assisted in their need'.

King Edward intended to incorporate Lancastrian Eton, which was still unfinished, into St George's Chapel, Windsor, and obtained a papal bull authorising him to do so in 1463. All Henry VI's grants were revoked in Edward's first parliament, and the building was stripped of its bells, furniture and other valuables. No more might have been heard of it, but in 1467 Edward suddenly relented, restored some income, and petitioned the Pope to cancel the bull. There is no direct evidence

Elizabeth Woodville (lower right foreground), Edward IV, Bishop Thomas Rotherham and Cecily Neville, kneeling with other members of the confraternity before the Trinity. The Luton Guild Book, c. 1475

that Elizabeth was responsible for his change of heart; but she could not have forgotten that her own family had once been deeply committed to Henry VI and may have wanted to preserve the best of his legacy. Present-day scholars may owe her more than they think.

One way in which the great and the good could express their devotion to their faith was by patronising religious institutions, and Elizabeth was no exception. She obtained a licence to establish a fellowship of the Trinity at Leadenhall in London intended to support sixty priests in March 1466, and later founded a chapel dedicated to St Erasmus (the protector of sailors and women in childbirth) in Westminster Abbey, almost certainly in gratitude for her husband's preservation during his nail-biting voyage into exile in 1470 and for the successful delivery of the Prince of Wales. Like earlier queens, she became an honorary member of religious guilds (including the London Skinners' Company's Fraternity of Our Lady's Assumption, and the Holy Trinity Guild, Luton), and took a close personal interest in the two great religious houses situated near Sheen Palace, the Carthusian charterhouse and the Bridgettine Abbey of Syon. In 1477 she was granted the privilege of attending services in all the Carthusian order's houses that had been founded by kings and queens of England, and two years later gave the prior of the Sheen charterhouse, John Ingleby (who was to become one of her executors), forty-three acres of land from her manor there.

Elizabeth also went on pilgrimages, partly to show her contrition for her failings, but perhaps equally to share in the camaraderie and 'holiday atmosphere' that characterised jaunts of this nature. Chaucer's pilgrims were journeying to St Thomas Becket's tomb for the good of their souls, but no one who reads *The Canterbury Tales* could doubt that they were determined to enjoy themselves in the process! Elizabeth's pilgrimages were restricted to holy sites in England – principally Canterbury and the shrine of Our Lady of Walsingham (Norfolk) – but Jerusalem, Rome and Compostela were magnets for her aesthetic brother Anthony. It was after visiting Rome in 1476 that he was robbed of his jewels and plate at Torre di Baccano, about twelve miles north of the city, and was obliged to delay his journey while efforts were made to recover them. Elizabeth sent him letters of exchange worth 400 ducats to help pay his expenses and assist his passage home.

A queen would not usually interfere in wider religious matters, but there was one occasion when Elizabeth was able to use her position and influence to extricate her subjects from a particular spiritual difficulty. The recently proclaimed feast of the Visitation of the Blessed Virgin Mary fell close to two other religious festivals observed in England, and in 1480 Elizabeth petitioned the Pope to allow English men and women to observe it in private without forfeiting any spiritual benefits. The Pope granted special indulgences to those who said the Angelical Salutation (Hail Mary) three times daily 'because the queen desires the devotion of the faithful of the realm for the said salutation to be increased'.

Medieval people sometimes had a rather mechanical approach to their faith – reflected in their routine offering of the mass-penny, for example – but no one thought that religion was an anachronism or that they would not be held accountable for their sins. It is never easy to decide how much of an individual's piety was conventional as opposed to profoundly personal, but there seems little doubt that Elizabeth's convictions were genuine and that she would have thanked God for the many blessings she believed He had bestowed upon her. Her worldly responsibilities and the unkind things said about her have tended to obscure this aspect of her character, and both her mother-in-law, Cecily Neville, and the 'Red Queen', Margaret Beaufort, have been more admired for their devotion to their religion. But no one fought harder for her son, the future Henry VII, than Margaret, and few died possessing greater wealth.

But could Elizabeth have been both a committed Christian *and* a witch who cast spells to achieve her objectives? We need, I think, to distinguish between witchcraft as an alternative religion, and the use of magic to foretell the future or harm an enemy. On one level, it allowed intelligent but unsophisticated minds to explain the otherwise inexplicable, while at the same time enabling them to rid society of those who (it was always assumed) were intrinsically evil. We saw in the first part of this book how, only a few years after Elizabeth was born, Eleanor Cobham, wife of Humphrey Duke of Gloucester, Henry VI's uncle and heir apparent, was accused of using dubious methods to discover if her husband would succeed to the throne and she would become queen. She failed to appreciate that such enquiries were tantamount to hoping that the king *would* die, and Duke Humphrey's enemies made the most of their opportunity. She was punished by being made to carry a lighted taper through London's streets before being consigned to life imprisonment, and the case shows how readily what may have been no more than idle curiosity could be misconstrued.

Eleanor's marriage to Duke Humphrey was dissolved on the grounds that she had used her secret powers to persuade him to marry her, and it is no coincidence that Elizabeth's mother Jacquetta faced similar accusations when Warwick the Kingmaker tried to destroy the Woodvilles in 1469. It was almost impossible to prove that such charges were untrue or unjustified, and they were music to the ears of those who wanted to discredit the victim and those associated with her. Elizabeth was not mentioned in the indictment brought against her mother, and was only implicated fourteen years later when Richard of Gloucester accused her of withering his arm and of using sorcery to bewitch King Edward. Richard, in the words of the Tudor historian Polydore Vergil, claimed that 'by the space of a few days past, neither night nor day can I rest, drink, nor eat, wherefore my blood by little and little decreaseth, my force faileth, my breath shorteneth, and all the parts of my body do above measure, as you see (and with that he showed them his arm), fall away; which mischief verily proceedeth in me from that sorceress Elizabeth the queen, who with her witchcraft has so enchanted me that by the annoyance thereof I am dissolved'.

No one believed him, of course – Thomas More remarked that his arm was 'ever such since his birth' and 'well they [the assembled lords] wist that the queen was too wise to go about any such folly' – but he returned to the attack in *Titulus Regius*, the statute that established his right to the throne. This declared that the 'ungracious pretensed marriage' between his brother and Elizabeth 'was made ... by sorcery and witchcraft, committed by the said Elizabeth and her mother, Jacquetta, Duchess of Bedford, as the common opinion of the people and the public voice and fame is through all this land'. He offered to prove this 'in time and place convenient', if anyone should doubt him – although that seems to have been the end of the matter, at least as far as he was concerned.

So was Elizabeth really a witch, or was this just another, rather crude, attempt to blacken her reputation? Her supposed descent from the water goddess Melusina may have made her more susceptible to such allegations, and her marriage to King Edward defied rational, logical explanation. But *suspicion* is, in the last resort, all we have to go on, and it would be both irrational and illogical to 'convict' her without a shred of real evidence. She had undoubtedly bewitched Edward, but perhaps not in the way that Richard and some of his contemporaries supposed!

ELIZABETH AND HER IN-LAWS

Elizabeth's relations with some of her in-laws, notably her mother-in-law Cecily Neville, her two brothers-in-law George Duke of Clarence and Richard Duke of Gloucester, and her son-in-law Henry VII, were – in time-honoured fashion – far from easy. This section will try to explain how the dissensions arose and assess the damage they inflicted, but will not seek to apportion blame for them. All four treated her harshly on occasion, and she had to contend with one or more of them for her entire reign and beyond.

Elizabeth's relations with her mother-in-law were probably always doomed to failure. Cecily and her husband, Richard Duke of York, would almost certainly have been crowned king and queen if the duke had not been slain at Wakefield on 30 December 1460, and her son Edward's victory could not entirely compensate for the cruel manner in which her own royal title had been snatched from her. The Yorkists might treat her with the respect due to a queen or queen-dowager, but she would have been acutely aware that this was a courtesy rather than a right.

Cecily would have been prepared to bow the knee to a daughter-in-law born into one of the great royal families of

Europe, but a Northamptonshire knight's girl was an entirely different matter. Dominic Mancini says she was so angry when Edward told her he had married Elizabeth that she 'fell into such a frenzy, that she offered to submit to a public enquiry and asserted that Edward was not the offspring of her husband the Duke of York, but was conceived in adultery, and therefore in no wise worthy of the honour of kingship'. The allegation that Edward was illegitimate (probably because he had been born at Rouen, outside England) was an old chestnut, and Mancini, who was writing in 1483, cannot have known what Cecily was supposed to have said almost twenty years earlier. But there is no reason to doubt his belief that there was animosity between the two women, or that frosty interviews like that described in *The White Queen* actually took place.

When news of Edward's victory at Towton on Palm Sunday 1461 was brought to Cecily, one of those present, Nicholas O'Flanagan, Bishop of Elphin, wrote to the papal legate Francesco Coppini urging him not only to send congratulations to the king but also to write to his mother 'who has a great regard for you, and can rule the king as she pleases'. Their relationship was bound to change, at least formally, after Edward married, but he acknowledged his mother's special position by building new apartments for Elizabeth at Westminster, presumably so that Cecily did not have to vacate the rooms she had occupied for the previous three years. It has been assumed that Cecily's absence from both Elizabeth's coronation in 1465 and her husband the Duke of York's reburial at Fotheringhay in 1476 was to avoid any dispute with Elizabeth over precedence, but this is by no means certain. Kings and queens did not usually attend their spouses' coronations or funerals at this period, and she may have deliberately absented herself to emphasise her queenly status in Yorkist eyes.

Cecily's influence may also have been at work when her younger son Richard of Gloucester and other lords and prelates met at her London town house, Baynard's Castle, to discuss the terms of Edward IV's will. They decided to deprive Elizabeth (and presumably her brother Anthony) of any role the late king had desired for them, and to effectively remove the young prince, now Edward V, from the influence of his mother's family. Baynard's Castle may have been no more than a convenient venue for these deliberations, but it is difficult to avoid the conclusion that Cecily concurred with this decision and was happy to facilitate it. Elizabeth Woodville would play no part in a minority government if she had any say in the matter, and she may not have been displeased when Richard deposed young Edward and took the throne.

Richard of Gloucester's relationship with his mother has itself been subject to debate and to differing interpretations. Remarkably, he first sought to justify his assumption of power by reviving the story that his elder brother King Edward had been conceived in adultery, before, apparently, changing his mind and basing his claim on the alleged invalidity of Edward's marriage to Elizabeth. Cecily would surely have resented having her reputation besmirched in this manner (which may be one reason why the excuse was altered), but she seems to have remained on good terms with Richard. A letter he wrote to her in 1484 asking her to appoint his chamberlain, Francis Lovell, to an office in Wiltshire was couched in the formal language a king would have used on every occasion but contains no hint of animosity:

Madam, I recommend me to you as heartily as is to me possible, beseeching you in my most humble and effectual wise [manner] of your daily blessing to my singular comfort and defence in my need. And madam I heartily beseech you that I may often hear from you to my comfort. And madam, I beseech you to be [a] good and gracious lady to my lord, my chamberlain, to be your officer in Wiltshire . . . I trust he shall therein do you good service and that it please you that by this bearer I may understand your pleasure in this behalf. And I pray God send you the accomplishment of your noble desires. Written at Pontefract the third day of June with the hand of your most humble son, Ricardus Rex.

Both Elizabeth and Cecily lived for another decade, but any contact between them was minimal. After a brief period of rehabilitation at the beginning of Henry VII's reign (see below) Elizabeth was sent to Bermondsey Abbey, while Cecily seldom left her home at Berkhampstead Castle after Richard was killed at Bosworth. Elizabeth stood godmother to her first grandson, her daughter Elizabeth's son Prince Arthur, when he was baptised in September 1486, but Cecily, the infant's great-grandmother, was again absent. Two mistresses in the house was perhaps always one too many!

George Duke of Clarence, Elizabeth's elder brother-in-law, had been born close to a throne but had no real prospect of inheriting it. He was his brother Edward's heir for most of the 1460s (it is unlikely that any of the king's three infant daughters would have been allowed to succeed him), but betrayed his dissatisfaction and impatience when he accepted his father-in-law Warwick's offer to make him king in 1470. Warwick failed to deliver however – the 'Lincolnshire Rebellion' ended in failure – and his subsequent reconciliation with Queen Margaret and the House of Lancaster meant that George would now realise his ambition only if Henry VI and his son Prince Edward both died childless. It was probably this, as much as any other factor, that persuaded him to rejoin King Edward before the battle of Barnet, and allowed him to finish on the winning side.

George resumed his position at court after his brother's final victory at Tewkesbury, but remained disgruntled and continued to look for ways of improving his prospects. As early as 1472 he was suspected of conspiring with his wife's surviving uncle, Archbishop George Neville, and the exiled Lancastrian Earl of Oxford, and when, in the next year, Oxford attempted to invade England, he assured Louis XI that he had the support of twenty-four lords, knights and gentlemen and *one duke*. He may have meant the Duke of Exeter, who had his own, distant Lancastrian claim to the throne and whom Edward IV had never trusted; but George Duke of Clarence cannot be ruled out.

George supposed that because he was married to the Earl of Warwick's elder daughter Isabel he would succeed to his late father-in-law's lands (on behalf of his wife), and that the vast Beauchamp-Despenser inheritance of the widowed Countess of Warwick would also pass to him. In normal circumstances, if there was no son to inherit, a deceased's property would be divided equally among his or her surviving daughters, but Anne, Isabel's younger sister, had been married to Prince Edward of Lancaster as part of the agreement reached between her father Warwick and the boy's mother, Queen Margaret, in France. Prince Edward's death at Tewkesbury had left Anne a young widow with no one to defend her interests; but all this changed when Richard of Gloucester, George's younger brother, announced that he intended to marry her and claim her half share of the inheritance. The Croyland chronicler says that George disguised Anne as a cookmaid to prevent Richard from finding her; but Richard sought her out, lodged her in sanctuary, and appealed to the king.

It would be tedious to describe the unedifying, often bitter, dispute between the two royal brothers, but the settlement which they and King Edward finally agreed between them was as immoral as it was illegal. We have already seen how young George Neville, Warwick's nephew, was prevented from succeeding to the lands his uncle had settled on him, and how the Countess of Warwick was declared to be *legally* dead so that her daughters (and their husbands) could inherit her lands immediately. The countess protested to anyone who would listen, but her husband had died a traitor and she had few friends.

Edward wanted to restore harmony in the royal family so that he could mount a new expedition to recover Henry V's French empire, and both George and Richard joined him in what proved to be an abortive sortie into France in 1475. They returned wealthier, bought off by Louis XI's offer of personal pensions coupled with lucrative trade and marriage agreements, but George was left to reflect that all the money in the world could not buy him the crown he so longed for. Matters finally came to a head when their brother-in-law, Charles of Burgundy, was killed in battle at Nancy on 4 January 1477. Duke Charles had fought long and hard to create a new 'middle kingdom' of Burgundy, independent of both Germany to the east and France to the west, and his widow Duchess Margaret suggested that Mary, her late husband's daughter and heiress, could secure her territories against King Louis by marrying George, whose wife, Isabel, had also died a few weeks before.

George was delighted with the prospect of cutting a figure on the European stage, perhaps even becoming *King* of Burgundy one day, and was mortified when King Edward refused to allow him to marry Mary. Edward knew only too well that if his brother became Duke of Burgundy English troops would be needed to prevent the French from conquering the duchy, and he could hardly expect to receive his generous annual pension from King Louis if their two countries were at war. Elizabeth would have shed no tears over George's departure in normal circumstances – on the contrary, she would probably have welcomed it – but she would have been alarmed by French-inspired rumours that he meant to use Burgundian arms to make himself king in England. Her sons by the king were aged only five and two, vulnerable to the ambitions of a powerful rival if their father happened to die prematurely, and she would have begged her husband to reject this and any scheme that would make George more formidable than he already was.

George responded by leaving the court in high dudgeon and by behaving lawlessly in his own territories. He had his wife's former servant Ankarette Twynho executed on the absurd charge that she had poisoned her mistress (everyone knew that Duchess Isabel had died in childbirth), and when one of his own supporters, a Thomas Burdet, was hanged for conspiring against the king and the young Prince Edward, George travelled to London and had Burdet's claim that he was innocent read before the royal council. No self-respecting king could tolerate such a blatant assertion that his justice was invalid, and George was arrested on, or soon after, 10 June 1477 and confined in the Tower of London. He was tried and condemned in parliament the following January (where, as the Croyland writer observed, 'not a single person uttered a word against the duke except the king [and] not one individual made answer to the king except the duke'), and executed on 18 February 1478, traditionally by being drowned in a butt of malmsey wine. This may have been a last, melodramatic request or gesture, but it is perhaps more likely that he used an old barrel for washing purposes and was unromantically drowned in his bath!

George had made a thorough nuisance of himself, but

none of the charges brought against him automatically warranted the death penalty. He had, allegedly, kept a copy of a document drawn up in 1470 naming him heir to the throne if Henry VI's line failed, and had spread rumours that Edward was illegitimate; but such misdemeanours could have been punished by imprisonment or the loss of his estates. Contemporaries could not understand why the king found it necessary to inflict the ultimate penalty on his own brother, and his decision has continued to baffle modern writers. It has been suggested that George had threatened to claim that Edward and Elizabeth had never been properly married and that none of their 'illegitimate' children had any right to the succession, but whatever the reason, he was clearly regarded as a serious risk.

So did King Edward make the final, fateful decision himself, or was Elizabeth instrumental in persuading him that she and their children would never be safe so long as George lived? Dominic Mancini, who came to England five years later in 1483, says specifically that she had 'concluded that her offspring would never come to the throne unless the duke of Clarence were removed, and of this she easily persuaded the king'. Mancini was probably handicapped by his unfamiliarity with English; but he had at least one reliable informant in the person of the royal physician John Argentine, and there is no reason to doubt that his statement reflects what people were thinking – and saying – at the time. Elizabeth's part in the process is, like so much else, ultimately unknowable, but few could blame her if she breathed a sigh of relief when George was finally no more.

Richard of Gloucester is said to have interceded with the king for their brother and to have been angered by his execution, but his feelings did not prevent him from asking Edward to adjust the Warwick inheritance settlement in his favour. Very little is known of Elizabeth's dealings with Richard in her husband's lifetime, but there is nothing to suggest that he was on openly bad terms with her or with other members of her family. Richard's biographer Paul Murray Kendall thought that 'the queen, beautiful and rapacious, would know how to show her haughtiness to the undersized lad from Yorkshire with the awkward torso and the solemn face', but this, like so much else in Kendall, is great literature but doubtful history. Richard spent much of the period from 1471 to 1483 serving as his brother's viceroy in the north of England, and would have encountered Elizabeth only on great ceremonial occasions or when he periodically attended court. Their relationship was perhaps distant rather than friendly, politely formal and tinged with caution. Richard had always been loyal to her husband, but had shown that he could be as ambitious and determined as his brother George.

King Edward's line looked set to reign long into the future, but everything changed when he died after a short illness on 9 April 1483. Elizabeth wrote to her brother Anthony Earl Rivers, the Prince of Wales's guardian, urging him to bring her son Edward from Ludlow to London so that he could be crowned as soon as possible, and to come accompanied by as many troops as he could muster. She knew only too well that her family was unpopular in certain quarters and was prepared to err on the side of caution; but some counsellors, notably her old enemy Hastings, feared that she was planning to establish a Woodville-dominated government and objected to the large number of soldiers. Elizabeth quickly realised that she was provoking, rather then deterring, opposition, and went out of her way to reassure everyone. She 'most beneficiently tried to extinguish every spark of murmuring and disturbance', in the words of the Croyland writer, and it was agreed that the young king's escort would be limited to 2,000 men.

When King Edward died Richard of Gloucester was in the north of England and immediately wrote to the queen and the council to express his condolences and declare his loyalty to his brother's heir. He also dispatched a letter to Anthony Earl Rivers at Ludlow, asking when and by what route he intended to bring Edward V to London, and suggesting that they rendezvous somewhere on the way. Anthony apparently replied amiably, proposing that they meet in the vicinity of Northampton about 29 May, although when Richard arrived there he found that the main royal party had pushed on to Stony Stratford, seventeen miles further south. Anthony and Lord Richard Grey, Elizabeth's younger son by her first marriage, returned to Northampton, where they were joined by the Duke of Buckingham, and the four noblemen passed a pleasant evening together. But next morning Anthony and Richard Grey were arrested, and Richard and Buckingham rode to Stony Stratford where they informed the young king that they had frustrated a plot to ambush them. Edward protested, but was powerless to prevent his uncle, his half-brother and other members of his entourage being sent to prisons in the distant north.

It is highly improbable that the Woodvilles intended to harm Richard – hard evidence is entirely lacking – but both parties feared the consequences if the other gained a controlling hand in government. Richard claimed that Edward IV's last will – or a codicil added to it – had named him protector of the realm if Edward died before his son reached maturity, but the will is missing and we can only speculate upon what it might, or might not, have said. Richard was just turned thirty, a man of considerable experience and proven ability, but who surprisingly had not been mentioned in the will Edward had drawn up before leaving for France in 1475. It was Elizabeth who had been given authority to arrange the royal children's marriages if their father failed to return safely, and whatever role Edward had proposed for Richard it is hard to believe that his wife (and her brother) were to be deprived of all influence. The problem was that the boy had been brought up by members of his mother's family, and would inevitably prefer them to an uncle he scarcely knew.

When Elizabeth heard what had happened at Stony Stratford she tried, unsuccessfully, to raise forces and then sought sanctuary at Westminster with her five daughters, her younger son by the late king, and her eldest son the Marquis of Dorset. It was here that Thomas Rotherham, Archbishop of York and chancellor, found her surrounded by 'much heaviness, rumble, haste and business, carriage and conveyance of her stuff, chests, coffers, packs, fardels [bundles], trusses all on men's backs, no man unoccupied, some lading, some going, some discharging, some coming for more'. Elizabeth 'sat alone low on the rushes all desolate and dismayed, whom the Archbishop comforted in the best manner he could, showing her that he trusted the matter was nothing so sore as she took it for'. He handed her the Great Seal of England – clear evidence that, as far as he was concerned, she still counted politically – although he then thought better of it and asked her to return it to him the following day.

Richard paid his young nephew every courtesy, and seemed content when the council formally appointed him Protector. He deferred to the assembled notables when they refused to have Anthony Earl Rivers, Richard Grey and the others arrested at Stony Stratford executed immediately, and although young Edward's coronation was postponed until 22 June there was no suggestion that it would not now happen. It is impossible to know if Richard was pursuing a carefully laid plan to its logical conclusion or whether, alternatively, he was responding to a changing situation; but on 10 June, some five weeks after reaching London, he sent urgently to the north for extra soldiers, seeking assistance 'against the Queen, her blood adherents and affinity, which have intended and daily doith intend to murder and utterly destroy us and our cousin the Duke of Buckingham and the old royal blood of this realm'.

It would have taken the northern troops between two and three weeks to reach London, and events appear to have moved faster than Richard had anticipated. Only three days later, on Friday 13 June, he had Lord Hastings arrested in the council chamber and instantly beheaded without trial. Word was spread that Hastings had been caught conspiring with Elizabeth against the protector and had paid the penalty – an allegation so improbable that historians have baulked at it ever since. Hastings and Richard had both shared the royal exile in 1470–1, and the former had taken the lead in urging Richard to seize the initiative after King Edward died. His poor relationship with Elizabeth has already been noted, and his decision to change sides – if change sides he did – seems inexplicable. One writer has suggested that Hastings had hoped to be as close to Richard as he had been to Edward and resented Buckingham's intrusion; but a more likely reason is that he had realised that Richard intended to make himself king. He would never have countenanced the deposition of young Edward, and his ability to summon a powerful retinue from his Midlands heartland meant that he had to be removed before Richard could proceed further. His 'crime', his unshakable loyalty to his late friend's son, was a crime in Richard's eyes alone.

Hastings's removal was Richard's second successful coup against those he knew would oppose him, but he had still another problem to deal with. He could not feel secure while the younger prince remained in sanctuary with Elizabeth, and on 16 June the Archbishop of Canterbury and a group of peers were sent to Westminster to persuade her to surrender him to them. They tried various ploys, arguing that the boy king was missing his brother and that Prince Richard could not claim sanctuary because he had committed no crime and no one was threatening him; but Elizabeth retorted that the first difficulty could be overcome by placing her elder son in her custody, and added that there was no reason why she and her children should not avail themselves of the Church's protection when the times were so uncertain. Eventually the archbishop, 'perceiving that the Queen began to kindle and chafe and speak sore biting words against the Protector', told her bluntly that if she would trust him and these other lords they would ensure that no harm came to Prince Richard, but that if she rejected their offer they would not attempt to influence or assist her on any future occasion. Elizabeth 'stood a good while in a great study'. She knew that Duke Richard could take her son from the sanctuary by force if he chose to, and was obliged to recognise that she had little alternative but to accept the lords' proposal. With many tears, she gave him to the archbishop, charging him that 'as far as ye think that I fear too much, be you well ware that you fear not as far too little'.

Prince Richard was sent to join his brother in the Tower, and six days later, Ralph Shaa, a Franciscan friar, preached a sermon at St Paul's Cross in which he claimed that all King Edward and Queen Elizabeth's children were illegitimate and that Richard of Gloucester was the rightful heir to the throne. This was based on a revelation made by Robert Stillington, Bishop of Bath and Wells, that Edward had contracted an informal – but still binding – marriage with Lady Eleanor Butler, a daughter of the late Earl of Shrewsbury, presumably at some time between the death of her first husband in 1461 and his wedding Elizabeth in 1464. The position was, apparently, that if Elizabeth had known of this, then her marriage to the king was, and would have remained, invalid; but if she was unaware of it (and Edward would almost certainly not have told her!), then their union could have been recognised after the Lady Eleanor died in 1468. This was important because the Prince of Wales was not born until 1470, but King Edward never supposed that a casual undertaking he had given years earlier (and had very probably forgotten) would one day return to haunt his son.

The lords who might have resisted Richard's take-over had been thoroughly cowed by the destruction of Hastings, and he began his reign as king on 26 June. His nephews, Elizabeth's two young sons, were seen playing in the constable of the Tower's garden some little time after, but were then 'withdrawn into the inner apartments of the Tower proper, and day by day began to be seen more rarely behind the bars and windows, till at length they ceased to appear altogether'. No one knows the answer to this, the most famous of all English historical mysteries, but one thing we can be sure of is that Elizabeth would have been desperate to learn what had become of them. She never said, nor so much as hinted, what she was able to discover, but her relationship with, and attitude towards, Richard III was bound to be affected by the extent to which she held him responsible. Did she think her sons were alive or dead, and if dead did she blame Richard or someone else?

The omens were not good. On 25 June, the day before Richard assumed the kingship, Anthony Earl Rivers, Lord Richard Grey and two other Woodville associates who had been arrested at Stony Stratford were executed at Pontefract, and Elizabeth lost both a brother and the younger son of her first marriage. The cheers and shouts of acclamation that greeted Richard's coronation on 6 July would have rung hollow in the Westminster sanctuary, but she neither gave way to sorrow nor ceased to plan for the future. Richard left London to 'progress' around his new kingdom two weeks after the coronation, but had scarcely departed when word reached him of a conspiracy designed to liberate the two princes. The Croyland writer heard that 'many things were going on in secret ... for the purpose of promoting this object *especially on the part of those who had availed themselves of the privilege of sanctuary*' (my italics), and that Elizabeth was being urged to disguise some of her daughters and smuggle them out of the country in case anything happened to her sons. The plot was nipped in the bud – four men were executed – and Richard ordered John Nesfield, a trusted supporter, to guard the sanctuary to ensure that only those with permission could enter or leave.

Richard's tour of his kingdom proceeded pleasantly until on reaching Lincoln on 11 October he learned of a new outbreak of trouble headed by his erstwhile ally the Duke of Buckingham. No one knows why Buckingham turned against the man he had helped to the throne a few short months earlier. It is possible that, like other kingmakers, he thought that the great rewards he had received ought to have been still greater, but it has also been argued that he had been alienated by the fate of the princes (whatever that was), and even that he had killed them in the hope of becoming king himself. The Croyland chronicler tells us that the aim of the uprising was again to restore one of the princes to the throne, but that when 'a rumour was spread that the sons of King Edward had died a violent death' the conspirators decided to invite Margaret Beaufort's son, Henry Tudor, the next male heir of the House of Lancaster, to return from exile and claim the kingdom. Richard was dismayed by Buckingham's defection, but he responded vigorously and luck was with him. The rebellion was poorly co-ordinated, and the foul weather that scattered Henry Tudor's little flotilla of ships also prevented Buckingham, who was in Wales, from crossing the River Severn into England. The Duke was captured and executed in Salisbury market place on 2 November 1483.

Margaret Beaufort had been one of the main instigators of the Buckingham uprising, and had gone to considerable lengths to persuade Elizabeth to become party to it. Margaret's doctor and confidant Lewis Caerleon had gained access to the Westminster sanctuary in his professional capacity, and had proposed to Elizabeth that Margaret's son Henry should marry her eldest daughter, Princess Elizabeth, when he had gained the kingdom. Dr Caerleon had the ticklish task of implying that Elizabeth's sons were dead without giving the impression that Margaret was glad of it (because it clearly improved *her* son's chances of becoming king), but he was as diplomatic as he was discreet. Elizabeth may, possibly, have agreed to the plan on the understanding that her own sons' claim to the throne would not be jeopardised if it turned out that one of them was still living, but Margaret's thoughts would have been for Henry alone.

The failure of the rebellion can only have added to Elizabeth's difficulties. She had now been implicated in three unsuccessful plots against Richard (with Hastings, in the July conspiracy, and most recently with Lady Margaret), and would have feared that his patience with her was all but exhausted. Christmas 1483 must have been a miserable occasion, a world removed from the gaiety of the last Christmas of her husband's lifetime, when the Croyland writer described the royal court as 'befitting a most mighty kingdom, filled with riches ... and (a point in which it excelled all others) boasting of those most sweet and beautiful children, the issue of his

[Edward's] marriage with queen Elizabeth'. Now, the fate of those children, even the very existence of two of them, was uncertain, and their mother was effectively a prisoner of the state.

Richard was undoubtedly angry with Elizabeth, but was obliged to recognise that his embarrassing public stand-off with his sister-in-law was not enhancing his reputation either at home or abroad. He seems to have adopted a carrot-and-stick approach, using 'frequent entreaties as well as threats' until, finally, Elizabeth agreed to leave the sanctuary around Easter 1484. The agreement drawn up between them stated that 'Dame Elizabeth Grey', as she was now called, would receive 700 marks (£466 13s. 4d.) annually for her maintenance, that Richard would treat her daughters as his own kinswomen, marrying them to 'gentlemen born' with appropriate dowries, and that he would not imprison or believe any ill report of them without first hearing their side of the story. It was guaranteed by an oath sworn on holy relics before an assembly of notables, in the words of one historian 'by the most solemn and public promise that Richard could contrive'.

The document did not mention the two princes, but it is unclear what conclusions should, or should not, be drawn from this. It is possible to argue that Elizabeth would never have negotiated with a man who had the blood of her sons fresh on his hands (what mother could have done so?), but that, alternatively, she had little choice. The sanctuary must have become increasingly cramped and uncomfortable during the nine months the six royal ladies had occupied it, and it is likely that their 'hosts', the Church authorities, were anxious to resolve the matter before it soured their own relationship with the new monarch. Elizabeth would also have known that Richard was some fifteen years her junior, and the fact that there would probably not be another king in her lifetime meant that she had no option but to deal with him. His execution of her brother and the younger son of her first marriage had not prevented her from coming to terms with him, and if she could overlook their deaths could she not overlook the princes' murders too?

But it is not quite that simple. Elizabeth may have 'done what she had to do' to improve the lot of her five daughters, but some little time after this she wrote to the elder son of her first marriage, Thomas Grey Marquis of Dorset, urging him to make his peace with Richard also. Dorset had found refuge at Henry Tudor's little court-in-exile in Brittany after the failure of Buckingham's rebellion, and it says much for his mother's persuasiveness that he now tried to abandon Henry only to be pursued and forced to return. It is possible that Richard compelled Elizabeth to write to him, but Dorset, who knew only too well what had happened to his brother Richard and uncle Anthony, would surely have suspected trickery. Whatever Elizabeth told him, it was enough to convince him that there had been a sea-change in her relationship with Richard, and that the Woodvilles were back in business. She never said why she had modified her opinion, but a logical explanation would be that she had discovered that one of her royal sons was still living or that Richard had persuaded her that he was not responsible for their fate.

There is, however, another possible explanation. We do not know precisely when the Marquis of Dorset tried to return to England, but contemporary writers imply that it was not long before rumours began to circulate that Richard intended to marry Elizabeth's daughter, his niece Elizabeth of York, when his sickly wife Queen Anne died. Richard thought that this would frustrate Henry Tudor's plan to marry her while compelling disaffected Yorkists to tolerate him for the girl's sake; but Sir Richard Ratcliffe and William Catesby, two members of his 'kitchen cabinet', told him bluntly – 'to his face' as Croyland has it – that such a union was incestuous and would never be accepted. They argued that many northerners had supported Richard out of loyalty to Anne, Warwick the Kingmaker's daughter, and that he would lose their backing if he married a Woodville. This was true to a point, although their real concern was that the younger Elizabeth would seek to punish them for their part in the deaths of her uncle Anthony and half-brother Richard Grey if she became queen.

Elizabeth of York. Bronze effigy by Torrigiani, Henry VII Chapel, Westminster Abbey

We might suppose that Princess Elizabeth would have recoiled at the prospect of being forced to marry an uncle who had indisputably ordered the execution of members of her mother's family, but remarkably, she embraced the plan with enthusiasm. Sir George Buck, Richard's earliest apologist, saw, 'in the cabinet of the Earl of Arundel', a letter she had written to Arundel's ancestor, the Duke of Norfolk, towards the end of February 1485 asking Norfolk to do all he could to hasten the matter. The letter has disappeared and Buck did not provide a full transcript, but in his words she 'prayed him [Norfolk] as before to be a mediator for her in the cause of her marriage to the king, who, as she wrote, was her only joy and maker in this world, and that she was his in heart and in thoughts, in body, and in all'. It is unlikely that she would have expressed these sentiments without her mother's approval and encouragement, but again, we should not assume that Elizabeth Woodville had genuinely forgiven Richard. She could have taken the view that it was the *surviving* members of her family who mattered, and that here was an opportunity they might never have again.

The moment never arrived, however. Queen Anne duly expired on 16 March, but two weeks later Ratcliffe and Catesby compelled the beleaguered king to stand up in the great hall of the Knights of Rhodes at Clerkenwell and declare publicly that he had no intention of marrying the younger Elizabeth. Richard went so far as to deny that he had even considered the possibility, although the Croyland writer was in no doubt that 'there were some persons, however, present who very well knew the contrary'. In the event Richard was destined to remain King of England for only five more months, and, long before this, it was known that Henry Tudor was planning an invasion from his new base in France. Henry, prudently, left Elizabeth's son Dorset behind when he sailed for England in early August, and on the 22nd defeated and killed Richard on Bosworth Field. Elizabeth cannot have mourned Richard any more than she had his brother George, and Henry's promise to marry her daughter meant that she would become queen mother after all.

So what did happen to the two 'Princes in the Tower'? It is often alleged that their disappearance was a mystery to everyone, but someone had to remove them from the Tower (dead or alive), and someone had to give the order. It is impossible to believe that Richard III and Henry VII (Henry Tudor) did not know – or care – what had become of them, or that close family members (including Elizabeth Woodville, princess – soon to be queen – Elizabeth and Henry's mother Margaret Beaufort) remained in complete ignorance. The implication is that they did know but chose to remain silent, something that would not have been necessary if both boys were dead and threatened no one. Edward V was being visited by his doctor in the summer and autumn of 1483 and could have succumbed to his malady; but there is no suggestion that Prince Richard was ill, and no evidence that King Richard or King Henry had him killed. The most likely scenario is that he was sent to a safe and secure place, his whereabouts and true identity known only to a handful of people, in order to ensure that, as far as possible, he posed no threat to the reigning monarch. Such a secret plan would have required Elizabeth Woodville's agreement, and could explain the apparent thaw in her relationship with King Richard in 1484 and 1485.

The boy had to 'disappear' then, but where did he go and was that the last the world heard of him? One possibility is that he was taken to Colchester Abbey after the battle of Bosworth and apprenticed to the abbey's master bricklayer, eventually re-emerging as 'Richard Plantagenet of Eastwell' after the dissolution of the monasteries in 1539. Alternatively, he may have been smuggled or sent abroad, reappearing as the young man known as Perkin Warbeck in Ireland in 1491. Warbeck is a plausible contender in that he actually resembled Edward IV, his 'father', and never, so far as is known, made an obvious blunder. But he always declined to explain where he had spent his 'missing' years (his claim that he wanted to protect those who had shielded him may have been genuine or may have been designed to avoid the one question everyone was bound to ask him), and he was finally hanged as a common criminal in 1499. Elizabeth Woodville, who died in 1492, would scarcely have heard of him, and there is no evidence that anyone sought the opinion of her daughter Elizabeth, his 'sister'. The younger Elizabeth would have seen him, if only from a distance, when he was first captured, and could surely have identified him if they had been allowed to converse privately. Henry may have been too afraid that she would recognise him to permit such a meeting, or alternatively, was so convinced that he was an impostor that there was no need.

The new reign began well enough for Elizabeth Woodville. King Henry married her daughter on 18 January 1486, and treated her with all the respect due to the queen's mother. The act of parliament that had invalidated her marriage to King Edward and bastardised their children was repealed, and on 5 March she was given an income consisting of annuities and a life interest in a raft of properties in southern England. She had lost many members of her family, but could look forward to a comfortable retirement and a peaceful old age.

King Henry had won a decisive victory at Bosworth, but was bound to face challenges from individuals who would have hoped to succeed Richard III if he had remained childless and from others who had been wholly committed to him. An insurrection mounted by Francis Viscount Lovell, the late king's chamberlain, in April 1486 was suppressed without difficulty, but later in the year Henry learned of a new and altogether more serious plot being hatched in Ireland. Polydore Vergil blamed an Oxford priest, one Richard Simons, who, he said, had trained a personable youth named Lambert Simnel to impersonate the Yorkist claimant Edward Earl of Warwick, the son of the executed George Duke of Clarence, who was then a prisoner in the Tower of London. Simons had taken his protégé to Ireland, where Richard Duke of York, Edward IV's and Richard III's father, had been a highly respected royal lieutenant in the 1450s, and where, according to Vergil, he convened an assembly of the Irish nobility and convinced them that Simnel was the real Warwick, who had somehow escaped from custody. The Irish lords responded enthusiastically, and began to plan an invasion of England that would restore the boy to his 'right'.

None of this is very plausible, however. Simons was an ordinary cleric who had probably never seen the real Earl of Warwick and had no direct knowledge of how he (or any other prince for that matter) conducted himself. He would have been ignorant of the small, personal details of the boy's life that could have come only from another member of the family, and would have needed help to produce an acceptable substitute. The same would have been true when the unlikely pair reached Ireland and began to publicise their 'mission'. Few would have taken them seriously, still less danced to their tune in the manner described by Vergil, unless some word of their coming had preceded them, and the vast probability is that they were part of a wider conspiracy organised by senior Yorkists in England. The Irish nobles had been well primed.

Vergil did not identify the leading conspirators, but the royal council, meeting at Sheen Palace in February 1487, took three crucial decisions. First, it was decided to offer pardon to all rebels who would throw themselves on the king's mercy; secondly, to allow the real Earl of Warwick to attend mass at St Paul's Cathedral and to speak with those who knew him (so that none could doubt that the boy in Ireland was an impostor); and thirdly, to deprive Elizabeth Woodville of all her properties and send her to Bermondsey Abbey. The first two decisions were direct responses to the Simnel conspiracy (as we may now call it), and it must be supposed that the same is true of the last, the one penalising Elizabeth, but that Henry did not care to acknowledge that his own mother-in-law had been conspiring against him. Vergil admits that Elizabeth was being punished, but says that it was because she had broken faith with Henry when she made her peace with Richard III three years earlier. He sidesteps the fact that Henry had been aware of this for his entire reign but had hitherto treated her kindly, and does not indicate why, if the reason was genuine, he chose this particular moment to accuse her. Lord Bacon's remark, that Elizabeth was so tainted with treason that 'it was almost thought dangerous to visit her, or see her', is almost certainly nearer the truth.

There had been no obvious, open quarrel between Elizabeth and Henry, so why would she have turned against him? Bacon was writing just over a century later, but there is no reason to doubt his assertion that she had been angered by Henry's treatment of her daughter and increasingly resented the overbearing attitude of his mother, Margaret Beaufort. Henry had been anxious to dispel any suggestion that his claim to the throne had only been accepted because he had married Edward IV's eldest daughter, and although the younger Elizabeth had given him a son she had still not been crowned. Henry always turned to his mother when he needed advice, and as Margaret assumed ever greater authority so Elizabeth Woodville thought her daughter 'not advanced but depressed'.

But would Elizabeth have sought to depose her daughter and her daughter's husband in order to make Edward of Warwick, the son of her old enemy George of Clarence, king? Some modern writers believe that she had no quarrel with King Henry, and surrendered her properties to her daughter Elizabeth and retired to Bermondsey as part of an amicable 'family settlement' that just happened to coincide with the Simnel rebellion. They suggest that she may have been ill or perhaps wished to spend her last years in religious contemplation; and maintain that Henry would not have referred to her in endearing terms in official documents or proposed her as a wife for James III, the King of Scots, if he thought her guilty of treason. What does the evidence really say?

Henry did indeed continue to behave as though everything was 'normal', even referring to Elizabeth as 'our right dear and right well beloved queen Elizabeth, mother unto our most dear wife the queen' when he gave her fifty marks in 1490. But any hint that he was on bad terms with his mother-in-law would have called the stability of his dynasty into question, and his actions speak louder than his words. Elizabeth Woodville was conspicuous by her absence when her daughter was finally crowned in November 1487 (Henry and his mother watched events from behind a lattice), and although Henry had little choice but to let her kinsman Francois de Luxembourg see her when he visited England in November 1489, they were not allowed to meet privately. Margaret Beaufort was present to hear all that was said.

Admittedly, Henry would not have proposed marrying

Elizabeth to James III in November 1487, five months after the Simnel rebellion, if he thought her guilty of treason, but how serious was he? The idea of a union between the Scottish King and the English queen-dowager can be traced to the 'Three Years' Truce' which the two countries signed in July 1486 (long before there was any trouble in Ireland), and it is likely that Henry continued the negotiations even if he had no intention of bringing them to fruition. The Scots would not cause trouble in northern England if they thought their king was about to marry into the English royal family, and Henry, who had troubles aplenty, would have seen it as a good way of keeping the border quiet. King James was murdered in June 1488 after the battle of Sauchieburn, so the subterfuge did not have to be maintained for long.

Elizabeth was no longer young by 1487, but the Scots would not have thought her a suitable bride for their king if she had serious health problems and few if any medieval aristocrats would have surrendered their lands willingly. On the contrary, they seized every opportunity to add to their acres by whatever means were available to them because wealth invariably enhanced status. Henry's mother, Margaret Beaufort, was pious even by contemporary standards, but her commitment to her religion never prevented her from acquiring money. She used it to found chantry chapels and university colleges, and still left the then vast sum of £14,724 when she died in 1509. Elizabeth, on the other hand, was restricted to an annuity of £400 (less than the settlement she had received from Richard III), and even this was not always paid promptly. King Henry would surely not have given her the properties in the first place if he had always intended them for Elizabeth of York.

Clearly, Elizabeth would *not* have wanted to depose her daughter (however much she wanted to remove Henry and his overbearing mother), but this is to assume that Elizabeth of York would have ceased to be queen when Henry was killed or at least toppled. She would never have contemplated making George of Clarence king, but Edward, his son, was young, possibly simple-minded, and malleable. There was, as yet, no precedent for a queen-regnant, but a papal dispensation would have allowed the younger Elizabeth to marry Edward, her first cousin, after Henry had been dealt with, and made Elizabeth Woodville the real power behind the throne. The claims of any children the young couple might have would conflict with those of their half-brother, the infant Prince Arthur, but recent events had shown how easily inconvenient royal children could be sidelined. Firm evidence that any of these thoughts actually formed in Elizabeth's mind is inevitably lacking, but she would, arguably, have been prepared to countenance such a scheme if it allowed her to regain the upper hand.

The other possibility is that Elizabeth knew by early 1487 that one of her sons was alive and in hiding, and that she intended to 'produce' him if the Irish rebellion succeeded. The conspirators would have considered the possibility of allowing the real prince to lead it in person, but concluded, regretfully, that his safety outweighed any additional support he might bring to their party. All Yorkists would have regarded a son of Edward IV as the rightful heir to the throne, and Warwick's claim would have been instantly superseded if one of the two missing 'princes' had emerged from the shadows. The Tudor writer Edward Hall says that the conspirators originally considered using Simnel as a stalking-horse for Prince Richard, but then apparently changed their minds.

Everything now turned on the success or failure of the rebellion, and Elizabeth could do nothing but sit quietly in Bermondsey and await the outcome. In April Henry clapped the Marquis of Dorset, the elder son of her first marriage, into the Tower 'to preserve him from doing hurt either to the King's service or to himself', as Bacon has it, and then moved into the Midlands, to Kenilworth Castle in Warwickshire, to await developments. The conspirators, reinforced by nearly 2,000 Continental mercenaries supplied by Margaret of Burgundy, Edward IV's and Richard III's sister, 'crowned' Simnel 'Edward VI' in Dublin on 24 May 1487, and their combined army, led by the Earl of Lincoln, the Yorkist kings' nephew, sailed for northern England eleven days later. They hoped that former supporters of Warwick the Kingmaker (the young Earl of Warwick's grandfather) would rally to them, but were doomed to disappointment. Perhaps, as one writer suggests, Englishmen had had enough of 'adventures in shining armour', and were apprehensive of a 'king' who needed foreigners to restore him to his own.

The Earl of Lincoln decided that his best chance was to march southwards as rapidly as possible in the hope of forcing a battle before all Henry's forces could reach him, but he was again thwarted. The king had allowed his soldiers to return home over the winter, but he was ever vigilant and, in the words of one commentator 'in his [Lincoln's] bosom, and knew every hour what the Earl did'. The rebels spread rumours that Henry had already been defeated in the hope that some of his friends would be dissuaded from joining him, and one contingent led by Lord Welles apparently panicked and fell back on London. Yorkists who were in sanctuary in the city emerged to assault known Tudor sympathisers, and Elizabeth must have heard and drawn comfort from the commotion. Everything might yet be well.

The Earl of Lincoln deployed his 8,000-strong army on some high ground to the south-west of the village of East Stoke in Nottinghamshire on 15 June 1487, and waited for the king's forces to advance towards him the following day. He tried to maximise his numbers by concentrating them in a single contingent or 'battle' which he hurled down the slope at Henry's vanguard; but probably half his soldiers were Irishmen whose rustic weapons and lack of body armour made them easy targets for the royal spearmen and archers. The Yorkists 'fought hardily and stuck to it valiantly', but as the morning lengthened the king was able to reinforce his forward division, and his soldiers' professionalism and superior equipment eventually told in their favour. Lincoln and most of his fellow commanders perished in the final, furious onslaught, leaving the priest Simons and the boy Simnel to face Henry's anger. The former disappeared into an ecclesiastical prison, while the latter became a scullion in the royal kitchen.

We will never know the precise role that Elizabeth played in the rebellion, but she may well have provided money, assisted with Simnel's 'education', and perhaps encouraged the Irish lords to use him as a substitute until the real Earl of Warwick – or one of her sons – could be liberated. No one recorded the moment when news of the disaster was brought to her, but it is possible to imagine the abbot, the trace of a smile playing about his lips, informing her of it in the days after the battle. Henry had wanted to capture the Earl of Lincoln alive so that he could 'learn from him more concerning the conspiracy' (Vergil), and could, arguably, have obtained at least some of this information from Elizabeth; but there is nothing to suggest that he asked her or that she subsequently co-operated with him. Perhaps, by this time, they knew each other all too well.

THE LAST PHASE

The Simnel conspiracy was Elizabeth's last throw of the political dice, and the remaining five years of her life were spent in virtual seclusion behind the abbey's walls. She was permitted to return to public life on rare occasions – the reception of her Luxembourg kinsman, for instance – but her absence from her daughter's coronation implies that such concessions were kept to a minimum. Her last years were further saddened by the deaths of her remaining two brothers and three of her four remaining sisters. Sir Edward Woodville was killed aiding the Duke of Brittany at the battle of St Aubin du Cormier on 28 July 1488; Richard, the third and last Lord Rivers, died in March 1491; and Anne Countess of Kent, Margaret Countess of Arundel, and Joan Lady Grey of Ruthin all passed away within the same period. She may not have been close to some of them – Sir Edward had fought for King Henry at Stoke, for example – but they were all members of her immediate family. Their funerals would have brought many of the great and the good together, but the probability is that Elizabeth was not allowed to travel around the country or communicate with whom she would.

We have already noted that Elizabeth's smaller allowance was not always paid on time, and this would also have made her last years more difficult. King Henry was something of a miser, but he would have had reason to ensure that she never had more money than she or those managing her affairs needed. A servant might carry a secret message for old loyalty's sake, but strangers could not be bribed, or rebellion contemplated, without funds. Elizabeth's situation is confirmed by her will, which she drew up on 10 April 1492, apparently because she was by then ill and did not expect to live for much longer. It is a pathetic document, quite unlike the will of a queen or a member of the aristocracy:

> In God's name, Amen. The 10th day of April, the year of our Lord God 1492. I Elizabeth, by the grace of God Queen of England, late wife to the most victorious Prince of blessed memory Edward the Fourth, being of whole mind, seeing the world so transitory and no creature certain when they shall depart from hence, having Almighty God fresh in mind, in whom is all mercy and grace, bequeath my soul into his hands, beseeching him, of the same mercy, to accept it graciously, and our blessed Lady Queen of comfort [the Virgin Mary], and all the holy company of heaven, to be good means for me. Item, I bequeath my body to be buried with the body of my Lord [King Edward] at Windsor, according to the will of my said Lord and mine, without pompous ceremony or costly expenses done thereabout. Item, where I have no worldly goods to do the Queen's Grace, my dearest daughter [Elizabeth], a pleasure with, neither to reward any of my children, according to my heart and mind, I beseech Almighty God to bless her Grace, with all her noble issue, and with as good heart and mind as is to me possible, I give her Grace my blessing, and all the foresaid my children. Item, I will that such small stuff and goods that I have to be disposed truly in the contentation [satisfaction] of my debts, and for the health of my soul, as far as they will extend. Item, if any of my blood [relations] will of my said stuff or goods to me pertaining, I will that they have the preferment before any other. And of this my present testament I make and ordain mine executors, that is to say, John

Ingilby, Prior of the Charterhouse of Sheen, William Sutton and Thomas Brente, doctors. And I beseech my said dearest daughter, the Queen's grace, and my son Thomas, Marquis Dorset, to put their good wills and help for the performance of this my testament. In witness whereof, to this my present testament I have set my seal, these witnesses, John, abbot of the monastery of Saint Saviour of Bermondsey, and Benedictus Cun, Doctor of Physic. Given the day and year abovesaid.

The will confirms both Elizabeth's deep personal piety – God is mentioned or appealed to on a number of occasions – and the state of abject poverty in which she found herself. Medieval testators routinely paid for the saying of hundreds, sometimes thousands, of the masses they believed would speed their souls to paradise, but Elizabeth could only ask that what little remained after her debts had been settled should be used for this purpose. She had nothing to leave to her daughter the queen, or any of her other children, and this was clearly a source of regret rather than something she had wished or intended. King Henry, her son-in-law, is nowhere mentioned, and it is difficult to avoid the conclusion that their relationship remained poor.

Elizabeth Woodville's signature, from a receipt for the annuity she received from Henry VII, 1491

It was not unusual for contemporaries to request a 'simple' funeral in the sure knowledge that their families would bury them with appropriate ceremony; but Elizabeth would have known that a deceased's estate bore the cost of this and that queenly obsequies were beyond her means. King Henry could have relented sufficiently to make a dignified ending possible, but the evidence is that everything was done 'on the cheap'. When Elizabeth died on Friday 8 June 1492 her body was placed in a wooden coffin, and taken by boat from Bermondsey to St George's Chapel, Windsor, two days later. It was received there by a single priest and a clerk ('prevely' – privately or secretly – at eleven at night), and interred almost immediately, without, apparently, the dean and canons being present. Her very existence had been an embarrassment, and there was to be no spectacle now that she was dead.

Her son the Marquis of Dorset, his half-sisters Anne, Katherine and Bridget, and some other family members reached Windsor on the following Tuesday and Wednesday, and that night the Bishop of Rochester conducted the service of *Dirige*, the Office of the Dead. Elizabeth's two eldest daughters did not attend – Elizabeth of York was heavily pregnant while Cecily was represented by her husband Lord Welles, the king's uncle – and the others present were almost all relatives of Edward IV or the Woodvilles. One of the heralds was shocked by the meanness of the arrangements, remarking that 'there was nothing done solemnly for her saving a low hearse such as they use for the common people with four wooden candlesticks about it'. There was, he adds, 'never a new torch, but old torches, nor poor man in black gown or hood, but upon [approximately] a dozen divers old men holding old torches and torch ends'. Dorset paid the 'dole' (the customary distribution of money to the needy) and gave forty shillings to the heralds, presumably out of his own pocket. It was all a far cry from the funeral of King Henry's mother seventeen years later, which cost an enormous – but affordable – £1,021!

What, then, can be said of this woman whose modest expectations had been transformed when she married King Edward but who had paid a high price for her new-found status? No other English queen had been deposed, *and* lost so many of her close family in bloody revolutions, *and* had her marriage declared invalid and her children bastardised, *and*, finally, suffered the indignity of being officially forgotten. Her Lancastrian rival Margaret of Anjou had also been deposed, exiled, lost her son and husband, and been compelled to resist those who wanted to supersede them; but throughout her troubles Margaret had a consolation always denied to Elizabeth – she was a French princess who could, in the last resort, expect her powerful kinsman King Louis to intercede for her. It is no coincidence that Henry VIII executed two of his English wives (and considered beheading a third); but that his two foreign-born queens – who had both in their own ways incurred his displeasure – both died in their beds. Elizabeth could flee into sanctuary, but she was still at the mercy of powerful enemies. Warwick the Kingmaker and Richard of Gloucester refrained from using violence against her in 1470 and in 1483, but on both occasions her safety hung in the balance. Ultimately, she had no one to help her but herself.

The real Elizabeth may not be too far removed from the plucky, pitiful queen Shakespeare depicted in *Richard III* and *Henry VI, Part 3*, but twentieth-century writers have not treated her kindly. Cora Scofield, whose admired biography of Edward IV was published in 1923, wrote that 'even wise heads have been known to be turned by a sudden elevation in rank, and Elizabeth Woodville's head, which was not wise, had evidently been badly turned. Worse still, love seemed to have turned her husband's head as well. For, not content with the folly of having married this "widow of England", there was no end to the favours Edward was ready to shower on her undeserving family'. To David MacGibbon, her 1938 biographer, she was 'a person of a cool calculating decision of character, without any deep affection, but of steady dislikes and revengeful disposition', while Paul Murray Kendall described her as the 'impelling spirit', the 'greediest and most wilful' of the Woodvilles, in his 1955 life of Richard III. Charles Ross, writing about the same king a quarter of a century later, remarked that 'her rather cold beauty was not offset by any warmth or generosity of temperament. She was to prove a woman of designing character, grasping and ambitious for her family's interests, quick to take offence and reluctant to forgive'.

But was she really like this? People were indeed surprised that Edward IV married for love rather than for money and influence, but his choice was not entirely without merit nor were Elizabeth's siblings undeserving of the favours they received from him. It is difficult to reconcile Miss Scofield's allegation that her head had been 'turned' with the 'cold' and 'calculating' traits observed by MacGibbon, nor does the latter's claim that she lacked 'deep affection' sit well with Professor Ross's 'grasping and ambitious for her family's interests'. All these writers, it is fair to say, take the view that Elizabeth and the Woodvilles were a 'bad lot' and interpret their actions accordingly, but if we approach the subject without preconceptions it is possible to see most of them in a quite different light.

The two men most responsible for blackening Elizabeth's character were Warwick the Kingmaker and Richard of Gloucester; but their opinions should not blind us to the fact that other contemporaries took a very different view of her.

The Croyland writer noted how she 'most beneficiently tried to extinguish every spark of murmuring and disturbance' when trouble flared in the council in the aftermath of Edward IV's death, and Speaker Alyngton had no reason to commend her 'great constancy' during the dramatic events of 1469–71 unless he genuinely admired her for it. A Londoner who wrote a poem celebrating Edward's recovery of his kingdom expressed similar sentiments:

> O Queen Elizabeth, O blessed creature,
> O Glorious God, what pain had she?
> What languor and anguish did she endure?
> When her lord and sovereign was in adversity,
> To hear of her weeping it was great pity,
> When she remembered the King she was woe
> Thus in every thing the will of God is do [done]

It could be argued that men who sought Edward IV's favour were unlikely to criticise Elizabeth, but they would have been inviting ridicule if they had written and said such things when everyone else thought the opposite. The same is true of the Tudor chronicler Edward Hall, who described her as 'a woman more of formal countenance than of excellent beauty, but yet of such beauty and favour that with her sober demeanour, lovely looking, and feminine, smiling (neither too wanton nor too humble) besides her tongue so eloquent, and her wit so pregnant'. Hall never knew Elizabeth and would perhaps not have spoken ill of Henry VIII's grandmother; but he had access to sources of information now lost to us, and there is something about his characterisation that rings true.

Elizabeth Woodville was not perfect – perhaps no one is – but she seems to have fulfilled her difficult and demanding role admirably. Her critics never questioned her competence or alleged that she had failed in her duty (as they surely would if she had presented them with an opportunity), and her devotion to her husband never faltered. Like every mother, she was ambitious for her family, but she cannot be accused of neglecting her brothers' and sisters' interests or of not doing her utmost to secure the throne for her son Edward. She never doubted Richard of Gloucester's true intentions – unlike her brother Anthony and Lord Hastings, who both walked blindly into the traps Richard had prepared for them – and would have been regarded as an astute politician if she had lived in the twentieth or twenty-first centuries. It was her misfortune to be born into a male-dominated society that allowed women no public, political role.

This, then, was Elizabeth Woodville, a woman who experienced greater vicissitudes of fortune than anyone of her generation and who was probably more sinned against than sinning. We can question her motives but not her ability, her judgement but not her loyalty. All in all, there is much to admire in the personality of the 'White Queen'.

NOTES AND SOURCES

The quotations from contemporary sources have been taken from the following:

Ross, C. *Edward IV*, 1974; Lander, J.R. *Government and Community*, 1980; *The Great Chronicle of London*, ed. A.H. Thomas and I.D. Thornley, 1938, reprinted Gloucester, 1983; *The Historie of the Arrivall of Edward IV in England and the Finall Recoverye of his Kingdomes from Henry VI A.D. M.CCCC.LXXI.*, ed. J. Bruce, Camden Society, 1838; British Library Add. MSS. 6113, f. 100b. *Calendar of the Patent Rolls, Edward IV 1467–77*, 1900; 'The Record of Bluemantle Pursuivant', in C.L. Kingsford, *English Historical Literature in the Fifteenth Century*, Oxford, 1913; Sutton, A.F., and Visser-Fuchs, L., with Hammond, P.W. *The Reburial of Richard, Duke of York 21–30 July 1476*, Richard III Society, 1996; Myers, A.R. 'The Household of Queen Elizabeth Woodville 1466–7', *Bulletin of the John Rylands Library*, 1 (1967–8); *Acts of Court of the Mercers Company*, ed. L. Lyell and F.D. Watney, 1936; *The Paston Letters 1422–1509*, ed. J. Gairdner, 6 vols, 1904; *More's 'History of King Richard III'*, ed. J.R. Lumby, Cambridge, 1883; Dominic Mancini, *The Usurpation of Richard III*, trans. C.A.J. Armstrong, 2nd edition, Gloucester, 1984; *The Memoirs of Philip de Commines*, ed. A.R. Scoble, 2 vols, 1855–6; *The Travels of Leo of Rozmital*, ed. & trans. M. Letts, Hakluyt Society, Cambridge,

1957; *The Stonor Letters and Papers*, ed. C.L. Kingsford, 2 vols, 1919–20; *Ingulph's Chronicle of the Abbey of Croyland*, trans. H.T. Riley, 1854; Twigg, J. *A History of Queens' College, Cambridge 1448–1986*, Woodbridge, 1987; Sutton, A.F., and Visser-Fuchs, L. 'A "Most Benevolent Queen": Queen Elizabeth Woodville's Reputation, her Piety, and her Books', *The Ricardian*, x (1995); *Three Books of Polydore Vergil's English History*, ed. H. Ellis, Camden Society, 1844; Hammond, P.W., and Sutton, A.F. *Richard III: The Road to Bosworth Field*, 1985; Nicolas, N.H. *Privy Purse Expenses of Elizabeth of York, Wardrobe Accounts of Edward IV*, 1830, reprinted 1972; Laynesmith, J. 'The Kings' Mother', *History Today* (March, 2006); *Calendar of State Papers and Manuscripts Existing in the Archives and Collections of Milan*, I, 1385–1618, ed. A.B. Hinds, 1913; Kendall, P.M. *Richard III*, 1955; Ross, C. *Richard III*, 1981; Buck, Sir George *The History of King Richard the Third*, ed. A.N. Kincaid, Gloucester, 1979; *British Library Harleian Manuscript 433*, ed. R. Horrox and P.W. Hammond, 4 vols, 1979–83; Bacon, Francis *The History of the Reign of King Henry VII*, ed. R. Lockyer, 1971; *Materials for a History of the Reign of Henry VII*, ed. W. Campbell, 2 vols, 1873–7; Trevelyan, G.M. *A Shortened History of England*, Harmondsworth, 1959; Hall(e), Edward *The Union of the Two Noble Families of Lancaster and York*, 1550, reprinted Menston, 1970; *Testamenta Vetusta*, ed. N.H. Nicolas, 2 vols, 1826; Sutton, A.F., and Visser-Fuchs, L., with Griffiths, R.A. *The Royal Burials of the House of York at Windsor*, 2005; *Political Poems and Songs Relating to English History*, ed. T. Wright, 2 vols, 1859–61.

Readers who would like to have a fuller account of Elizabeth's life are referred to my *Elizabeth Woodville: Mother of the Princes in the Tower*, third edition, Stroud, 2010. The standard biography of her husband is Ross, C. *Edward IV*, 1974, while the most recent is the book of the same title by H. Kleineke, 2009. M. Hicks's study, *False, Fleeting, Perjur'd Clarence*, Gloucester, 1980, remains the only life of George, Elizabeth's elder brother-in-law, but Richard, the younger, has attracted much greater attention. P.M. Kendall's *Richard the Third*, 1955, relies heavily on informed guesswork but is a great 'popular' biography, M. Hicks's *Richard III*, Stroud, 2000, offers a valuable reassessment of its subject's motives, and the present author's biography of the King will be published in 2012. Hicks, M. *Warwick the Kingmaker*, Oxford, 1998, and Pollard, A.J. *Warwick the Kingmaker: Politics, Power and Fame*, 2007, have re-evaluated the life of Elizabeth's other great antagonist, while H. Maurer has charted the career of her Lancastrian rival in *Margaret of Anjou: Queenship and Power in Late Medieval England*, 2003. Henry Tudor's reign is assessed in S. Cunningham's *Henry VII*, 2007, while M.K. Jones and M.G. Underwood tell the story of his mother Margaret Beaufort in *The King's Mother*, 1993. The fate of the Princes in the Tower is the most famous of all historical mysteries, and two contrasting theories can be found in A. Wroe's *Perkin: A Story of Deception*, 2003, and in my *The Lost Prince*, Stroud, 2007. For the Lambert Simnel rebellion and the battle of Stoke, see my *Stoke Field: The Last Battle of the Wars of the Roses*, Barnsley, 2006.

A number of contemporary documents relating to Elizabeth have been printed. G. Smith has transcribed a fifteenth-century account of *The Coronation of Elizabeth Wydeville*, 1935; a description of her churching banquet held after the birth of Elizabeth of York can be found in *The Travels of Leo of Rozmital*, ed. & trans. M. Letts, Hakluyt Society, 2nd series, cviii, Cambridge, 1957; and *The Record of Bluemantle Pursuivant* (in Kingsford, C.L. *English Historical Literature in the Fifteenth Century*, Oxford, 1913), records the care she lavished on the welcome given to Louis de Gruthuyse when he visited England in 1472. Three of her letters survive, in *The Stonor Letters and Papers*, ed. C.L. Kingsford, 2 vols, 1919, in *The Paston Letters*, ed. J. Gairdner, 6 vols, 1904, and in *The Coventry Leet Book*, ed. M.D. Harris, 4 parts, Early English Text Society, 1907–13; her will is transcribed in Nicolas, N.H. *Testamenta Vetusta*, 2 vols (1926), and an account of her funeral is included in Sutton, A.F. and Visser-Fuchs, L., with Griffiths, R.A. *The Royal Funerals of the House of York at Windsor*, Richard III Society, 2005.

Useful articles, some of them based on original documents, are:

Fahy, C. 'The Marriage of Edward IV and Elizabeth Woodville: a new Italian source', *English Historical Review*, lxxvi (1961)

Harrod, H. 'Queen Elizabeth Woodville's visit to Norwich in 1469', *Norfolk Archaeology* 5 (1859)

Myers, A.R. 'The Household of Queen Elizabeth Woodville, 1466–7', *Bulletin of the John Rylands Library*, I (1967–8)

Scofield, C.L. 'Elizabeth Wydevile in the Sanctuary at Westminster, 1470', *English Historical Review*, xxiv (1909)

Sutton, A.F. and Visser-Fuchs, L. 'A "Most Benevolent Queen" Queen Elizabeth Woodville's Reputation, her Piety and her Books', *The Ricardian* x, 129 (1995)

Sutton, A.F. and Visser-Fuchs, L. 'The Cult of Angels in Late Fifteenth-Century England: An Hours of the Guardian Angel Presented to Queen Elizabeth Woodville' in *Women and the Book*, ed. L. Smith and J.H.M. Taylor (1996)

Sutton, A.F. and Visser-Fuchs, L. 'The Device of Queen Elizabeth Woodville: A Gillyflower or Pink', *The Ricardian* xi, 136 (1997)

Sutton, A.F. and Visser-Fuchs, L. 'The Entry of Queen Elizabeth Woodville over London Bridge, 24 May 1465', *The Ricardian* xix (2009)

MARGARET
BEAUFORT

1443–1509

Michael Jones

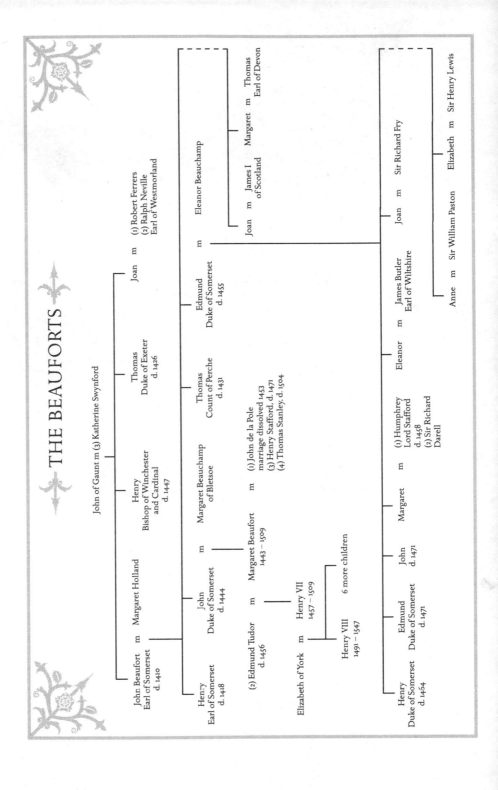

THE BEAUFORTS

John of Gaunt m (3) Katherine Swynford

John Beaufort m Margaret Holland
Earl of Somerset
d. 1410

Henry
Bishop of Winchester
and Cardinal
d. 1447

Thomas
Duke of Exeter
d. 1426

Joan m (1) Robert Ferrers
(2) Ralph Neville
Earl of Westmorland

Henry
Earl of Somerset
d. 1418

John m Margaret Beauchamp
Duke of Somerset of Bletsoe
d. 1444

Thomas
Count of Perche
d. 1431

Edmund m Eleanor Beauchamp
Duke of Somerset
d. 1455

Joan m James I
of Scotland

Margaret m Thomas
Earl of Devon

Margaret Beaufort m (1) John de la Pole
1443 – 1509 marriage dissolved 1453
(3) Henry Stafford. d. 1471
(4) Thomas Stanley. d. 1504

(2) Edmund Tudor m Henry VII
d. 1456 1457 – 1509

Elizabeth of York m Henry VII
1457 – 1509

Henry VIII
1491 – 1547

6 more children

Henry
Duke of Somerset
d. 1464

Edmund
Duke of Somerset
d. 1471

John
d. 1471

Margaret m (1) Humphrey
Lord Stafford
d. 1458
(2) Sir Richard
Darell

Eleanor m James Butler
Earl of Wiltshire

Joan m Sir Richard Fry

Anne m Sir William Paston

Elizabeth m Sir Henry Lewis

THE FAMILY STORY

Lady Margaret Beaufort's life is a dramatic and moving story of a woman in the late Middle Ages who never saw herself as a victim, someone who suffered greatly and bore terrible dangers yet fought like a tigress to advance the fortunes of her only son, Henry Tudor. When that son became Henry VII of England on 22 August 1485, after vanquishing his rival Richard III in battle at Bosworth, it was as much Margaret's triumph as the king's. Margaret was courageous, intelligent and astute, a formidable plotter during the Wars of the Roses, a woman whose deep personal piety never interfered with her political pragmatism. She was strong-willed and ambitious and reached the pinnacle of her power and influence during the reign of her son, when she was known simply as 'the King's Mother'.

Lady Margaret Beaufort was born on 31 May 1443, the only child and heiress of John Beaufort Duke of Somerset and his wife Margaret Beauchamp of Bletsoe. Margaret was born into a major aristocratic family, closely related to the ruling Lancastrian dynasty, a guarantee of social pre-eminence and landed wealth. Indeed, her father – one of Henry VI's military commanders – had been elevated to his dukedom two months before her birth, as he prepared to lead a major expedition to France in the closing stages of the Hundred Years' War. But Margaret had no memory of him. Somerset's campaign was a fiasco, and the duke returned home in disgrace, was banished from court and then – rumour had it – committed suicide, unable to brook his calamitous fall from favour. He died a day before Margaret's first birthday and was buried with little ceremony in Wimborne Minster in Dorset.

The story of Margaret's father was a tragic one. John Beaufort was captured at the disastrous English defeat at Baugé in 1421, when Henry V's younger brother Thomas Duke of Clarence impetuously attacked a much larger Franco-Scottish army during a raid into Anjou. Baugé was one of the worst English defeats in the Hundred Years' War. The English commander's behaviour was so reckless that a mutiny nearly broke out in his ranks. According to the chronicler John Hardyng, a number of the assembled English aristocrats began a heated discussion of Thomas's impulsive decision even as his army began to form up, for the order to ride into battle had been issued during an early-evening banquet, when a supposed informer announced the proximity of a French army, reinforced by a large contingent of Scottish soldiers (who were fighting as their allies, against the English). Halfway through a meal, Thomas believed he had a chance to surprise and overwhelm his foes – and, throwing all caution to the wind, commanded his surprised followers to saddle up, and led a mounted charge in the direction of his opponents.

However, the full English army was not ready to go into battle and Thomas rode off at speed without his archers, who formed the majority of his raiding force and whose dreaded longbow had been one of the principal reasons for Henry V's stupendous victory against the French at Agincourt in 1415, some six years earlier. Thomas had not been present at that great battle: he had contracted dysentery during the siege of Harfleur, and – like many others in the English army – had been forced to return home. This clearly rankled with him, and on the spur of the moment Thomas now decided that he would win a victory even greater than that of Henry V.

In Agincourt's aftermath, some of the French nobility had taunted the victors that the English aristocracy was no match for them, and had won only because of their reliance on a mass of peasant soldiers and a killing weapon that had no chivalric merit. This was desperate stuff, for the French had been out-generalled and out-fought at Agincourt, and Henry V had cleverly used his archers as part of a highly effective battle plan. But Thomas let this slight by the enemy go to his head, refusing to wait for his archers to form up behind him, and instead charging off into the gathering gloom with only a mounted force of knights accompanying him. Margaret's father, John Beaufort, was one of his unfortunate companions.

John Beaufort, who at this stage held the title and rank of Earl of Somerset, had a grandstand view of the débâcle that followed, for the English commander was his stepfather. After the death of his own father in 1410, his mother, Margaret Holland, had remarried Duke Thomas and her Beaufort children had been brought up in the duke's own household. John would have been riding in Thomas's personal retinue, close to his stepfather, pell-mell towards the village of Baugé, across ground that had not been properly reconnoitred and towards an army of whose size and strength the English were entirely ignorant. What his thoughts were during this twilight charge can only be imagined.

Tragically for the Beaufort family, the course of battle that followed was all too predictable. Thomas Duke of Clarence careered across a shallow river and into the village of Baugé, where fighting with a surprised Scottish advance guard flared up around the church and principal buildings. Part of

Thomas's small force then pushed on to the ridge above the village. By now the alarm had been raised and a much larger army of French and Scots had gathered to meet them. The English had lost any semblance of battle formation and were rapidly overwhelmed. Duke Thomas was killed and most of his aristocratic followers captured, John Beaufort among them. It was an utter disaster.

Our modern understanding of battles is very much an analytical one, based on a study of the strategy and tactics of the rival commanders and their grasp of logistics and planning. A medieval audience would have seen things rather differently, for to them a battle was very much a trial by combat and its result a judgement from God on the merits of each side. A calamitous battle was a source of stigma, just as a resounding victory was a source of pride and affirmation. The battle of Baugé, in 1421, left a troubling legacy for the Beaufort family, just as the battle of Wakefield, in 1460, bequeathed a similarly disturbing one to the House of York, many years later. The image it held – reflected in poetry composed within the family circle – was one of fortune's wheel, a wheel that could raise those astride it to power, influence, wealth and the zenith of success, then suddenly turn, casting those at its top to the ground in a complete and bewildering fall from grace.

Margaret's father was now a prisoner of war and would remain one for the next seventeen years. This was an exceptionally long period of imprisonment for a nobleman to endure. Initially, there were hopes for his speedy release, but all negotiations came to nothing. There was a particular reason for this. Beaufort fell into the hands of the French House of Eu, who bought his rights from his original captor, a Scottish captain. Buying and selling of ransom rights was a lucrative source of profit during the Hundred

Years' War, very much in the way that successful commodities trading is now. But the House of Eu wanted John Beaufort in order to arrange a prisoner swap, an exchange between John and the head of their own family, Charles Count of Eu, who had been captured by the English at Agincourt.

In normal circumstances this would have been brought about easily and quickly. But Henry V in his will of 1422 – drawn up shortly before his death at the château of Vincennes – forbade the release of either Eu or another French aristocrat, Charles Duke of Orléans, until they recognised the Treaty of Troyes, the settlement that vested the rights to the kingdoms of England and France on the House of Lancaster. This veto effectively blocked Eu's release, and doomed Margaret's father to an equally lengthy period of captivity.

These political factors were important. They overrode chivalric convention, which believed it unreasonable to place additional obstacles in the way of a nobleman's release. John Beaufort had every reason to feel aggrieved. He grew into manhood and middle age as an exile and captive. Among the many documents concerning his ransom negotiations one stands out. It is dated in the year 1427 and concerns his fresh hopes for a prisoner exchange, one between Beaufort and John Duke of Bourbon, who had also been captured by the English at Agincourt. John Beaufort was dispatching a messenger to the English government, appealing for a speedy release of the Duke of Bourbon. His missive had been drawn up by a clerk, and was clearly and carefully formulated. But as the messenger was about to ride off, Beaufort was overcome with emotion. Hastily he scrawled a postscript in his own hand, pleading, almost begging for his freedom. But once again negotiations broke down and nothing came of his desperate appeal.

John Beaufort endured the longest term of imprisonment of any English aristocrat in the Hundred Years' War. According to his own statement, his captivity ruined his health and left him burdened with crippling debt. Over the years, as his hopes of release were continually dashed, his outlook became bitter and disillusioned. The impasse over his ransom was eventually broken through the personal intervention of Henry VI, who overturned the restriction of his late father and authorised Eu's release, an act of clemency that at last ensured Beaufort regained his freedom.

Henry VI disagreed with the war policy Henry V had so dramatically begun at Agincourt and continued with the conquest of Normandy, and was now seeking an end to the Hundred Years' War through a negotiated peace treaty. His willingness to release the Count of Eu – and the Duke of Orléans two years later – signalled a break with the past. It was an act of kindness remembered with particular gratitude by Margaret Beaufort, who believed that Henry VI had saved her father from almost certain death in captivity and who as a result revered the Lancastrian King throughout her life.

However, by the time of his release in the autumn of 1438, John Beaufort was an angry man, intent on recouping the large ransom that he had been forced to pay. His marriage in 1442 to Margaret Beauchamp of Bletsoe was a relatively humble one for an aristocrat of his standing – a further consequence of his long captivity in France, for when he finally came home there were no suitable candidates for a man of his rank, which infuriated him still further. Margaret Beauchamp was quickly made pregnant, and subsequently saw little of her new husband as he returned to France as a Lancastrian commander with the sole intention of amassing as much profit as possible. Henry VI was generous, granting Beaufort a stream of lands and offices, and in 1443 he was given a major new command, to lead a substantial army into territory held by the Valois regime of Charles VII and bring the French to battle.

Much was hoped from this new military initiative. Charles VII had roused himself from the lethargy of his early years and was now conducting his affairs with energy and purpose. In 1442 he had led an expedition into English-held Gascony. The new campaign was intended to be a decisive rejoinder to this Valois revival. Henry VI invested more than £26,000 in Beaufort's expedition, more than half his annual income, at a time when the Lancastrian regime was becoming increasingly short of money. Beaufort negotiated long and hard with the king, demanding a host of lands, titles and offices in England and France. His rewards were lavish, and included promotion to the dukedom of Somerset.

But Beaufort wanted to recoup even more of his ransom. He showed little ability or skill in his command, for – after sailing from Portsmouth to Cherbourg with his army – he quite incredibly made no effort to liaise with the English commander already in Normandy, Richard Duke of York, a course of action that caused Duke Richard considerable offence. The chronicler Thomas Basin was in Rouen at the time Beaufort's army landed in the duchy, and he reported a joke current among Lancastrian captains: the purpose of the expedition had become so secret, it was said, that its commander was no longer aware of it himself. Richard Duke of York, the king's lieutenant in France, was reduced to sending out a stream of messengers trying to find out where the new army actually was.

However, the sole purpose of Beaufort's meandering raid into French territory in 1443 was to fill his own coffers with plunder and loot. He created a diplomatic incident by entering the territory of the neutral duchy of Brittany, besieging its frontier town of La Guerche and then forcing the Breton duke to pay him a substantial sum of money to lift the siege, an abuse of power and office so flagrant that it enraged even the placid Henry VI. Despite being fully paid for his war transport, Beaufort demanded additional payments from all the Norman towns that he passed through, again provoking a storm of protest – his levying of illegal taxes was later the subject of a full government inquiry. No meaningful military success was garnered from his campaign, and – to add insult to injury – Beaufort disbanded his troops early and pocketed the remainder of their wages.

John Beaufort's conduct provoked outrage, and when he returned home he met with an exceptionally hostile reception.

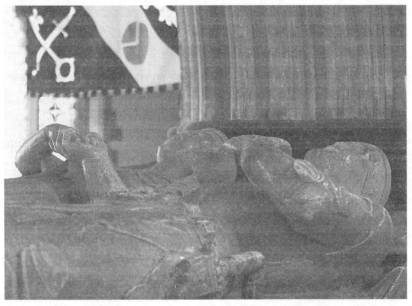

The tomb of Margaret's father, John Beaufort Duke of Somerset, at Wimborne Minster in Dorset. The legacy of this disgraced war commander and suicide was a deeply troubling one, but it fuelled Margaret's powerful ambition, and she constructed this memorial during the reign of her son, Henry VII

An infuriated Henry VI banished him from court and ordered a full investigation by the English treasury of his financial malpractice. According to the Croyland Chronicle, a well-informed contemporary source whose author knew Beaufort personally, the gravity of his wrongdoing now hit home. Keenly feeling his disgrace, and unable to bear it any longer, John Beaufort committed suicide on 30 May 1444, almost a year after Margaret's birth.

A disgraced war commander and a suicide was the worst stigma an aristocratic house could possibly bear. Beaufort was quietly buried in Wimborne Minster and his family put out the story that he had succumbed to ill-health. But as Margaret grew up she would have learned the truth about her father's fate. In this intensely religious age, death at one's own hand cast the soul of the suicide from the protective mantle of the Church's intercession. The pious yet pragmatic Margaret found this prospect too painful to bear, and over time constructed a different reality, one that focused on the injustice of her father's long captivity and heavy ransom, and portrayed him as an innocent victim of vengeful fate.

Some lines of verse on John Beaufort's death – commissioned by the family – caught the same theme, reciting: 'When he was wedded, and in estate most high, fortune – to ground him – cast him down most cruelly'. Margaret later confided to her confessor, John Fisher, her fear of the mutability of worldly fortunes, the turn of fortune's wheel, that when great success had been achieved all might be taken away. Fisher was struck by Margaret's extreme emotional distress – her convulsive sobbing and weeping – as she shared this recollection. It was made in the privacy of the confessional chamber, when Margaret was an elderly lady and matriarch of the House of Tudor. She had always impressed Fisher with her composure and presence of mind, her calm – almost icy –

deliberation when dealing with matters of state or political intrigue. By then Margaret had witnessed many turns of fortune's wheel herself. But this torrent of emotion had a quite shocking power, as if a deeply buried secret had suddenly been uncovered.

If Margaret perceived her father as a victim, over time, as she grew into adulthood, she cast herself as a survivor, a survivor who would right the wrongs of fortune and master the storms that had wrecked his reputation and standing. She would hazard all to advance the prospects and reputation of her family. This guiding principle held an almost redemptive power for her.

Although John Beaufort had been cast from royal favour, at the time of Margaret's birth the Beaufort family still dominated the politics of Henry VI's government. Her great-uncle Cardinal Beaufort was the most important statesman in the land, an experienced diplomatic negotiator and chief money-lender for the war effort in France. Her uncle Edmund Beaufort was another of Henry's leading war commanders, soon to become his chief lieutenant in France. But Margaret became aware, over time, that this powerful position within the Lancastrian realm could prove transient. The king's authority was weak and the war in France was going badly.

There were deeper reasons for the Beaufort family's ambition and vulnerability, and to fully understand Lady Margaret's own life it is important to explore them. To do so, we have to pull back in time from the tragedy of Margaret's father and look at the family's pedigree. For its origins in the late fourteenth century set the Beauforts apart from other aristocratic families. And here lay the source of another stigma. The Beauforts were originally bastards, the illegitimate offspring of John of Gaunt's adulterous liaison with Katherine Swynford.

This earlier history is important. In the early 1370s, John of Gaunt – the rich and powerful uncle of King Richard II – had turned from his second wife Constance of Castile and begun an affair with Katherine, the governess of his children. Gaunt's conduct quickly gained notoriety. This 'scandalous affair' – as one chronicler bluntly described it – produced four bastard children – three boys and a girl – who were named Beaufort after Gaunt's French castle and lordship in the Champagne; the oldest of them was Margaret's paternal grandfather.

The issue of bastardy was complex in the late Middle Ages. It was a time of increasing social mobility, with a land-based economy being replaced by a land-and-cash one, and a rising merchant class buying property and acquiring aristocratic titles. The de la Poles, Earls then Dukes of Suffolk in the fifteenth century, had risen to prominence 100 years earlier as a successful family of Hull merchants. It was possible for those of relatively humble stock to rise more quickly up the social ladder, whether through profits of trade or war. And this fluidity meant that the stigma of bastardy was lessening – within aristocratic and gentry families bastard offspring were more frequently mentioned in wills and granted money and even property.

To a certain extent, this social mobility benefited the Beauforts. John of Gaunt immediately recognised them as members of his broader family, and after the death of his wife Constance of Castile he chose to marry Katherine Swynford, his former mistress, at Lincoln in early 1396. This remarkable decision showed that Gaunt genuinely loved Katherine, and it paved the way for the elevation of the Beaufort family. In September 1396 the Pope ratified the marriage – despite the couple's earlier adulterous affair – and declared all its offspring, past and future, legitimate. The following year Gaunt had the Beauforts' legitimacy confirmed by act of parliament, and subsequently the family was granted a stream of lands and titles.

But the stigma of bastardy still remained. Gaunt's marriage to Katherine elicited much comment, and little of it was approving. One contemporary noted: 'the wedding caused many a man's wondering, for, as it was said, he had held her long before.' And when the Lancastrian King Henry IV took the throne in 1399 he confirmed the legitimacy of his family of the half-blood, but inserted a clause barring the Beauforts from succession to the throne. The three words – inscribed in Latin in the act of patent – *excepta dignitate regali* planted a lasting slur on the family. While the Beauforts were loyal servants of the new dynasty, and active in their military and civil responsibilities, they were barred from ever bearing the crown of England.

It is worth speculating on the effect this had on the family, for the decision would have powerfully impacted on the Beauforts' sense of identity. In the medieval age individuals saw themselves within a larger family story, one that for the English nobility was mapped out in lavish pedigrees and genealogies, where rights were borne from generation to generation, and where the 'livelode', the family livelihood and its line of inheritance, was defended almost as a sacred trust. The mocking nickname for the Beaufort family, 'Fairborn', was still in regular use in the fifteenth century, not only in the gossip of taverns and dining halls, but even inscribed – slightingly – in the pedigrees of rival aristocratic families.

A common perception in the mid-fifteenth century was that the Beauforts were becoming increasingly acquisitive and ambitious, eager to grasp money and property in whatever fashion – however unscrupulous. Such a view would further explain the reckless greed of Margaret's father on his military campaign in 1443, but it had a wider impact.

Chroniclers were struck above all by the family's ruthless self-interest. The charge of avarice was first laid against Margaret's great-uncle, Cardinal Beaufort, and then her own father and her uncle, John and Edmund Beaufort, successively promoted to the dukedom of Somerset. Prejudice against the Beauforts' bastard origins remained – with hostile observers and rival magnates perceiving them as upstarts, seizing an undue share of royal patronage at the expense of more established aristocratic families. This grievance fuelled Richard Duke of York's bitter animosity towards his rival Edmund Beaufort Duke of Somerset, for Duke Richard went to great lengths to stress, in his writings and political proclamations, the purity of his own blood line and lineage.

For the Beaufort family, the amassing of lands, wealth and titles may have been a palliative, as it almost certainly regarded the bar on succeeding to the throne as a considerable injustice. If so, this anger would have fuelled an abiding desire to overturn the prohibition and reinstate the Beauforts at the heart of the Lancastrian dynasty.

This powerful family ambition was certainly picked up by contemporaries and it was a formative experience in Lady Margaret's own political education. It was masked in the reigns of Henry IV and Henry V, for these kings had sons and brothers to succeed them, but was flung dramatically to the fore during the reign of Henry VI, when the king's marriage to Margaret of Anjou in 1445 failed, for eight years, to produce any children, and it was rumoured that the pious and unworldly monarch – who flew into a paroxysm of terror and moral consternation when confronted with naked female bathers on a visit to Bath, and who banned all low-cut blouses and dresses from the Lancastrian court in case he caught sight of a woman's cleavage – was incapable of begetting any.

At a time of uncertainty about the succession, what one Lancastrian king could prohibit, another could remit, and Henry VI – whose grasp of royal patronage was as uneasy as his sexual confidence – was at this time dominated by the court favourite William de la Pole Duke of Suffolk, a close ally of the Beauforts who was working to further their cause. Some observers voiced a very real concern that the king, manipulated by Suffolk, might now choose to overturn the clause barring the Beauforts from the throne.

This fear was expressed openly in 1450, when the Duke of Suffolk acquired Margaret's wardship and hastily arranged her marriage to his son and heir John. The country was in turmoil. The last English possessions in Normandy were being lost to the Valois armies of King Charles VII and parliament sought a scapegoat. The king's chief minister was an easy target. The House of Commons was virulently hostile to Suffolk and prepared impeachment charges against him. Strikingly it declared that the marriage between his son and Margaret Beaufort was proof of a wish to gain the crown for his own family through Margaret's rights as a Lancastrian heiress. Since the Beauforts were at this stage still barred from the succession, the accusation made little sense unless the Commons feared that the stipulation was about to be removed by the king, perhaps as a mark of favour to the Duke of Suffolk. This concern was never put to the test, for Suffolk – forced into exile – was captured in the English Channel by a privateering ship and brutally murdered later the same year.

Yet the dynastic issue remained, and with Henry VI suffering increasingly poor health and the government of the country in a state of collapse, the lack of a clearly designated succession posed a very real threat to political stability. There were a number of dynastic contenders – Richard

Duke of York, the wealthiest magnate in the realm and the key political figure in the early 1450s, was the most prominent; there were also the senior members of the Holland and Stafford families. Yet after the death of the Duke of Suffolk in 1450, it was not Duke Richard but Margaret's uncle Edmund Beaufort Duke of Somerset who became Henry VI's principal counsellor. The signal favour shown to Edmund Beaufort was ill-deserved – he had presided over the last disastrous English defeats in Normandy, a source of fury to Richard Duke of York, who now suspected that the Beauforts might be nominated as heirs to the crown ahead of him and the other candidates, an accusation he made openly in articles drafted against Edmund Beaufort in 1452.

I have taken time to rehearse these broader family issues because I believe they strongly shaped Lady Margaret's own identity. Embedded within it was an overarching theme – powerful yet thwarted ambition and a deep desire, almost a yearning, for the throne of England itself. By harnessing this ambition Margaret sought an opportunity to right a family wrong and to remove the stain on its reputation caused by her own father's disgrace and death.

By early 1453 political tension was running high: Richard Duke of York and Edmund Beaufort Duke of Somerset were jostling for influence with the king, and the country was facing armed insurrection and revolt. It was at this dangerous time that the nine-year-old Margaret was summoned to court by Henry VI. The Beaufort family story was now to take a new turn, as Margaret made her first entry on to the political stage.

THE VISION

Margaret Beaufort's early childhood had been a quiet one, lacking the show and ostentation normally associated with the wealthy heiress to a duke, the highest aristocratic title in the land. After the death of her father John Beaufort Duke of Somerset, on 30 May 1444, she had been brought up by her mother, Margaret Beauchamp, at her house at Bletsoe in Bedfordshire, and at the Beaufort castle of Maxey in the Lincolnshire Fens. These were small residences; indeed Maxey was little more than a fortified manor house, which Margaret shared with the two sons and three daughters of her mother's first marriage to Sir Oliver St John. Margaret Beaufort always had an enormous affection for the St John family, and from this one imagines that the first part of her life was happy and untroubled. She clearly enjoyed the company of her half-brothers and -sisters and, for a time at least, was sheltered from hearing about her father's tragic death and the dangerous intrigues of high politics.

In January 1450, with Margaret still only six years old, came the first sign that this idyllic period would not last. Henry VI's favourite and chief minister William de la Pole Duke of Suffolk was fighting for his very survival. William de la Pole had enjoyed a remarkable pre-eminence in the Lancastrian regime, able to easily manipulate the king and dominate the political stage, but now the House of Commons was determined to make him the scapegoat for the disastrous reopening of the Hundred Years' War, a resumption of hostilities against the Valois regime of Charles VII that had seen much of English-held Normandy lost to the French, and the

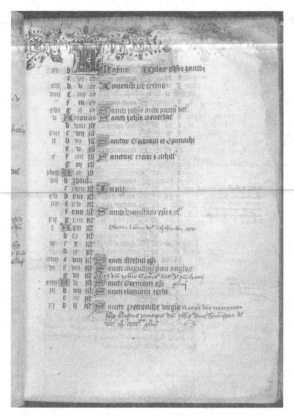

Margaret's date of birth, on 31 May 1443, from the Beaufort Hours

duchy's capital, Rouen, surrender after putting up only token resistance. Failure abroad and government mismanagement at home had created a volatile and angry mood in London, where a turbulent parliament was now in session.

In the same month the House of Commons brought a stream of accusations against William de la Pole, ranging from corruption to high treason, and despite William answering these allegations he was arrested and imprisoned in the Tower of London on 28 January. New charges were drafted, and it must have become clear to the beleaguered royal favourite that the Commons intended to impeach him and that his position was now desperate. His thoughts turned to his seven-year-old son and heir, John de la Pole. By 7 February he had arranged a marriage for him, to the six-year-old Margaret Beaufort.

This child marriage was a hasty measure, put in place by a desperate man who feared for his own future. As William secured it, he was negotiating with the king for an act of royal clemency in which he would be banished from the kingdom but allowed to keep his life. Yet, amid such terrible concerns, it was significant that he chose Margaret for his son. Appearances can always be deceptive in politics and Margaret – despite her relatively humble lifestyle – was a wealthy heiress, and thus a significant acquisition in the medieval marriage market. And William de la Pole, intensely ambitious for his family, well knew Margaret's dynastic position and that – most important of all – in the right circumstances she could hold a claim to the throne herself.

There is no evidence that Margaret ever met William de la Pole or his son. But she would certainly have been told about him, and the contract that now existed between her and John de la Pole, although because it was a child marriage it would only be formally ratified when Margaret was twelve. What would she have made of it all?

For this young girl, the idea of marriage did not yet have any meaning or reality. She would have been delighted and flattered that she had been chosen by a duke, a royal minister and the most prominent politician in the country. William de la Pole had been one of the principal English captains in the Hundred Years' War and was an accomplished and charming courtier. Margaret's mother would have told her pleasing tales of William's chivalric gallantry. Less welcome would have been news of the English military defeats in France, which Margaret would have also learned about at this time. These distant yet unsettling reports were not only threatening the life and career of Margaret's prospective father-in-law but also that of her uncle, Edmund Beaufort Duke of Somerset, for Edmund Beaufort was now the king's lieutenant in France, and Henry VI's principal commander in Normandy.

After this brief hiatus, Margaret's life continued very much as before. However, she had become aware of her own dynastic importance, even though such concepts would have been fleetingly grasped by a young child. But Margaret was no ordinary child. She had a precocious sense of a great destiny being mapped out for her, a sense that was powerfully strengthened by a fresh series of political developments.

Early in 1453 the nine-year-old Lady Margaret was summoned to the Lancastrian court of Henry VI and his queen, Margaret of Anjou. The king instructed Margaret's mother, Margaret Beauchamp of Bletsoe, to come to London at Shrovetide (14 February) and wait there at his command. Towards the end of February the child marriage between Margaret and John de la Pole was annulled, and King Henry authorised a payment of 100 marks (almost £67) to 'his right dear and well-beloved cousin Margaret' for her clothing to attend upon him in state. This was a sumptuous gift, worth over £25,000 in today's money, so Margaret would have been dressed magnificently, in fine cloth embroidered with jewels. Being fitted for such wonderful garments, and then making her entrance at the royal court, would have been an extraordinary experience for a young girl. She would have known that everyone's attention was on her as she was thrust into the political limelight. The king was planning to dissolve Margaret's child marriage to John de la Pole, and arrange another one in its place, to his half-brother Edmund Tudor. Only Edmund Tudor was not a child, but a 22-year-old man.

Margaret had a clear memory of the events that followed, one that she later shared with her confessor and spiritual adviser John Fisher. In her recollection, the events took place with the court in full session at the royal palace of Westminster in mid-May 1453, when she had been forced to choose between two suitors, John de la Pole and Edmund Tudor. The king, Henry VI, had urged her to consider the merits of Edmund, his half-brother. But Margaret had been unable to decide. So she decided to pray to St Nicholas, 'who was the patron and helper of all true maidens', appealing to him to show by a sign what was right for her to do. That night she had a vision of St Nicholas, 'dressed in white, as if he were a bishop', who advised her to choose Edmund for her husband. Margaret duly did.

This is a remarkable account. Since it was confided to her spiritual adviser, who only made it public in his sermon on the month's anniversary of her death as a tribute to her piety, there is no reason to doubt its basic authenticity. It shows that Margaret already had a highly developed and unusually powerful sensitivity to religious experience, one that belonged among the mystical tradition of women visionaries of the late Middle Ages. Only Margaret was not a recluse, but a wealthy heiress with a blood-link to the throne, lavishly fêted at the Lancastrian court.

It is worth rehearsing the sequence recalled by her. Margaret asked directly for guidance from a particular saint. She then saw the saint in a vision, and since he instructed her on what to do it seems likely that she also heard his voice. It immediately evokes the life of another astonishing woman who also appealed for help from named saints – Michael, Margaret and Catherine – and then saw them and heard their voices: Joan of Arc, who experienced her first vision at around the age of eleven. Joan was not an aristocrat but from the French peasantry; however, like Margaret she was a woman of action rather than contemplation, ready to fight for her cause.

In more general terms, Margaret's vision shows that she had a strong sense of personal destiny. The harsh political reality was that this young girl had little say in what was happening around her. It was the king and his advisers who had decided to annul Margaret's child marriage to John de la Pole, and she would simply have been required to take part in a ceremony in which the match was formally dissolved. But Margaret invested that ceremony with great mystical significance and power. She did not ask advice from a bishop or priest, a representative of the English Church or of the ruling Lancastrian government. By appealing directly to a Christian saint she took command of the situation and reclaimed that decision as her own. It gives us an intimate insight into the way she thought and made sense of the world.

Margaret would now marry Edmund Tudor, and it was decided that the marriage would take place after two years, when she was twelve and her husband twenty-four. Margaret's childhood was now coming to an end, and although – after her appearance at the royal court – she returned home with her mother, her life was different. She now received a much more intensive education, instruction in etiquette and would have been regularly informed of the news at court and of the kingdom as a whole. She would have learned of the king's breakdown that summer, how he had fallen into a stupor, unable to recognise anyone or anything, not even his own son, Prince Edward, born to his queen Margaret of Anjou in October 1453. And with the king sick, Margaret would have been told of the two great factions within the realm, the one clustered around the greatest aristocrat in the land, Richard Duke of York, the other around the party of her own uncle, Edmund Beaufort Duke of Somerset.

The House of York was in the ascendant. In 1454 it was Richard Duke of York who governed the realm as Protector and consigned his rival Edmund Beaufort to the Tower of London. When Henry VI recovered his health early in 1455, released Edmund from imprisonment and restored him as chief minister, York went into open revolt. He raised an army and confronted the king and his supporters at St Albans, where a confused skirmish took place amid the city's streets. When Edmund was cut down and killed, the fighting ceased. Margaret would have received this news with horror. In her eyes her uncle, the family's most senior representative, was a loyal and devoted servant to the House of Lancaster. His pre-eminence within the realm showed the power the Beauforts could wield, a power that Margaret would also come to enjoy, but his fate also warned of terrible danger.

On 1 November 1455 the marriage between Margaret and Edmund Tudor took place at Bletsoe, and then the couple left for Tudor's residence at Lamphey in Pembrokeshire. In the spring of 1456 Margaret became pregnant. She was twelve years old and small in build for her age. Her 24-year-old husband chose not to wait until she was older and physically stronger before consummating the marriage, but put the life of his young wife at risk to ensure that she would become pregnant as quickly as possible. His motives were entirely mercenary, for by right of the 'courtesy of England' as long as Margaret produced an heir Edmund would enjoy a life interest in her estates, whatever the subsequent fate of mother and child. It was a rape within marriage, deeply shocking by modern standards and surprising and harshly inconsiderate by medieval ones, for even in this far more ruthless age it was normal practice to wait until a young wife was at least fourteen before having sex with her. The experience caused Margaret lasting physical and emotional damage.

In the Middle Ages, a dutiful Christian wife would not be expected to ever openly criticise her husband. But there is compelling evidence that Margaret knew, or came to know, that what had happened to her was morally wrong. Many years later, when Margaret's own son – Henry VII – was on the throne, she strongly intervened to delay the marriage of her granddaughter, also named Margaret, to the Scottish King James IV. Her reason was that the Princess Margaret was too young, and that her intended husband could not be trusted to wait before consummating the marriage. It was a striking echo of her own experience, and such was her authority with her son, the king, that her wishes were immediately respected.

Margaret's pregnancy was deeply frightening for her. This brave young woman had to come to terms with constant physical and emotional pain, and also her fears for the well-being of her husband, Edmund Tudor, the man who had violated her. For Tudor remained her husband and protector in a lawless region of Wales, a country entirely alien to Margaret, and his life and safety were now in jeopardy. Tudor was acting as Henry VI's lieutenant in the region and as he took up the reins of power he clashed with local supporters of Richard Duke of York. It was the Yorkists who proved the stronger. One of York's retainers, Sir William Herbert, captured Tudor and imprisoned him in Carmarthen Castle in August 1456. As Margaret's pregnancy developed, the news about her husband became more and more alarming. She first learned that he had been taken captive, then that he had fallen dangerously ill – a victim of a local outbreak of the plague – and finally there came the hammer blow. Margaret learned that Edmund Tudor had died in Carmarthen on 1 November 1456.

Margaret was more than six months pregnant. She could not risk the dangerous journey back to England, and was now alone, a young widow, vulnerable and terribly afraid. Her confessor John Fisher later spoke of this time, almost certainly drawing on information Margaret had shared with him. Fisher recalled that she had been terrified – in this violent and remote place – fearful for her own safety and that of the child she was carrying. She dreaded the real danger that they both could fall victim to the plague that had killed her husband. In the circumstances, Margaret did the only thing possible – she sought the protection of her brother-in-law, Jasper Tudor, and took up residence in his nearby seat at Pembroke Castle. She gave birth to a son there on 28 January 1457, and named him Henry in honour of the Lancastrian King Henry VI.

The recollections of John Fisher – an invaluable and intimate source about Margaret's life – make clear that the birth was a very painful one because of her small build and young age. It must have been a terrible experience for her. But soon after her recovery from this ordeal, Margaret made a striking decision, to negotiate another match as quickly as possible. This was a quite remarkable course of action, for Margaret's experience of sex within marriage at the age of twelve had damaged her and left her physically unable to bear any more children. It was likely to have put her off sex completely – indeed any form of close physical intimacy may have repelled her. One of the religious books owned by Margaret and later bequeathed to Christ's College, Cambridge, contained a chapter on the spiritual responsibilities of marriage. The section on frigidity had been annotated, probably by Margaret herself or a scribe under her instruction, and a question was posed in the margin. It asked if it was a sin to find sex abhorrent. The thought clearly troubled Margaret, and almost certainly encapsulated her own experience.

And yet, in March 1457, less than two months after the birth of her son, Margaret rode with Jasper Tudor from Pembroke Castle to the Duke of Buckingham's manor of Greenfield, near Newport in Gwent. Not yet fourteen, Margaret could easily have chosen to stay at Pembroke with her young son and, for a time at least, keep away from high politics. But she decided to embark upon a different path. Humphrey Stafford Duke of Buckingham was the most important member of the Lancastrian court and the only English magnate as powerful as Richard Duke of York. Margaret's chief aim was to gain the duke's protection, safeguard her interests and those of her infant son, and avoid another husband being forced upon her. She resolved to do this as quickly as possible.

This was a political transaction, and yet it was also a remarkable personal moment. Margaret, a thirteen-year-old girl, was not intimidated by the prospect of negotiating with a 54-year-old duke, a man who had held most of the important posts of the realm, including the captaincy of Calais and the constableship of England. There was a family entrée, because the duke's oldest son, also named Humphrey, had married another Margaret Beaufort, Margaret the daughter of Edmund Beaufort Duke of Somerset. But these discussions also required poise and confidence. Margaret was now seeking to arrange a marriage between herself and the duke's younger son, Henry Stafford. Her efforts were crowned with success. Bishop Reginald Boulers of Coventry and Lichfield granted dispensation for the match on 6 April 1457, necessary because Margaret Beaufort and Henry Stafford were second cousins. The marriage was celebrated at Humphrey Duke of Buckingham's lavish residence at Maxstoke in Warwickshire soon afterwards.

This was a triumphant outcome, placing Margaret once again at the centre of court and government. For the Lancastrian court had rejected London for Coventry, Kenilworth and the Midlands, and the Duke of Buckingham's estates lay in the centre of its area of influence. Margaret had already acquired a taste for the machinations of court politics. Lady Margaret Beaufort's early biographers, obsessed by her piety, downplayed her political skill and powerful ambition. Yet these attributes formed the heart of her identity.

SUN OF YORK

In normal circumstances, Margaret Beaufort could now have looked forward to a period of stability, as her new husband Sir Henry Stafford served the Lancastrian regime and enjoyed the fruits of its patronage. But these were not normal circumstances. The dramatic events that led to Richard Duke of York's son Edward Earl of March being crowned King Edward IV have already been told elsewhere, and will only be repeated briefly here.

A topsy-turvy period of politics saw first the Yorkists routed at Ludford in October 1459, and then the return of Richard Neville Earl of Warwick and Edward Earl of March from Calais in the summer of the following year. They landed at Sandwich and, gathering a small army, marched to Northampton and demanded an audience with Henry VI. Humphrey Duke of Buckingham, the commander of the Lancastrian forces, refused to grant them one. On 10 July

1460 both sides prepared for battle, and the Duke of Buckingham drew up his will, settling 400 marks of land on Margaret and her husband. In the confused fighting that followed, marred by the treachery of one of Henry VI's followers, the Yorkists were triumphant and Duke Humphrey was slain trying to protect the king from his assailants.

Margaret would have been shocked by the news of Northampton. She had chosen Humphrey Duke of Buckingham as a powerful protector for herself and her son, and now that protector had died violently in battle. For a while, it seemed possible that the Lancastrians might still triumph, as Margaret of Anjou gathered a fresh army and defeated the Yorkists in clashes at Wakefield and the second battle of St Albans. But Queen Margaret's failure to occupy the capital lost her the military advantage, and Edward Earl of March now seized his opportunity. Edward had defeated a Lancastrian army raised by Jasper Tudor and his father Owen at Mortimer's Cross – on the Welsh Marches near Wigmore in Herefordshire – on 2 February 1461. Before the battle Edward had drawn encouragement from an unusual meteorological phenomenon, a parhelion, whereby three suns had appeared in the sky, and later made the sun in splendour his royal badge in celebration of his victory.

Margaret would have drawn little solace from the three suns. At the close of the battle the House of Tudor had been decimated: Owen Tudor was executed and Jasper forced into flight, leaving the fortunes of Margaret's son Henry Tudor increasingly vulnerable. Edward now entered London, claimed the crown of England and then marched north to do battle with the Lancastrians. The two sides met at Towton in Yorkshire on 29 March 1461. This bloody battle, fought in a blinding snowstorm, ended in a complete rout of the Lancastrian army and established Edward IV on the throne.

The battle was a body-blow for Lady Margaret, for in its aftermath she discovered the remainder of her Lancastrian friends and allies had either been slain or driven into exile. It was a grim roll-call. Her mother's third husband, Lionel Lord Welles, was killed in the fighting. Her cousin Henry Beaufort Duke of Somerset, and his younger brothers Edmund and John, had been forced to flee the country – first to Scotland, and then to France. It was rumoured that Jasper Tudor had also gone into exile in France.

Margaret quickly realised that the only way to safeguard her fortunes was to seek a *rapprochement* with the Yorkist king. Accordingly, her husband Sir Henry Stafford, who had fought with the Lancastrians at Towton, quickly made his peace with the new regime, securing a general pardon, first for himself and later his wife. Henry Stafford's reconciliation protected Margaret's estates, which were saved from confiscation in the acts of resumption of two successive parliaments. But Margaret was unable to prevent a long-term separation from her son, and this was a terrible blow for her. On 30 September 1461 Edward IV granted the wardship and marriage of Henry Tudor to his loyal supporter William Lord Herbert. The four-year-old Henry would now be transferred to Herbert's keeping at his Welsh castle of Raglan.

Henry Tudor was brought up with care and consideration by Lord Herbert. Edward IV's close ally had paid the king no less than £1,000 for the rights of his wardship and intended, when he came of age, to marry him to his eldest daughter Maud. Raglan was a fine residence to grow up in, magnificently rebuilt by Herbert himself and, as described by one Welsh poet, with its 'hundred rooms filled with festive fare, its towers, parlours and doors, its heaped-up fires of long-dried fuel'.

Herbert's wife Anne Devereux supervised Henry's

upbringing with real kindness. Lady Margaret could have had few qualms about her son's treatment, nor about his political future under the Yorkists, for both Herbert and Margaret were united in hoping that Edward IV might eventually restore Henry Tudor to the earldom of Richmond, the title held by his father. But it was an emotional blow none the less, the harsh reality that she would now miss much of his childhood, and only hear about it at second hand. Although rights of wardship were part of the reality of medieval life, this separation would be particularly hard for Margaret to bear.

Lady Margaret adjusted to the new situation as best she could. She sent regular messengers to Raglan to gain the latest news about her son's upbringing, and negotiated with Herbert so that she could pay him the occasional visit. On one of these she toured her West Country estates with her husband, and then travelled to Bristol, where the small party accompanying her was ferried across the River Severn to Chepstow. Here they were met by a band of Herbert's followers and escorted to Raglan Castle, where they stayed a week, before returning to England. The details of the itinerary are set out in the household documents belonging to Margaret, but beneath this dry record one can easily imagine her excitement and anticipation as she crossed the Severn and drew closer to her son, and her deep sadness as she parted from him.

In the early years of Edward IV's reign, Margaret and her husband Sir Henry Stafford chose to set up their home in the castle of Bourne in Lincolnshire. The castle was pleasantly situated, set in parkland bordered by water, its roof-gardens offering striking views across the Fens, and it was in a part of the country Lady Margaret already knew well, and was happy in, conveniently close to her mother's own residence of

Maxey. Bourne belonged to Margaret as part of the Holland inheritance that had descended to her through her paternal grandmother, and was a reminder that in her marriage to Stafford she was a great landed heiress and he, although the son of a duke, was only a younger son – with just a small estate to his name. The couple's wealth and standing depended on Margaret's properties, and the security of these was reliant on the goodwill of Edward IV, the new Yorkist king.

Such support was by no means guaranteed in the complex politics of the Wars of the Roses, for Margaret, despite her marriage to Stafford, remained a Beaufort, and the Beauforts had been bitter opponents of Edward's father, Richard Duke of York. Edward IV, however, was ready to be conciliatory to his father's former enemies. The king was young, personable and charismatic, and sought to win over the remaining supporters of the exiled Lancastrian King Henry VI to his cause. Foremost among them was Margaret's own cousin, Henry Beaufort Duke of Somerset.

Henry Beaufort was one of the leading members of the Lancastrian party. After the death of his father, slain at the first battle of St Albans in 1455, he had become one of Henry VI's most prominent war captains, and had fought against the Yorkists at Wakefield, the second battle of St Albans and Towton. He cut a dashing chivalric figure and was a notable jouster – well known in the courts of Burgundy and France. In the aftermath of the Lancastrian defeat at Towton, Beaufort had been sent to France by Margaret of Anjou to recruit fresh military aid for the embattled queen and her supporters. But his diplomatic mission did not go according to plan. Henry Beaufort arrived in Paris to find the French King Charles VII on his deathbed. Charles had been preparing an invasion army to support the Lancastrians, but he fell

ill, and passed away before the force could set sail. Charles's
successor, Louis XI, did not wish to antagonise England's
new Yorkist government, and disbanded the soldiers. He also
arrested Beaufort and threw him in jail.

After a spell of captivity in a French prison, Henry
Beaufort was eventually freed, and allowed to take refuge in
Bruges, under the protection of Charles Count of Charolais,
the son and heir of Philip the Good, Duke of Burgundy. But
Beaufort seems to have become demoralised by the collapse
of French backing for the Lancastrian cause, and, isolated
from other Lancastrians, began negotiations with Edward IV
and his chief aristocratic supporter the Earl of Warwick.
Although at the end of 1462 he joined a Lancastrian invasion
of north-eastern England, he showed little stomach for a fight
and quickly came to an agreement with the Yorkists – dramatically defecting to Warwick's army.

Edward IV was initially cautious in his treatment of this
prominent former Lancastrian. However, by the summer of
1463 a remarkable *rapprochement* had taken place. All Henry
Beaufort's lands and annuities (annual cash payments,
charged on the royal exchequer) were restored, and the king
displayed a considerable show of trust in a man who had
once been one of his most bitter opponents, inviting Beaufort
to joust in royal tournaments, going hunting with him and
even allowing him on a number of occasions to share the
royal bed. In medieval society such an act did not have the
sexual connotations we would find today, but it was a signal
mark of royal favour, and many were taken aback that it was
now being bestowed so lavishly – one source, Gregory's
Chronicle, noting of Henry Beaufort in surprised indignation: 'the king made full much of him'.

But in the aftermath of this extraordinary charm offensive
by the Yorkist king a full reconciliation with the Beaufort

family occurred. In July 1463 Henry Beaufort's younger brother Edmund, held in the Tower of London for more than two years, was released from captivity. His widowed mother Eleanor Duchess of Somerset – Lady Margaret's aunt – was given a royal pardon and her annuities restored to her. Trusted servants were also welcomed back into the fold. John Martyn of Deptford, who had been the estate manager of Margaret's late father, received a pardon, as did Henry Court, who had served the Beaufort family loyally for two generations. Lady Margaret must have viewed these developments with surprise and delight, for the reappearance of her own family on the political stage was almost miraculous. And if Henry Beaufort had remained loyal to Edward IV she would have benefited not only politically but also financially from the Beauforts' new position within the Yorkist regime, and gained a powerful protector at court. But her joy was to be short-lived.

At the end of July 1463 Henry Beaufort accompanied the king on a progress into the Midlands. But at Northampton local townspeople, infuriated at seeing him in the royal party, rioted and very nearly killed him. Deeply shaken, Beaufort left Edward IV's entourage and retired to his castle of Chirk in north-east Wales. Once away from the seductive charm of the new monarch, he began to reconsider his political future, remembering his family's long tradition of loyalty to the House of Lancaster and regretting his sudden conversion to the Yorkist cause. In the autumn of 1463 Henry Beaufort reopened communications with the exiled Lancastrians, and at the end of the year he fled to Scotland to join them.

Edward IV was incensed by Beaufort's action, which he regarded as both a political betrayal and a deeply personal one. He had after all showered his former enemy with honours and gone out of his way to welcome him into the Yorkist regime. His generosity now appeared a serious miscalculation, and he had lost face through a very public courting of Beaufort's allegiance. The king was enraged. When Henry Beaufort returned to northern England with a small Lancastrian army, and was defeated and captured at Hexham in May 1464, the king ordered him to be stripped of all aristocratic insignia and then summarily executed. Edward took a vindictive pleasure in Beaufort's humiliation and death, and according to one chronicler, his executioner – the Earl of Warwick's brother, John Lord Montagu – was promoted to the earldom of Northumberland solely because he had captured and then beheaded him.

Edward's breach with the Beauforts was now permanent. Henry Beaufort's younger brothers Edmund and John had escaped the rout at Hexham and went into exile abroad, joining the household of Charles Count of Charolais in Flanders. Charolais had earlier sheltered Henry Beaufort and now took his brothers under his protection. Edward – unable to reach them – took out his fury against the family by imprisoning their mother, the elderly Eleanor Duchess of Somerset, and confiscating all her possessions, a spiteful act against a defenceless and vulnerable widow. But the warning for Lady Margaret was clear.

In 1465 Margaret was admitted with her mother to the confraternity of the Abbey of Croyland (or Crowland). Joining a confraternity – a voluntary association of lay people supporting and faithful to a particular religious institution – was not an unusual occurrence in the late Middle Ages, but what was more significant was Margaret's young age when she chose to do so – she was only twenty-two. The Fenland Abbey of Croyland was reasonably close to her principal residence of Bourne Castle, but more importantly it was the chronicler of the abbey who had recorded details of the fall from royal favour of Margaret's father, from the pinnacle of regal trust to disgrace, banishment and suicide. Margaret would have known of this already, but her decision to involve herself more closely with the abbey at this time suggests that recent political events may have painfully reminded her of his tragic fate.

For Henry Beaufort's bloody execution by the Yorkists, less than a year after basking in the sumptuous favour of Edward IV, was once again unsettling proof of the impermanence of worldly power. The Act of Attainder passed against the Beauforts in the parliament of 1465 – which formally confiscated all their landed possessions – showed the depth of the king's anger against them. Its wording was surprisingly personal: Henry Beaufort had broken his oath to the king, 'against all nature of gentilesse' – he had acted dishonourably by breaking his word and abusing royal trust. By doing so he had brought dishonour and shame upon his family name. Against such treachery, the harshest punishment was justified. Fortune's wheel had turned again – and done so with rapidity and violence.

With Edward IV pursuing a vendetta against the Beaufort family, Margaret must have feared for her own future, and in the face of such danger may have considered retreating from the political arena altogether, as she joined another confraternity at this time, the Order of the Holy Trinity, near Knaresborough in Yorkshire, a religious body concerned with freeing captive Christians imprisoned by the Turks. On this occasion she also obtained admission for her son, Henry Tudor. While England was afflicted by civil war and political unrest, eastern Europe was succumbing to the onslaught of the Ottoman Turks, led by the Emperor Mehmed II – aptly named 'the Conqueror' – who had besieged and captured

Constantinople in 1453 and in the following decade annexed most of Greece and Serbia.

Margaret's interest in the Order of the Holy Trinity shows her breadth of thinking, and that she was capable of seeing beyond the misfortunes of her family to a broader vista, the threat to European Christendom from the Islamic Turks. One senses she was deeply fearful for the future, yet determined to face its challenges as best she could. Contributing to the ransoms, and helping to free those Christian knights captured and imprisoned by the Ottomans, held the moral equivalence in the late Middle Ages of participating in a crusade, and receiving an absolution for past sins. It is striking that Margaret's primary concern was to gain the admission of her eight-year-old son into the order alongside her. By associating herself and Henry Tudor with such a worthy cause she may have hoped to break a chain of punishment for past wrongdoing, and gain spiritual protection from present menace.

By 1465 Queen Margaret of Anjou's exiled Lancastrian court had departed from Scotland and settled at the castle of Koeur in Alsace. Lady Margaret was well aware that the queen was now living in poverty with her son Prince Edward and a clutch of die-hard Lancastrian noblemen and household officials. The queen's chancellor Sir John Fortescue described a hand-to-mouth existence, apologising to another exiled Lancastrian – John Butler Earl of Ormonde – that the bearer of a letter sent to him had only been given two French crowns for his costs 'because we had no more money [to give him]'. Henry VI was not among these penniless refugees; he had been discovered in northern Lancashire in 1465, leading the life of a fugitive in the aftermath of his flight from the battle of Hexham, and was now securely locked up in the Tower of London.

However, Margaret's remaining male cousins Edmund and John Beaufort were living in better conditions, attached to the household of Charles Count of Charolais in Flanders, and receiving regular financial payments. Other exiled Lancastrians were drawn to Charolais's service on a more occasional basis, and these included John Courtenay Earl of Devon and Henry Holland Duke of Exeter. But Edmund Beaufort and Charolais had become firm friends, and the two fought side by side at Montlhéry on 16 July 1465, when Charolais defeated the forces of Louis XI of France. The presence of Edmund Beaufort – who now styled himself Duke of Somerset – at this battle attracted considerable interest and was noted by a number of foreign chroniclers. It was Beaufort – in Flanders – who would become a rallying figure for Lancastrian exiles, a fact all the more galling for Edward IV, who had let him out of prison in the first place, and the king's anger against all members of the Beaufort family ran unassuaged.

Margaret Beaufort was well aware of this, and in the aftermath of Montlhéry may have despaired of her own future. Yet she was pragmatic and astute, and above all a fighter, and with the dispersal of the Lancastrian cause her chief concern remained – as always – to protect the interests of her son, still in the wardship and keeping of William Lord Herbert, one of Edward IV's closest supporters. The Beauforts were now the king's irreconcilable enemies, but Margaret sought the support of the Stafford family of her husband. Her ability to cultivate alliances and negotiate with shrewdness and courage first tempered Edward's suspicion of her, and then gave her an entrée into the Yorkist court.

An opportunity to do this certainly existed. In 1465 Sir Henry's nephew, Henry Stafford Duke of Buckingham, had married Katherine Woodville, the younger sister of Edward

IV's now queen. And Margaret's mother-in-law, Anne Neville, had also remarried Edward's treasurer and close supporter, Walter Lord Mountjoy. It was the Stafford connection that gave Margaret a chance to win back the trust of the Yorkist king. This course of action required patience and prudence, but Margaret was intelligent enough to see where her best chance lay. Walter Lord Mountjoy was a close friend of Edward IV, and Margaret – who had a good relationship with her mother-in-law, Anne Neville, with whom she shared literary and religious interests – enlisted her support. By cultivating this connection Margaret gained Walter Lord Mountjoy's advocacy and in late 1466 Mountjoy interceded with the king on her behalf. Edward's hostility began to lessen.

In December 1466 Edward IV granted Margaret and her husband the Beaufort manor of Woking in Surrey, an estate that had been in royal hands since the attainder of Henry Beaufort Duke of Somerset. It was a highly symbolic act of patronage, for the fine manor house and its surrounding lands – in open countryside alongside the River Wey, but conveniently close to the capital – had been a favourite residence of the Beaufort family. But Edward was now treating Margaret as a Stafford rather than a Beaufort, and restoring both her and her husband to political influence. As a result of the king's change of heart, Woking now became Margaret and Sir Henry Stafford's principal residence.

Lady Margaret's surviving household accounts give us a snapshot of the couple's journey south. A flurry of improvements to Woking's manor house took place in January 1467 before Margaret and Sir Henry Stafford moved in. The counting-house was re-roofed, stables repaired and a new larder built. Carts and extra staff were hired from the Abbot of Bourne to speed the transfer. The moated manor house

The ruins of the fine manor house at Woking in Surrey that became Margaret's principal residence, and a reconstruction of its appearance in the fifteenth century

lay a mile south of the town of Woking, screened by a copse and surrounded by parkland. Entrance was commanded by a gatehouse and drawbridge, leading to an outer courtyard, with its lodgings and stables. A second gate opened out on to the great hall, with adjoining pantry and buttery, the chapel and the private chambers of lord and lady. Beyond the moat were sheds for horses, sheep and cattle, and gardens, bordered by the fruit trees of the orchard, which ran down to a large fishpond and the winding river.

Margaret moved into this new residence with an enlarged household establishment, its strength doubled to between forty and fifty, with an influx of Stafford servants personally recommended by Anne Neville, Margaret's mother-in-law, who had very much taken the couple under her wing. These included men of particular quality: William Wisetowe, who was appointed their steward, Thomas Rogers, their auditor, and – most important of all – Reginald Bray, who would become their estate manager and Margaret's most trusted and loyal servant. After all the difficulties of the preceding years, Lady Margaret must have felt an astonishing surge of hope as she set up home at Woking. Fortune at last seemed to be turning her way.

Sir Henry Stafford now enjoyed a far more active political role. In May 1467 he rode to a royal council meeting at Mortlake; on another occasion he was summoned to attend the king at Windsor. In May 1468 both he and Margaret came up to stay in London during the meeting of parliament, arriving in the capital by boat and lodging at the Mitre in Cheapside. Edward IV, whose foreign policy – with Woodville support – had become increasingly hostile to France, was considering sending a military expedition against Louis XI, led by Walter Lord Mountjoy. In retaliation, Louis backed a small invasion force commanded by Jasper Tudor. In July 1468 Tudor landed in the Dyfi Estuary, close to the castle of Harlech, which remarkably had never been reduced by the Yorkists and was still in Lancastrian hands, and then launched a raid across north Wales. Edward responded quickly, ordering William Lord Herbert to raise an army and deal with this threat. Herbert chose to take young Henry Tudor with him, and Margaret – anxious for his safety – sent out a stream of messages enquiring after his well-being. In the event, the eleven-year-old Henry Tudor was safe enough. He witnessed the destruction of his uncle Jasper's forces at Twt Hill near Caernarfon, and then saw his guardian Herbert finally capture the Lancastrian stronghold of Harlech, which surrendered to his army on 14 August. But Jasper Tudor himself was able to escape Herbert's soldiers and sail back to France.

Lord Herbert had once again performed stalwart service for his master. However, Edward IV's rule was becoming increasingly unpopular, and unrest within the realm was growing. Law and order was beginning to break down in the localities, and – faced with a threat to some of their properties in Kendal – Margaret and Sir Henry Stafford now sought a stronger demonstration of Edward's favour. In December 1468 they took a remarkable step, inviting the king to hunt at Woking park, and afterwards to dine with them at their lodge at Brookwood. Edward accepted their invitation. Lady Margaret – chief heiress of the Beaufort family, enemy of the House of York – was now to entertain a Yorkist king to supper.

The lordship of Kendal had been granted to Margaret's father on the eve of his great expedition to France in 1443, and she felt honour-bound to protect her lands there. Estate management was a vital skill in the late Middle Ages, particularly as Lady Margaret's properties were, like many aristocratic holdings, scattered over a wide geographical area. She held a clutch of estates in the West Country, and another in the eastern Midlands. But it was her manors in north-west England, around the Cumbrian town of Kendal, that were now at risk. In the summer of 1468 the Parr family – enjoying the support of the powerful magnate Richard Neville Earl of Warwick – had challenged Margaret's legal right to hold these properties and also stirred up unrest among her tenants. Storm clouds were gathering over the Yorkist polity: Warwick's relations with the king were deteriorating, and this ambitious nobleman – known to posterity as 'the Kingmaker' – was very much pursuing his own agenda. In November Margaret's estate manager Reginald Bray had ridden north with a trusted group of servants in an attempt to collect arrears of rent. Conditions were dangerous, and the men received extra financial reward because, as one document noted tellingly, 'of the trouble now in the world'. But the rents remained unpaid.

Margaret and Sir Henry Stafford sought the backing of the king. But they also judged the opportunity was right to personally meet and entertain Edward IV, and build a deeper relationship with him. While Stafford would receive the king at Guildford, hunt with him and escort him to Brookwood, Margaret took charge of organising the festivities. In 1453 she had been bought fine clothing to meet the Lancastrian Henry VI. Now, in 1468, as she prepared to receive a Yorkist monarch, she chose her own, a dress of fine velvet and high-quality Flemish cloth. A pewter dinner service was bought in from London, servants carefully transporting its five dozen dishes and four dozen saucers to Brookwood. Further provisions were acquired in Guildford: wildfowl and a variety of fish, including pike, lampreys, several hundred oysters and eel, 'half a great conger for the king's dinner', to be washed down by five barrels of ale.

As Margaret prepared to receive Edward IV she was fully aware that she was entertaining a man who had ordered the execution of her cousin and was the implacable enemy of the remainder of her family. Yet she must have felt an extraordinary sense of pride and excitement. On this December night the king, Sir Henry Stafford and Lady Margaret dined together under a magnificent canopy of purple silk, especially made for the occasion, with music provided by the royal minstrels. That such a meal had happened at all was tribute to Margaret's perseverance, prudence and courage. But it was also proof of a ruthless pragmatism. She would stop at nothing to further the interests of her son. He – and he alone – commanded her abiding loyalty.

A FATEFUL YEAR

The magnificent banquet at Brookwood considerably strengthened Margaret and Sir Henry Stafford's standing with the king. In settled times, entertaining an English monarch would have reaped a handsome dividend of royal patronage. But the Yorkist regime was close to fracture, with Edward IV's authority under increasing threat. In the summer of 1469 the realm of England underwent a new period of political upheaval, one that would test the qualities of Lady Margaret to the utmost.

In the early 1460s the new Yorkist dynasty had successfully defeated its Lancastrian rivals. But now it was divided among itself, and by July 1469 the king had lost the allegiance of his chief aristocratic supporter Richard Neville Earl of Warwick, who began plotting with Edward's younger brother George Duke of Clarence. Warwick's resentment had been festering for some time, but Edward IV was slow to respond to the danger, and when he did so he completely underestimated the peril he faced. Warwick cleverly orchestrated a major rising in the north of England, led by one of his own retainers, Sir William Conyers – acting under the assumed name of Robin of Redesdale – and the king advanced north with insufficient troops to put it down. The Yorkist king had been outmanoeuvred, and was caught unprepared at Nottingham Castle between the rebels in the north and the forces of Warwick and Clarence moving up from the south. In desperation, Edward appealed to William Lord Herbert – newly promoted to the earldom of Pembroke after his successful reduction of Harlech Castle – to come to his assistance. Once more Herbert left Raglan Castle with a formidable array of Welshmen, and once more young Henry Tudor accompanied him. But Herbert – hitherto always victorious against Edward's Lancastrian opponents – was now marching towards disaster.

On the evening of 25 July William Lord Herbert's soldiers made contact with the rebels under Sir William Conyers at Edgecote, six miles north-east of Banbury. But that night Herbert quarrelled with his fellow aristocratic commander Humphrey Stafford Earl of Devon, who withdrew with his force of archers, leaving the royal army split in two. Realising this, Conyers attacked Herbert the following morning. The fighting that followed was confused. Herbert, without his archers, was quickly in difficulties and his battle line was pushed back, but showing considerable bravery he then rallied his men, and was beginning to turn the tables on Conyers when a fresh band of rebels entered the fray, bearing Richard Neville Earl of Warwick's livery of the bear and ragged staff. Believing that Warwick himself was about to join battle, the royal army broke in panic. Herbert was captured, and led to Northampton, where he was executed the next day.

When the first reports of this disaster reached Margaret and Sir Henry Stafford at Woking, a host of frantic messages was sent out in an attempt to ascertain the whereabouts of Herbert, Henry Tudor and the king himself, now rumoured to be in Neville custody in Warwick Castle. It soon became clear that Herbert had suffered an awful fate. For a brief but heart-rending period Margaret feared that her son had also been killed. But then news reached her that Henry Tudor was safe. He had been led from the battlefield by the Shropshire knight Sir Richard Corbet, and escorted to the residence of Herbert's brother-in-law Lord Ferrers at Weobley in Herefordshire. But Margaret could never put her initial shock and torment out of her mind, and nearly forty years later, it ran deep enough for her to share it with her confessor John Fisher, who recalled that Henry's wardship had been granted to those caught up in 'fierce and terrible warfare', a clear reference to Edgecote and its aftermath.

The battle was a chaotic affair – but its emotional repercussions were harsh enough, not just for Lady Margaret but also for the twelve-year-old Henry Tudor, who was led away from the field of combat in a state of terror, having seen his guardian – a man of whom he was personally fond – overwhelmed by a band of rebels and hauled off to captivity and certain death. Margaret now rallied, and sent a party of eight trusted servants to Weobley, where they found Henry and Herbert's widow, Anne Devereux, sheltering under the protection of Lord Ferrers. Handsome rewards were distributed to those caring for Henry Tudor, including one of twenty shillings to his personal attendant, a man named 'Davy', and a present was bought for Henry himself, in an effort to cheer him up; but the purchase of bow and arrows – although well intended – was not a happy gift for a young man who had just witnessed his guardian's army defeated through lack of archers.

The broader political picture was also confused. Warwick

and Clarence were unable to rule the kingdom using the captive king as a figurehead, and by the end of September 1469 Edward IV had regained his freedom. Margaret's concern was to secure the freedom of her son, and although Henry was well cared for by Anne Devereux, in October she began negotiations with Herbert's widow over the terms of his wardship. On 21 October at the Bell in Fleet Street, bread, mutton, ale and cheese were consumed as the legal councils of Lady Margaret and Anne Devereux met to try and reach an agreement over the matter. Margaret was nothing if not thorough – the records of Chancery and Exchequer were searched, the wording of the original grant was examined in detail and one servant was even dispatched to south Wales in search of further evidence. But the award could not be overturned.

The realm remained troubled, and fresh unrest flared up early in 1470, with a series of uprisings in Lincolnshire. Edward IV marched out of London to deal with the rebels, and Margaret's husband was summoned to join him, reaching the king at Stamford on the morning of 12 March 1470 with a fighting retinue of thirty men. Not much fighting occurred. Sir Henry Stafford arrived to see one of the plotters, Richard Lord Welles, executed in front of the royal army, after which the rebel force of his son and heir Sir Robert fled in panic, jettisoning their livery tunics, which gave the engagement the derisory nickname of 'Losecote Field'. Stafford remained with Edward as he marched north into Yorkshire to quell fresh insurrections stirred up by the Nevilles. On this occasion the king was successful, and in April Warwick and Clarence – aware that their support was fragmenting – decided to flee the country, crossing the Channel before Edward could intercept them, and taking shelter in France under the protection of Louis XI.

This period of wildly fluctuating politics continued. The French King Louis brokered a remarkable agreement at Angers between Warwick and Clarence and Margaret of Anjou, in which this prominent Yorkist magnate and Edward IV's own brother would now support a Lancastrian restoration. In September 1470 Warwick sailed for England with an army and quickly chased a surprised and disorganised Edward out of the country. Edward IV was now forced into political exile in Holland, and a surprised and bewildered Henry VI was freed from the Tower of London and restored to the throne.

Margaret of Anjou and her son Prince Edward were still in France, but Warwick – effectively governing the country in the king's name – was joined by a number of Lancastrian peers, including Jasper Tudor, and it was Jasper who now secured Henry Tudor's freedom. It was Sir Richard Corbet who once again escorted Henry Tudor, this time on a journey from Weobley to Hereford, where Jasper met him and brought him to London. And here Margaret and Henry were at last reunited.

Lady Margaret must have been astounded by the sequence of events that brought her son back to her, as if they formed the miraculous workings of providence. One of her first actions on Henry's return was to arrange for the thirteen-year-old to receive an audience with Henry VI. On 27 October 1470 Henry Tudor was rowed in Stafford's barge from London to Westminster to meet with the Lancastrian king. Afterwards, young Henry dined with Margaret, Stafford, Jasper Tudor and Henry VI's chamberlain, Sir Richard Tunstall. This meeting was later invested with much significance, for the Tudor court historian Polydore Vergil – a well-informed source – related how Henry VI made a miraculous prophecy concerning Tudor's future role in healing the divisions of civil war. John Fisher, in a Cambridge oration delivered before Margaret Beaufort and her son, was even more specific: the Lancastrian king had miraculously foretold Henry VII's own accession.

Henry VI had of course arranged the marriage between Margaret and Edmund Tudor, and it was natural enough that he should be interested in their sole offspring, the child that had been named after him. In the intervening years the Lancastrian king had suffered two major breakdowns, exile and finally a long period of captivity, and was clearly not in any state to exercise any semblance of power or authority. Yet something evidently happened at this audience, something – a remark or observation made by Henry VI – that led Margaret to believe that her son's destiny would be entwined with the throne of England, and that she had an important part to play in ensuring this came to pass.

After the audience with the Lancastrian king, Henry Tudor, his mother and her husband Sir Henry Stafford returned to Woking, where they spent several weeks together. The household records only briefly hint at their activities. On 5 November the three paid a visit to Guildford; a few days later they travelled to Maidenhead and Henley. At the end of the month Henry accompanied his uncle Jasper to south Wales. Margaret had every expectation of seeing him again shortly, and after Henry's departure she began negotiations with George Duke of Clarence, who held the honour of Richmond, to secure a landed settlement for her son. On 27 November a meeting was held with George at Baynard's Castle in London, and it was agreed that Henry would succeed to the honour on George's death.

In January 1471 Margaret's cousins Edmund and John Beaufort returned to England from Burgundy. Their friend and supporter Charles Count of Charolais had succeeded to the dukedom of Burgundy in 1467, and had kept his faith with the Beauforts in the years that followed, even after his marriage to Edward IV's sister Margaret of York in 1468. Edmund and John were sent away from the Burgundian court at the time of the marriage festivities, but were soon allowed to return, and continued to play an important role in Burgundian political life. In October 1470 Edward IV, his youngest brother Richard Duke of Gloucester, the Lords Hastings, Rivers and Say and some 400 household men had arrived in Holland, and were staying at The Hague, enjoying the hospitality of Louis of Gruthuyse. But Duke Charles was unwilling to support these exiles openly.

On 7 January 1471 Edmund Beaufort had visited the duke at St Pol and urged him to support the restored Lancastrian regime of Henry VI. Edward IV was allowed to put his own case to his brother-in-law and press for Burgundian support to restore him to the throne of England. But in the short term Charles decided in the Lancastrians' favour, allowing the Beauforts, and other exiled magnates – including Henry Holland Duke of Exeter and John Courtenay Earl of Devon – to return home. Remarkably, the prospects for the Lancastrian regime and its coalition of Yorkist supporters looked bright. Edward IV lacked substantial foreign backing and was not strong enough to mount an invasion without it, and Margaret of Anjou and her son Prince Edward would soon be sailing for England.

In one extraordinary year the political landscape of England had entirely changed. Margaret could now take her place in a Lancastrian court – nominally presided over by Henry VI – among her Beaufort cousins Edmund and John, and her brother-in-law Jasper Tudor, confident of a secure and important future for her son. It was a remarkable turn-around of events, and one that would have been impossible to predict even a few years earlier. Lady Margaret must now

have hoped that the wheel of fortune had found its perma
nent resting place.

REALPOLITIK

The adage a month is a long time in politics holds true for the
fifteenth century just as much as the present day. At the end
of January 1471 it seemed as if a restored Lancastrian government would once more rule over England. At the end of
February the situation was once again completely unclear. It
was the meddling of the French King Louis XI that damaged
the Lancastrian cause, for the ever-suspicious Louis insisted
that Richard Neville Earl of Warwick – who was in effect
ruling England in the name of Henry VI – wage war on his
arch-rival Charles Duke of Burgundy before he allowed
Margaret of Anjou's fleet to set sail. Warwick's declaration of
war – on 12 February 1471 – forced Charles to provide assistance to Edward IV, at last giving him the ships, men and
money to invade England. In March, when Edward's small
army landed in Yorkshire, Margaret's force still had not
embarked.

Warwick was reluctant to confront Edward's army immediately, and this proved another mistake. The delay allowed
the Yorkist king to open negotiations with his brother George
Duke of Clarence and win him back to his cause. Edward
now seized the military initiative, boldly marching on
London, held by Edmund Beaufort Duke of Somerset and
John Courtenay Earl of Devon. But these Lancastrian lords
were not prepared to remain in the capital, and instead

moved towards the West Country, to await the arrival of Margaret of Anjou's fleet. On 24 March Edmund Beaufort arrived at Woking with a retinue of forty men and stayed with Margaret and Sir Henry Stafford for four days. Edmund Beaufort was heading towards Salisbury, which he intended to use as a recruiting base for a small army. Stafford would not commit himself to joining it. Beaufort was forced to leave Woking on 28 March without any firm assurance of support.

We have reached a pivotal point in our story. As a historian my responsibility is to weave together a narrative based on my knowledge of the source material, the accounts of chroniclers and writers of the time, and the more impersonal documentary records. In the fifteenth century we have relatively few letters, which would reveal what a person wished to communicate to another, and those collections that do exist are mainly for gentry rather than aristocratic families. And we have no diaries, which would show us what a person really thought. So I base my story on the content of the sources, my interpretation of what they may or may not tell us and a broader reading of the personalities and politics of the period.

However, with Margaret Beaufort we also have an unusual and particularly valuable source, the recollections of her confessor and spiritual adviser John Fisher. These allow us a more intimate personal portrait, and also reflect back on key moments in Margaret's life, which she later shared with Fisher and gave him permission to use after her death. And as I have already mentioned, Fisher saw that Margaret was a deeply emotional person, but that emotion was masked by an icy self-control in matters of state. Here she was skilled, highly effective – with remarkable presence and force of personality – and above all absolutely ruthless.

I believe that Margaret was possessed of remarkable qualities, and learned or drew upon these skills at a relatively young age, then honed them as her political education and experience deepened. In my view of her, which is based on a considerable body of evidence, she never let her emotions cloud her political judgement. She was pragmatic, and concerned more than anything else to protect the interests of her son. The following two paragraphs are on balance what I believe happened. But here – more than anywhere else in the story – an alternative, more speculative reading of evidence and character is possible. So first of all, let me rehearse my preferred reading of events, and then I will once again briefly take the reader behind the scenes.

Margaret and her husband were dismayed by the confident generalship of Edward IV and the defection of George Duke of Clarence. Both knew that if they supported the Lancastrians and Edward emerged victorious the Yorkist king would be an implacable opponent. There would be no more second chances. In the circumstances Margaret temporised. On 2 April a body of Stafford's household servants travelled from Reading to Newbury for further discussions with Beaufort. Meanwhile Sir Henry Stafford rode off in the opposite direction, towards London. When Edward IV marched south – past Warwick's force at Coventry – determined to force entry to the capital, Stafford resolved to join his army. Margaret and her husband were now preferring Edward's chances to those of the Lancastrians, and on 13 April, as Edward prepared to confront Warwick at Barnet, north of London, chain-mail and plated armour was hastily brought to Sir Henry, camping on the field of battle. The following day, in a bloody but confused battle fought in swirling mist, Warwick was defeated and killed. That evening Margaret of Anjou's forces finally landed in the West Country.

Lady Margaret had preferred cold calculation to heady emotion, and pragmatism over loyalty to the House of Lancaster. It was a ruthless choice, but her instinct for political survival was acute and her decision was soon vindicated. After his triumph at Barnet, Edward moved swiftly against Margaret of Anjou. He was determined to cut off and defeat her force before she could gain further reinforcement – either in Wales or in the north of England. He trapped her army against the River Severn and on 4 May Margaret of Anjou's supporters were routed at Tewkesbury. John Beaufort was slain in the fighting. In the battle's aftermath, Edmund Beaufort and a number of other Lancastrians sought sanctuary in Tewkesbury Abbey. Edward IV granted a free pardon to all those within consecrated ground. It was a promise the Yorkist king had no intention of keeping, and two days later his soldiers broke into the abbey. Edmund Beaufort was hauled out and executed on 6 May.

The key source materials I have drawn upon here are Margaret's household accounts. These documents are very useful, as they show us the comings and goings at Woking, who visited, and how long they stayed. They also allow us to chart the couple's political strategy, but this can only be done if we assume that Margaret and Sir Henry Stafford were working in unison, with a shared sense of purpose. Most of the time they were – but these were not ordinary times. In the two paragraphs above I have told the story as if they were in complete agreement about what to do.

But suppose they were not. In this case the documents would only show us the man's side of events. It was Sir Henry Stafford who was master of the household, Stafford who would have to ride into battle, who would have to fight. The documentary material would record his movements, his decisions. If the political situation lay on a knife edge, Stafford's

instinct would always have been to support Edward IV.
Margaret's motivation was more complex. She had learned to
work with Edward, but probably also feared him. And now
her Beaufort cousins – at last restored to power and influence
within the realm – were appealing for her support.

Documentary evidence, however valuable, can take us only
so far. From the household records we know what Lady
Margaret bought when Edward IV came to supper, but we
do not know what her personal impressions were, what she
thought about him – as a man and as a king. And when
Edmund Beaufort rode into the great courtyard at Woking,
with his riding household of forty servants, with the world
once again in turmoil, we know that he stayed for four days,
from 24–28 March 1471, but nothing about what was said
during his visit. So we can imagine one scenario – rehearsed
above – with Beaufort urgently and emotionally appealing for
support for the Lancastrian cause, and Margaret and Sir
Henry Stafford listening courteously and attentively, but in
their inner thoughts and private conversations weighing the
chances of the rival sides, and deciding the advantage now lay
with Edward IV.

However, we could also imagine an alternative sequence,
with the couple in disagreement, and arguing passionately
and bitterly: with Margaret – more than at any other time in
her life – swayed by loyalty to her family; and Stafford calm,
rational and immovable, unwilling to support the Lancastrians – believing such a course of action was too risky,
and too dangerous. If this was the case, Margaret's impas-
sioned pleas, her anger, her tears, would find no place in the
records.

Then there was the safety of Margaret's son, Henry Tudor,
to consider. He was now in south Wales with his uncle Jasper,
and Jasper would almost certainly attempt to join Margaret of

Anjou's army. We can assume that Edmund Beaufort would have argued that the right course of action was to throw every man, every retainer, into battle for the Lancastrian cause, and this was the only way to achieve Henry's security. Was Margaret swayed by this emotional appeal? Or did she draw back, realising that if the Lancastrians lost the battle Stafford's support for Edward IV would give the only real guarantee of her son's political survival?

John Fisher, Margaret's confessor, came to know an old lady in her sixties, the mother of the Tudor king and matriarch of the House of Tudor. The Margaret that he met would have mastered her emotions in March 1471, and calculated the best course of action from her head rather than her heart. I have shown you that woman here. But people – in the Middle Ages as now – are complex and never entirely consistent. If Margaret had once powerfully surrendered to her feelings, and then realised with hindsight that the actions she had advocated, however understandable, were misjudged and mistaken, she would have redoubled her self-possession and self-control. We will never know.

I will continue my narrative. In the aftermath of Tewkesbury Edward IV was now determined to wipe out his opponents once and for all. The Lancastrian Prince Edward had been slain attempting to flee the battlefield, and on the Yorkists' return to London the hapless Henry VI was almost certainly murdered in the Tower on Edward IV's orders. Resistance in other parts of the country quickly collapsed. In south Wales, Jasper and Henry Tudor briefly held Pembroke Castle for the Lancastrians, but in September 1471 they fled abroad. They had hoped to reach the shelter of France, but instead storms blew them to the duchy of Brittany, and here they would remain for the next thirteen years.

On 4 October 1471 Margaret's husband Sir Henry

Stafford died. He had been wounded fighting at the battle of Barnet, and was never able to recover from his injuries. Margaret's estate manager and loyal servant Reginald Bray took care of the details of Stafford's burial at Pleshey in Essex. After her husband's death Margaret left Woking for a while – perhaps finding the memories of her time there too painful – and moved into her mother's London house 'Le Ryall' with a reduced household of sixteen, headed by three of her ladies-in-waiting.

In January 1471 Margaret's fortunes had been in the ascendant. She had been reunited with her son, a Lancastrian king was on the throne and, in her perception at least, the Beaufort family had been restored to its rightful position within the realm. In October 1471 they had reached a nadir. Her son was now in exile in Brittany, kept in captivity, under guard, and Margaret had no idea whether she would see him again. The Lancastrian King Henry VI, whom she revered as a saint, had almost certainly been murdered in the Tower of London. Her male Beaufort cousins had been wiped out, and Edmund Beaufort – whom she had come to know – had been hauled from the protection of religious sanctuary and executed. And now her husband for the last fourteen years – with whom she had enjoyed a companionable and affectionate relationship – had died. Margaret must have felt utterly bereft.

In May 1472 Margaret drew up her first will, and in it, she tried to make sense of her life so far. She sought reconciliation with her first husband, Edmund Tudor, whose body she wished to be moved from the House of the Grey Friars in Carmarthen and reinterred in Bourne Abbey, so that she could be laid to rest beside him. And she thought deeply about her exiled, captive son. She instructed her trustees to preserve an estate – drawn from her landed wealth – for the use of Henry Tudor, so that he could have an inheritance should he ever return to England and be restored to favour in the Yorkist realm. Sadly, this prospect seemed far distant.

Another aristocratic woman, faced with these traumatic experiences, might well have retired from active life alto-gether and joined a religious community. Margaret herself probably thought hard about taking such a step, in the autumn of 1465, and again in the autumn of 1471. Her sense of personal destiny, the vision of St Nicholas that she had seen as a child, the miraculous prophecy of Henry VI that she had heard as an adult, must at such times have seemed a mockery to her. Instead she had faced the bewildering turns of fortune's wheel, and watched as those around her met with violence and death. A genuinely pious woman and intelligent thinker, Margaret must have wondered if she was being pun-ished for some terrible sin, and as she did so, her thoughts would have returned again and again to the suicide of her father.

But Lady Margaret remained a fighter, and the drawing up of her will, far from turning her into a recluse, galvanised her once more into action. She resolved to return to court and find herself a new husband, and her sights were now set on one of the most powerful magnates in the kingdom, Thomas Lord Stanley, the steward of Edward IV's household. In June 1472 the marriage took place at Stanley's residence of Knowsley Hall in Lancashire. It was an arrangement of mutual interest. A carefully worked-out marriage contract guaranteed Margaret an annual income of 500 marks from Stanley's estates in Cheshire and north Wales. For Stanley, the match expanded his territorial influence, giving him a life interest in Margaret's substantial properties. The contract made no provision for issue, the most likely explanation being that Margaret wished to live a celibate life, rather than the later legend that Edward IV only allowed the union of Lady Margaret and Stanley on the condition that no children were produced.

Margaret now divided her time between Stanley's Lancashire and Cheshire properties and the demands of court activity in the capital. Thomas Lord Stanley quickly came to respect his wife's forceful personality and also her understanding of the law. In November 1473 a property dispute in Liverpool was delegated to an arbitration panel headed by Lady Margaret, and in August 1474 a dispute between two of Stanley's tenants, Thomas Ashton and Richard Dalton, was referred to Margaret's own legal counsellors. Lady Margaret was a frequent visitor to London, and early in 1475 she witnessed preparations for Edward IV's expedition to France. Stanley was one of Edward's principal captains, and in a flurry of activity craftsmen were paid for garnishing his armour and providing crimson and blue silk for his standards. Other servants went further afield, one, Edward Fleetwood, being given £50 to buy horses for Stanley in Flanders. The gathering of this great army, comprising almost half the English aristocracy, must have left a powerful impression on Lady Margaret.

Margaret's marriage strengthened her connection to the powerful and influential Woodville family. By the mid-1470s the Stanleys and the Woodvilles worked in close co-operation in the administration of Cheshire and north Wales, a partnership cemented by family alliances. Sir James Molyneux, chancellor to Anthony Earl Rivers, was Lord Stanley's nephew. Stanley's son and heir George had married Joan, the queen's sister, daughter of John Lord Strange and his first wife Jacquetta. Lady Margaret now benefited from these contacts, particularly in the arena of court ceremony. In July 1476 Margaret played an important part in the reburial of

Richard Duke of York, the king's father, at Fotheringhay, in attendance upon the queen and her daughters. In November 1480 Margaret was honoured in the celebration of the birth of the seventh royal princess, Bridget, at the newly refurbished palace of Eltham, acting as godmother and carrying the child in the procession.

A measure of mutual respect and affection grew between Margaret and Stanley. In 1478 she commissioned a selection of prayers of the Passion and the Holy Name for her husband, with four charm-like formulae placed in the middle of the book. It was believed that whoever recited these prayers would not perish in battle, was assured immunity from the plague, and – in the case of women – protection during pregnancy. It is highly likely that Margaret had used these charms during her own dangerous pregnancy, and recognising

Margaret's badges and coat of arms and the badge of her husband Thomas Lord Stanley from their book of prayers

Stanley's fear of death in battle (his reluctance to commit his
forces during the Wars of the Roses gave him a reputation for
political guile that would last for centuries) deemed this an
appropriate gift.

By the beginning of June 1482, ten years after her marriage
to Lord Stanley, Margaret had established herself at the heart
of the Yorkist court, wielding considerable political influence.
She now used this power in an effort to secure the return of
her son, who was still in exile in Brittany. A remarkable
document was drawn up in the presence of Edward IV and
Stanley at the Palace of Westminster on 3 June 1482. It laid
out arrangements for the disposal of the properties of
Margaret's mother, who had died a month earlier. They were
reserved for Henry Tudor's use, on certain conditions, the
principal being that Henry now return from exile 'to be in the
grace and favour of the king's highness'. Edward added his
royal seal in confirmation of the agreement. The pious hope
expressed in Margaret's will of May 1472 had now become a
reality. A place had been found for Henry Tudor within the
Yorkist realm.

Greater honour was envisaged. Lord Stanley later recalled
that towards the end of Edward IV's reign discussions were
held about the possible marriage of Henry Tudor to one of
the king's daughters. If a York–Tudor marriage was to take
place, a major restoration to Henry of aristocratic title and
lands would have followed, and draft documents preserved in
Lady Margaret's archives suggest that after Edward IV
granted Henry Tudor a royal pardon his promotion to the
earldom of Richmond (the title held by his father Edmund)
was anticipated. These arrangements show Edward now conciliatory towards the exiled Tudor, and were a remarkable
triumph for Lady Margaret. Fortune's wheel had turned
once more.

CONSPIRATOR

All rested on how Henry Tudor would react to the new arrangement. Margaret had not seen her son for nearly twelve years – and the thirteen-year-old boy she had last met was now a 25-year-old man. Edward IV was now ready to welcome Tudor back to England, yet it was hard to put aside the legacy of years of suspicion and mistrust. The Tudor court poet Bernard André described an earlier occasion, in 1476, when Henry had been warned by his mother not to come back to England if the king offered him one of his daughters in marriage. Margaret's doubts were well founded – at this stage Edward IV had other plans for all his daughters – and a year earlier another Lancastrian claimant, Henry Holland Duke of Exeter, had died in the most suspicious of circumstances, being pushed off a boat and drowning on his return from France in the royal expedition of 1475.

In November 1476 Henry Tudor managed to escape the clutches of an English embassy sent to Brittany, slipping away from his escorts and seeking sanctuary in the church of St-Malo. Polydore Vergil gave a vivid description of this incident, almost certainly derived from Henry himself, that he was terrified, fearing for his life, and clearly believing that he would suffer a similar 'accident' to Henry Holland once he was shipped to England. Even though Margaret was now vouching for Edward IV's good faith, the indenture of June 1482 also made provision for the possibility that Henry would choose not to return, despite these reassurances. Henry Tudor would bitterly tell the chronicler Philippe Commynes that most of his life had been spent as a captive or fugitive, and the result of such experiences was an almost pathological suspicion.

The lack of response from Henry Tudor cast a shadow over Margaret's achievement, although the new arrangement was never fully put to the test, for on 9 April 1483 Edward IV suddenly died – having fallen ill after a boating trip on the Thames, in which he contracted a serious chill. His son and heir was recognised as Edward V and a governing council, dominated by the Woodvilles, was set up to rule the country until the young king could be crowned, then replaced by a protectorate under Edward IV's younger brother, Richard Duke of Gloucester. The protectorate itself abruptly ended when Richard dramatically announced that his brother's marriage to Elizabeth Woodville was invalid and that the couple's two sons – Edward and Richard – were in fact illegitimate. Richard Duke of Gloucester now claimed the throne himself, accepting kingship by proclamation on 26 June and being crowned as Richard III on 6 July.

The circumstances of Richard's seizure of the throne were bloody and confused. Edward IV's two sons were confined to the Tower, William Lord Hastings executed for treason and Edward IV's queen forced to withdraw into sanctuary at Westminster Abbey with her daughters. Yet at this stage Lady Margaret's intention was to seek an accommodation with Richard III and safeguard the arrangements for Henry Tudor's return, drawn up a year earlier. She had opened negotiations with Richard in late June, using Henry Stafford Duke of Buckingham as an intermediary, and again the prospects of a marriage alliance for Tudor were discussed. On 5 July, the day before the coronation, Stanley and Margaret secured a private meeting with Richard and his chief justice William Hussey at Westminster. The following day Margaret played a prominent part in the coronation ceremony itself, bearing Queen Anne's train in the procession to Westminster Abbey, and serving at the banquet afterwards.

Richard III now undertook a royal progress throughout the realm. Thomas Lord Stanley was commanded to join him, and Lady Margaret, who had remained behind in London, began to have second thoughts about the wisdom of supporting Richard. She may have been informed by Jasper and Henry Tudor that they would never be willing to support such a scheme, and begun to despair of ever securing her son's return. Whatever the reason for it, Margaret now took a calculated but highly dangerous step, abandoning her allegiance to Richard III and beginning to plot against him. At the end of July 1483 she may have even participated in a plot to rescue the princes from the Tower, in which a newly restored Edward V would be supported by an invasion force led by Jasper and Henry Tudor. Information on this early conspiracy is fragmentary, being confined to a brief comment in one contemporary source, the French chronicle of Thomas Basin, and material gathered by the early-seventeenth-century antiquary John Stow. According to Stow, an attempt to storm the Tower failed, and Basin added that about fifty people were arrested and executed in London for their involvement in this rescue attempt.

The evidence for Margaret's plotting later in the summer is much firmer. The princes had now been withdrawn to the inner recesses of the Tower and their servants dismissed. By September 1483 most people feared that they were dead. Exactly what had happened to them, and – if they were murdered – who was responsible for it, has never been fully established. Chief suspicion rested on Richard himself, though some contemporary chroniclers also pointed an accusatory finger at Henry Stafford Duke of Buckingham, and in the early Stuart period researchers such as William Cornwallis and Sir George Buck even suggested that Margaret Beaufort herself may have decided to kill them, in order to further Henry Tudor's chances of taking the throne. Such a possibility cannot be entirely ruled out, and if so it would represent the darkest and most terrifying fruit of her remorseless ambition for her son.

However, while a motive for Lady Margaret existed – albeit a profoundly disturbing one – hard evidence for her involvement in such a scheme is scant indeed. Buck claimed to have found proof 'in an old manuscript book', but as he never cited its provenance or quoted from it, its existence remains a mystery. And no contemporary chronicler or source blamed Margaret for the princes' disappearance. Most believed Richard III himself was guilty of the crime. It is Margaret's motives for joining a rebellion against Richard that smack of opportunism, particularly since she had sought to co-operate with him at the start of his reign.

What is clear is that once the princes were assumed dead, with many contemporaries believing – rightly or wrongly – that Richard had murdered them, a major uprising was planned against the new Yorkist king, and Margaret herself took a leading role in its organisation. As Polydore Vergil said, she was 'commonly called the head of that conspiracy'. Her ambitions for her son's future now reached a dramatic and powerful culmination. Henry Tudor, united with the Woodville faction through a proposed marriage to Elizabeth of York, would claim the throne of England itself. Negotiations with Elizabeth Woodville were carried out by Margaret's physician, Lewis Caerleon, while contact with Henry Tudor in Brittany was undertaken by her servant Hugh Conway. Margaret's communication with the chief aristocratic supporter of the rebellion, Henry Stafford Duke of Buckingham, remained more ambiguous, and it was uncertain whether the duke fully knew of or supported Henry Tudor's bid to claim the throne.

In the event, all these plans came to nothing. In October 1483 separate risings against Richard III began in different parts of the country. They were badly co-ordinated, and the Kentish rebellion was promptly crushed by Richard's staunch supporter, John Howard Duke of Norfolk. Henry Stafford's tenants in Wales deserted him in large numbers, allowing Richard to move down on the rebellion in south-west England in considerable force. By the time Henry Tudor and his small fleet appeared off the coast of Dorset in early November, the rebel cause was all but lost, and Tudor prudently beat a hasty retreat.

The failure of the rebellion of 1483 placed Lady Margaret in considerable personal danger. Richard III was soon aware of the extent of her plotting, and – in his rage – may initially have considered executing her for treason. The later recollections of Henry Parker Lord Morley, who served as a cupbearer in Margaret's household, made clear that 'in Richard's reign, she was often in jeopardy of her life, yet she bore patiently such trouble in a manner that is extraordinary to think of'. After reflection, the king chose to spare her life because of the loyalty of her husband, Thomas Lord Stanley, who had maintained his allegiance to Richard throughout the uprising. In the parliament of 1484 she was remitted the full rigour of attainder, 'remembering the good and faithful service that Thomas Lord Stanley has done us, and for his sake'. Yet she was to forfeit all right to aristocratic titles and estates, the annual income that she enjoyed from her husband was declared void and the lands that she had conserved for the use of her son were now confiscated and dispersed among others. Stanley was instructed to keep her confined without household servants. In a life rich in triumph and adversity, it was the lowest point of her fortunes.

And yet – even in failure – the conspiracy initiated by Margaret began to develop a momentum of its own. Exiled Woodvilles, fleeing from England in the aftermath of the revolt, now clustered around Tudor in Brittany, and on Christmas Day 1483 in Vannes Cathedral Henry solemnly promised to return to England as king, vanquish Richard III and marry Elizabeth of York. By 1484 he was using the regal style of a king of England in messages and proclamations to his supporters and in 1485 his claim to the throne was recognised by the French, who provided the ships and soldiers for a small invasion fleet. At the beginning of August 1485 he landed in Wales with a small army, marched into England and confronted Richard III in battle. And at Bosworth on 22 August the numerically smaller army of Tudor triumphed over the larger one of Richard, with the Yorkist king slain in combat as he tried to cut down his challenger. Against all expectations, and against all odds, Margaret Beaufort's son Henry Tudor had won the throne of England.

THE KING'S MOTHER

The month of September 1485 saw a highly emotional reunion of mother and son. The victorious army of the new Tudor monarch reached London on 7 September, and two weeks later Henry VII left the capital and travelled to Margaret's manor house of Woking, which he had last visited nearly fifteen years before. It was a deliberate recreation of their previous meeting together in November 1470, before political fortune drove them apart. It was a long visit – the king staying for nearly three weeks – but they had much to talk about.

Henry's incredible victory at Bosworth would have been top of the list. The new Tudor king would have shared details of the campaign and battle, the difficult negotiations with the Stanleys, the sudden and decisive intervention of Thomas Lord Stanley's younger brother Sir William on the field of combat, Richard's dangerous last charge, in which the Yorkist monarch slew Henry's standard bearer William Brandon and was only a few feet from Tudor himself. Henry VII would have praised the performance of his French mercenaries, and their captain Philibert de Chandée, whom he elevated to the earldom of Bath in gratitude for his stalwart service. And more than anything, he and Margaret would have marvelled that, faced with Richard's much larger army, his small force had triumphed at all.

Henry had a present for his mother, taken from the spoils of Richard's war tent – the late Yorkist king's book of hours, his personal prayer book. It was a telling gift, and a well-chosen one. In public, the Tudor view of Richard was that he was an embodiment of evil, a man who had put himself beyond the pale through a series of horrifying killings. But many of these killings – the executions of Earl Rivers, Lord Hastings, Sir Richard Grey and Sir Thomas Vaughan in June 1483 – had taken place before Lady Margaret met with the king in the Palace of Westminster on 5 July, and discussed her son's future with him. Now that son had unseated him on the field of battle.

When Margaret very publicly assisted in Richard III's coronation on 6 July 1483, the day after this conversation, an Italian visitor to London, Dominic Mancini, related that

Later Tudor portraits of Margaret and her son, Henry VII

people in the street already openly feared for the safety of the young princes in the Tower, adding that some believed they were already dead, and others thought they would soon die. Yet this fact did not stop Margaret lending her support to Richard's cause. It is probable that she chose to rebel against him later that summer not out of a sense of moral outrage over the way he had seized the throne but because it seemed a more powerful and effective way of advancing the interests of her son.

In private, it is more likely the king and his mother were struck by the late king's piety, and that a genuinely religious person could be politically ruthless none the less, and on occasions take that ruthlessness to terrible extremes. As Henry and Margaret talked about past events and shared their hopes for the future, the king had already granted her a fine new London house at Coldharbour. Locked securely in one of its rooms was Edward Plantagenet, the son of Edward

IV's brother George Duke of Clarence. One of Henry's first actions after winning Bosworth was to send an armed retinue to seize Plantagenet and bring him to the capital. Both Henry VII and his mother knew that his own claim to the throne was weak, and that Clarence's son was a dangerous dynastic rival. He was a ten-year-old child, innocent of wrongdoing, but a dangerous child, and Margaret was now in effect his jailer. He was soon transferred to the greater security of the Tower of London, from where – like the princes – he would never reappear. The Tudor monarch lambasted Richard 'for the shedding of innocent blood' (a veiled reference to the murder of the princes) then cynically waited until the equally innocent Edward Plantagenet came of age before executing him on trumped-up charges.

Henry's Beaufort lineage gave him a royal pedigree, but one not strong enough in itself to justify a claim to the throne. To effect this, Henry duly married Elizabeth of York, the match that his mother had laboured hard to bring about. But the king's mother remained a dominating presence. At the Tudor court, Margaret's standing was as great as the queen's. In 1488 both she and Elizabeth were issued with liveries of the Order of the Garter, a sign of special standing, and a song was composed to celebrate their wearing of robes together. At the ceremony Margaret wore identical robes to the queen, cloth furred with miniver and woven with garter letters of gold, and in her heraldic insignia she used the royal coronet with its fleurs-de-lys. Royal household ordinances made provision for Lady Margaret's accommodation at all the palaces and residences used by the Crown. And contemporaries noted the frequency with which Margaret accompanied the king and queen on royal visits or progresses.

Their close relationship was reflected in the architecture of royal palaces. At Woodstock Margaret's lodgings were placed close to her son's, linked by a 'withdrawing chamber', a room that was built between the king's rooms and his mother's, one that allowed them to be together in utmost privacy, whether to discuss affairs of state or relax at cards or chess. And in the Tower of London Margaret's rooms were to be found next to the king's own bedchamber. And their remarkable intimacy and sense of common cause were reflected in their personal correspondence.

In a letter to his mother Henry VII wrote: 'I shall be glad to please you as your heart desirest, and I know well that I am as much boundeth to do so as any creature living for the great and singular motherly love and affection that it have pleased you at all times to bear me.' Margaret responded in equally fulsome fashion, addressing Henry as 'my own sweet and most dear king and all my worldly joy, my good and precious prince, king and only beloved son'.

Lady Margaret maintained an active political role. A post-script to a letter of hers, written in 1488 to Richard Fox, keeper of the privy seal, requested the latest news from Flanders, well aware that Margaret of York, the Dowager Duchess of Burgundy, was sheltering opponents of the new Tudor dynasty. At the times of Henry VII's expedition to France in 1492 it was the king's mother who made the greatest financial contribution and also donated large supplies of grain. In April 1497 the return of an embassy from the Burgundian court occasioned a typically sardonic gift. She was unable to resist a weighted jibe against the pretensions of Margaret of York, whose glittering court continued to support a host of plotters against her son's regime.

'I thank you heartily for the gift of gloves that you have brought from her,' she began, 'which are finely chosen, except that they are far too large for my hand. I think the

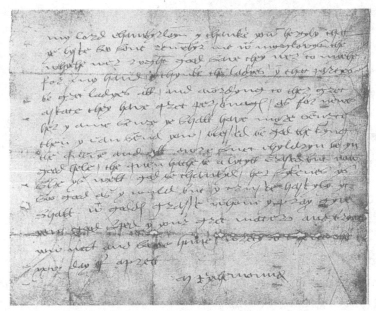

A letter written by Margaret in her own hand, to the Earl of Ormonde in 1497

women of this court are great ladies, one and all, and as befits their great estate, they are great in size also.' Beneath the mockery one senses the bitterness she felt towards the duchess, who had sheltered the pretenders Lambert Simnel and Perkin Warbeck, and encouraged their plots against the Tudor dynasty.

Margaret now became a great landowner, renegotiating her marriage contract with Thomas Lord Stanley so that she could hold her properties in her own right and acquiring plentiful estates from the king, whose income funded a substantial household, building projects, and her acts of religious and educational patronage. She built a fine palace at Collyweston in Northamptonshire where she entertained the king and great aristocrats of the realm but also held a court of equity, and a governing council of the Midlands, where she arbitrated in disputes on Henry's behalf. Here, in the summer of 1503, Henry's court stayed for three weeks, as Margaret's granddaughter, the Princess Margaret, made her way north to marry James IV, King of Scotland. Lady Margaret's choristers sang, acted and performed for her many guests.

Margaret's wealth allowed her to sponsor works of devotional literature, such as the printing of Walter Hilton's *Scala Perfectionis* or Sebastian Brandt's *Ship of Fools*, and she also tried her hand at translating, most notably the fourth book of the *Imitation of Christ* by Thomas à Kempis. Her educational patronage culminated in her Cambridge foundations of Christ's and St John's colleges. But these good works, which attracted the interest of her early biographers, were not undertaken in religious seclusion but from an active and highly pragmatic involvement in worldly affairs. Lady Margaret's household contained a full range of personalities: the scholarly, cultural presence of her confessor John Fisher or the dean of her chapel, Henry Hornby, contrasting with servants such as Reginald Bray – described as 'plain and rough in speech' – and John Hussey, an estate official notorious for his strong-arm rent-collection tactics. Lady Margaret respected Bray and Hussey because they were tough, practical and got things done – and she did not ask too many questions about how they did it. And among all these men Margaret exerted a commanding influence. Fisher said simply that, if division or strife arose among any of her household, 'she with great policy [forcefulness] did bolt [sort] it out.'

And such forcefulness was more than necessary. The turns of fortune's wheel did not end with Henry VII's accession. The court poet Bernard André likened the first twelve years of the Tudor dynasty to the labours of Hercules as a series of dangerous threats were beaten off, at home and abroad. Lady

Margaret's book of hours, her own prayer book, was not divorced from this world, and in it she recorded her son's victories against his assailants, in 1485 at Bosworth, where he won the throne, Stoke in 1487, when he defeated his first major rebellion, and in 1497 Blackheath, where he vanquished the last.

On 14 November 1501, when the marriage of Henry VII's oldest son Arthur to Katherine of Aragon in St Paul's Cathedral was lavishly celebrated by the king and his mother, it appeared that the Tudor dynasty had fought its way through such trials and won diplomatic and political acceptance on the European stage. But then fresh calamity struck. Only six months later the fifteen-year-old Arthur fell suddenly ill, and died at Ludlow on 2 April 1502. As the king's youngest son Edmund had succumbed to an outbreak of the plague two years earlier, and Prince Henry's health was at this stage not robust, the dynasty's hold on power began to appear fragile, and a new round of conspiracies started, initiated by the de la Pole family. A final blow fell on 11 February 1503 when the 37-year-old Queen Elizabeth of York died, shortly after giving birth to another daughter, Katherine. The king was stricken with grief, his mother drew up ordinances for the court to dress in black, the colour of mourning, and the unfortunate court astrologer William Parron, who a few months earlier had unwisely predicted that the queen would live to at least eighty, hurriedly left the country.

In the event, the fresh crisis was mastered, and Lady Margaret had the pleasure of watching her grandson Henry grow into a strong and athletic young prince. Henry's youthful athleticism was particularly encouraging as her son, the king, was succumbing to increasing ill-health, finally passing away on 21 April 1509. Margaret outlived him, participating in the festivities that marked the marriage of Henry VIII to Katherine of Aragon on 23 June. It was her last appearance at court, but a highly symbolic one – the Tudor dynasty was now fully established. She fell ill shortly afterwards, and died on 29 June 1509.

'All England on her death had cause of weeping,' said John Fisher in his funeral sermon, and it was indeed an extraordinary life. Margaret had fought long and hard to further the interests of her son, and the creation of the Tudor dynasty was in large part her achievement. And it is her fight that I have sought to recreate here. Margaret's early biographers paid little attention to her early career, instead becoming fascinated by her religious and educational patronage. For those interested in learning more about this, I have added their works in my bibliography, and the subject is also covered in the study of Margaret's life that I jointly undertook in 1992 with the archivist at St John's College, Cambridge, Malcolm Underwood. But it is the political arena – particularly in the period up to 1485 – that particularly fascinates me, and it is this I have focused on, in order to mirror Philippa Gregory's powerful historical novel *The Red Queen*.

Readers wishing to gain a full sense of Lady Margaret as a person are often confronted by a series of rather bland late-Tudor copied portraits. Here Margaret is presented in the wimple or headdress of widowhood, in the black cloth of mourning, plain, as if she were a nun. In some of these images she reads from a devotional book, in others she kneels at prayer. She appears to have retired from the world, to live the life of a spiritual recluse. The face is soft and featureless. The power and purpose of her life, and the dark, driving passion of her ambition, are nowhere to be seen.

To reconnect with that ambition, I recommend a visit to Margaret Beaufort's tomb in Westminster Abbey. Here, in

the effigy strikingly fashioned by the Florentine sculptor
Pietro Torrigiano from an exact likeness, one sees the
strength of character in her face. The sharply etched lines,
the pronounced cheekbones and slightly hooded eyes convey
considerable force of personality. Her features are intelligent,
but worldly and astute, an impression reinforced by the
coats-of-arms and badges that surround them. It is the face
of a political survivor.

The sense of destiny that Margaret experienced as a child
took her on a long and perilous journey. It was a journey of
darkness more than light, yet as her life drew to its close, she
saw that destiny reach its fruition. In 1499, as Margaret began
to build her impressive palace at Collyweston, and govern the
east Midlands on behalf of her son, she changed her signature from 'M Richmond' to the regal 'Margaret R'.
Contemporaries – with a mixture of awe and respect –
referred to her simply as 'the King's Mother'.

Margaret Beaufort's signature (from 1499)

NOTES AND SOURCES

Readers wishing to find out more about Margaret's remarkable life are recommended, as a first port of call, the author's own biography, co-written with Malcolm Underwood, the archivist at St John's College, Cambridge: Jones, Michael, and Underwood, Malcolm *The King's Mother: Lady Margaret Beaufort, Countess of Richmond and Derby*, Cambridge, 1992. But I would also like to discuss its major predecessors. The first major study was Halsted, Caroline *Life of Margaret Beaufort, Countess of Richmond and Derby*, London, 1839. Halsted, who also undertook a biography of Richard III, was perceptive in some of her judgements, but while she praised Margaret's moral qualities and patronage of learning, she neglected her political ambition and ruthlessness, and quite wrongly believed that she retired from the political scene once her son took the throne. The Cambridge antiquary Charles Cooper, in his *The Lady Margaret: A Memoir of Margaret, Countess of Richmond and Derby*, Cambridge, 1874, also focused primarily on Margaret's educational achievements and religious patronage, and largely neglected her early life. Routh, Enid *A Memoir of Lady Margaret Beaufort, Countess of Richmond and Derby, Mother of Henry VII*, Oxford, 1924, was the first biography to draw on Lady Margaret's household accounts – held in the archives of Westminster Abbey – but while she drew a fuller picture of Margaret's domestic routine and position at court, she again underplayed her political acumen. Simon, Linda *Of Virtue Rare: Margaret Beaufort, Matriarch of the House of Tudor*, Boston, Mass., 1982, while adding little new information to Margaret's life, was the first biography to emphasise the difficulties she faced as a woman in the world of fifteenth-century politics. For a good, readable recent study that pays proper tribute to her political role, readers are recommended Norton, Elizabeth *Margaret Beaufort: Mother of the Tudor Dynasty*, Stroud, 2010.

For a fuller picture of the life and reign of Margaret's son Henry VII, there is the standard biography by Stanley Chrimes, *Henry VII*, London, 1977, but far more accessible – and particularly good on Henry Tudor's early life – is Griffiths, Ralph, and Thomas, Roger *The Making of the Tudor Dynasty*, Gloucester, 1985. And for a valuable recent survey of the king's rule I highly recommend Cunningham, Sean *Henry VII*, London, 2007. The best introduction to the wider Beaufort family is the excellent biography of Margaret's great-uncle: Harriss, Gerald *Cardinal Beaufort*, Oxford, 1988; and see also my entries on Margaret's cousins, Henry and Edmund Beaufort, in the *New Oxford Dictionary of National Biography*.

On the politics of the fifteenth century that Margaret charted her course through there is a mass of material. For the troubled reign of Henry VI there are two major biographies: Wolffe, Bertram *Henry VI*, London, 1981; which is an easier read than the nevertheless valuable Griffiths, Ralph *The Reign of Henry VI*, London, 1981. Since much of the material that follows has already been discussed I will simply list the main secondary sources I have used.

BIBLIOGRAPHY

Baldwin, David *Elizabeth Woodville: Mother of the Princes in the Tower*, Stroud, 2002

Bennett, Michael *The Battle of Bosworth*, Gloucester, 1985

Coward, Barry *The Stanleys, Lords Stanley and Earls of Derby, 1385–1672: the Origins, Wealth and Power of a Landowning Family*, Manchester, 1983

Crawford, Anne (ed.) *Letters of the Queens of England, 1100–1547*, Stroud, 2002

Goodman, Anthony *The Wars of the Roses*, London, 1981

Hicks, Michael *False, Fleeting, Perjur'd Clarence*, Gloucester, 1980

Hicks, Michael *Richard III*, Stroud, 2000

Horrox, Rosemary *Richard III: A Study in Service*, Cambridge, 1989

Jones, Michael *Bosworth 1485: Psychology of a Battle*, Stroud, 2002

Kleineke, Hannes *Edward IV*, London, 2008

Lander, Jack *Crown and Nobility, 1450–1509*, London, 1976

Maurer, Helen *Margaret of Anjou: Queenship and Power in Late Medieval England*, Woodbridge, 2005

Pollard, Anthony *Richard III and the Princes in the Tower*, Stroud, 1991

Rawcliffe, Carole *The Staffords, Earls of Stafford and Dukes of Buckingham*, Cambridge, 1978

Rosenthal, Joel *Nobles and the Noble Life*, London, 1976

Ross, Charles *Edward IV*, London, 1975

Ross, Charles *Richard III*, London, 1981
Santiuste, David *Edward IV and the Wars of the Roses*, Barnsley, 2010
Storey, Robin *The End of the House of Lancaster*, London, 1966
Tyerman, Christopher *England and the Crusades, 1095–1588*, Chicago, 1988

Finally, quotes from primary sources and references to source material have been drawn from the following:

André, Bernard 'Vita Henrici Septimi' in *Memorials of King Henry VII*, ed. J. Gairdner, Rolls Series, London, 1858
Basin, Thomas *Histoire des règnes de Charles VII et Louis XII*, ed. J. Quicherat, 4 vols, Paris, 1933–44
Buck, Sir George *The History of King Richard III*, ed. A.N. Kincaid, Gloucester, 1979
Chronicles of London, ed. C. Kingsford, Oxford, 1905
An English Chronicle of the Reigns of Richard II, Henry IV, Henry V and Henry VI, ed. J.S. Davies, Camden Society, o/s, 64, 1856
English Historical Literature in the Fifteenth Century, ed. C.L. Kingsford, Oxford, 1913
Excerpta Historica, ed. S. Bentley, London, 1831
Historical Collections of a Citizen of London, ed. J. Gairdner, Camden Society, n.s., 17, 1876
Ingulph's Chronicle of the History of Croyland, ed. H.T. Riley, London, 1854
Letters and Papers Illustrative of the Reigns of Richard III and Henry VII, ed. J. Gairdner, 2 vols, Rolls Series, London, 1861–3
Materials for a History of the Reign of Henry VII, ed. W. Campbell, 2 vols, Rolls Series, London, 1873–7
'Mornynge Remembraunce had at the moneth mynde of the

Noble Prynces Margarete Countesse of Rychemonde and Darbye' in *The English Works of John Fisher, Part One*, ed. J.E.B. Mayor, *EETS*, 27, 1876

Original Letters Illustrative of English History, ed. H. Ellis, 11 vols, London, 1824–46

The Paston Letters, 1422–1509, ed. J. Gairdner, 6 vols, London, 1904

Rotuli Parliamentorum, ed. J. Strachey, 6 vols, London, 1767–77

Stow, John *The Annals or General Chronicle of England*, London, 1615

Vergil, Polydore *Three Books of English History*, ed. H. Ellis, Camden Society, o/s, 39, 1844

Warkworth, J. *A Chronicle of the First Thirteen Years of the Reign of Edward IV*, ed. J.O. Halliwell, Camden Society, o/s, 83, 1863

ILLUSTRATION ACKNOWLEDGEMENTS

ENDPAPERS
The Lady and the Unicorn: 'Sight' (tapestry) by French School (fifteenth century), Musée National du Moyen Age et des Thermes de Cluny, Paris/Giraudon/The Bridgeman Art Library

Page 48, Medieval Luxembourg, as imagined in the nineteenth century, published in Arendt, Charles *Hypothetischer Plan der ehemagligen Schlossburg Lützelburg auf dem Bockfelsen zu Lützelburg*, Luxembourg, 1895
Page 115, Parhelion © Erik Axdahl
Page 116, Sun in Splendour in eastern window, Great Tattershall Church © Revd Gordon Plumb
Page 135, Stained-glass window in the Large Hall of the Company of Stationers and Newspaper Makers in London showing printer William Caxton (c. 1422–91) presenting his first printed page to King Edward IV and his queen c. 1475 © Getty Images
Page 138, Jacquetta's signature, provided by Geoffrey Wheeler
Page 151, Garter Stall Plate of Richard Woodville from St George's Chapel, Windsor, provided by Geoffrey Wheeler
Page 157, Richard Neville, Earl of Warwick, the 'Kingmaker', and his wife Anne Beauchamp, from *The Rous Roll*, provided by Geoffrey Wheeler
Page 168, Elizabeth Woodville portrayed in her coronation robes as a member of the London Skinners' Company's Fraternity of Our Lady's Assumption, probably c. 1472, provided by Geoffrey Wheeler
Page 185, Elizabeth Woodville (lower right foreground), Edward IV, Bishop Thomas Rotherham and Cecily Neville, kneeling with other

members of the confraternity before the Trinity c. 1475, from The Luton Guild Book (now in the Luton Museum), provided by Geoffrey Wheeler

Page 208, Elizabeth of York. Bronze effigy by Torrigiani, Henry VII Chapel, Westminster Abbey © Warburg Institute, University of London

Page 221, Elizabeth Woodville's signature, provided by Geoffrey Wheeler

Page 240, The tomb effigy of Margaret's father, John Beaufort Duke of Somerset, at Wimborne Minster (Dorset) © Peter Booton Photography

Page 249, Calendar of the Beaufort Hours, showing the date of Lady Margaret's birth, 31 May 1443 © The British Library Board, BL Royal MS 2A XVIII, fol. 30

Page 270, *top*, Ruins of Woking Palace, by Giles Pattison and Surrey County Archaeological Unit. Reproduced by permission of Surrey History Centre © Copyright of Surrey History Centre; *bottom*, Reconstruction of Woking Palace's appearance in the fifteenth century © Kevin Wilson

Page 290, Margaret's badges and coat of arms and the badge of her husband Thomas Lord Stanley from their book of prayers, Westminster Abbey, MS 39, fol 1

Page 299, Half-length portraits of Margaret Beaufort and Henry VII, artist unknown © National Portrait Gallery, London

Page 302, Letter by Margaret Beaufort to the Earl of Ormonde, 1497, The National Archives UK

Page 306, Margaret Beaufort's signature (from 1499), provided by Geoffrey Wheeler

COLOUR INSERT

1 A 1410 painting of Melusina, one of sixteen paintings by Guillebert de Mets, c. 1410, original held by the Bibliothèque Nationale, Paris

2 John Duke of Bedford receiving a book from Jean Galoys in a contemporary painting, Ms 326 f.1 from *Pelerinage de l'Ame* by Guillaume de Digulleville (vellum) by French School (fifteenth century) © Lambeth Palace Library, London, UK/The Bridgeman Art Library

3 Melusina's crest on the heraldry of the Counts of St Pol. Original is in the Pavillon de l'Arsenale, Paris

4 Elizabeth Woodville, panel portrait, provided by Geoffrey Wheeler. Queens' College, Cambridge

5, 6 Elizabeth Woodville (detail) and Edward IV (detail), stained glass, Martyrdom Chapel, Canterbury Cathedral c. 1482, both provided by Geoffrey Wheeler

7 Edward, Prince of Wales, afterwards Edward V (contemporary stained glass at Little Malvern Priory, Worcestershire), provided by Geoffrey Wheeler

8 Richard III (oil on panel) by English School (sixteenth century) © Society of Antiquaries of London, UK/The Bridgeman Art Library

9 Calendar of the Beaufort Hours, showing the date of Henry VIII's birth and victory over Yorkist rebels at Stoke© The British Library Board, BL Royal MS 2A XVIII, fol. 30v

10 Full-length portrait of Margaret Beaufort by Rowland Lockey. Original is at St John's College, Cambridge

11 Tomb effigy of Margaret Beaufort at Westminster Abbey © Werner Forman Archive

12 Portrait bust of Henry VII, Pietro Torrigiano © Getty Images

INDEX

(EW = Elizabeth Woodville; JL = Jacquetta of Luxembourg;
MB = Margaret Beaufort)

DR PHILIPPA GREGORY was an established historian and writer when she developed an interest in the Tudor period and wrote the internationally bestselling novel *The Other Boleyn Girl*. She is currently writing a series of books on the Plantagenet family, of which the first two – *The White Queen* and *The Red Queen* – were number-one bestsellers in the UK. She lives in England and welcomes visitors to her website: www.philippagregory.com

DAVID BALDWIN taught history at the Universities of Leicester and Nottingham for many years and is the author of five books, including *Elizabeth Woodville: Mother of the Princes in the Tower*.

MICHAEL JONES taught at the University of South West England, the University of Glasgow and Winchester College. He is a Fellow of the Royal Historical Society and now works freelance as a writer and media presenter. He is the author of seven books, including *The King's Mother*, a highly praised biography of Margaret Beaufort shortlisted for the Whitfield Prize.